Appraising
The Graduate

Appraising *The Graduate*

The Mike Nichols Classic and Its Impact in Hollywood

J.W. WHITEHEAD

McFarland & Company, Inc., Publishers
Jefferson, North Carolina, and London

All photographs provided by Photofest.

LIBRARY OF CONGRESS CATALOGUING-IN-PUBLICATION DATA

Whitehead, J.W., 1962–
    Appraising The graduate : the Mike Nichols classic and its impact in Hollywood / J.W. Whitehead.
        p.   cm.
    Includes bibliographical references and index.
    Includes filmography.

    ISBN 978-0-7864-6306-0
    softcover : 50# alkaline paper ∞

    1. Graduate (Motion picture)   I. Title.
PN1997.G665W45   2011
791.43'72—dc22   2010046317

British Library cataloguing data are available

© 2011 J.W. Whitehead. All rights reserved

No part of this book may be reproduced or transmitted in any form or by any means, electronic or mechanical, including photocopying or recording, or by any information storage and retrieval system, without permission in writing from the publisher.

Front cover: Anne Bancroft and Dustin Hoffman in *The Graduate*, 1967 (Embassy Pictures Corporation/Photofest)

Manufactured in the United States of America

McFarland & Company, Inc., Publishers
   Box 611, Jefferson, North Carolina 28640
   www.mcfarlandpub.com

For John Jr. and Nancy,
who always knew;
for Betsy and Caroline,
who helped me know;
and for Kathryn and Jessica,
who know best.

Table of Contents

Acknowledgments — ix
Preface — 1

Part I. Introduction

1. "Plastics" — 15
2. Post-*Graduate* — 26
3. The Graduates — 50

Part II. Seeing *The Graduate*

4. "The Sounds of Silence": Of Human Baggage (00:00–03:00) — 69
5. The Graduation Party (03:00–06:30) — 76
6. The Locked Womb (06:30–16:30) — 83
7. "Ben? You'll Never Be Young Again." (16:30–21:00) — 94
8. The Birthday Party (21:00–24:00) — 99
9. An "Affair" at the Taft Hotel (24:00–38:00) — 104
10. "Drifting" (38:00–46:00) — 113
11. "Conversation"-Stopper (46:00–55:00) — 121
12. Elaine (55:00–1:10:30) — 128
13. "Scarborough Fair": The Berkeley Stalker (1:10:30–1:26:00) — 137
14. "Mrs. Robinson": The Loneliness of the Long-Distance Runner (1:26:00–1:41:00) — 137 / 145
15. More "Sounds of Silence": The Finishing Kick (1:41:00–1:46:00) — 154

Part III. Valediction

16. The Legacy of *The Graduate*   171

Chapter Notes   195
Filmography   201
Bibliography   203
Index   207

Acknowledgments

The first words I ever wrote about *The Graduate* no longer survive, and that is no doubt a mercy; they were written on assignment for a film studies class during the night in 1979 after I first saw Mike Nichols's 1967 film in the auditorium of my undergraduate school. (We watched the films on Monday nights, wrote and handed in two-page reflections to be discussed on Tuesdays, and — my favorite part — wrestled the unwieldy reels of the films onto a projector for frame-by-frame study in the classroom on Thursdays.) My professor was Caroline Cherry, an English Renaissance scholar doing generalist duty at a small, private liberal arts college. I loved film before I took that class; I loved it like I loved literature by the time the semester was over.

The first words of this book about *The Graduate*, roughly corresponding to the first chapter of Part I and the first half of Part II, were the product of a semester's sabbatical granted to me by Wheeling Jesuit University. I wish to thank Letha Zook, Faculty Council, and the long-suffering members of my department, especially Joe Brumble, Richard Cain, Paula Makris, and Kate Voorhees, for their encouragement and support in making a half-year's paid leave a reality. Literally, I could not have done this without the largesse of a sabbatical. Others have also been valuable to various phases of my growth as a scholar, critic, and writer, especially Betsy Morgan, Tim Corrigan, Dick Kennedy, Dan O'Hara, Peter Staffel, Kris Willumsen, and John Folger, all of whom have read or listened to things I should have had the sense to refine further before handing over to them, and all of whom have had the generosity to tell me so in the encouraging manner of true teachers. (Do not blame anyone named above for any errors of fact or judgment found within these pages.) I also wish to thank the librarians at WJU and at Bellaire (OH) Public Library, who make yearned-for nuggets of scholarly work efficiently appear, conjured from the smallest scraps of bibliographical shorthand. (A soapbox moment: Support your local libraries now or regret their reduced circumstances later.)

And in a study as focused as this one is on reading and interpreting point of view, it seems particularly appropriate to acknowledge my students. Over the years, they have routinely helped me to see more clearly not only through *their* eyes but also through my own.

As for the friends not already named above, and especially for my family: these are the people who have always believed in me, which creates its own pressures, but also mysteriously makes easier taking necessary chances. I can only hope I have shown them the sort of faith they have always shown me.

Preface

In late 1968, Mike Nichols was the hottest, coolest director in Hollywood. He'd made two films: *Who's Afraid of Virginia Woolf?* (1966) and *The Graduate* (1967), each of which had been a box-office success while garnering scores of nominations and awards. The Academy of Motion Picture Arts and Sciences had nominated Nichols as Best Director for both films, and in March 1968, he'd collected the Oscar for his work on *The Graduate*. The film, starring an unknown New York stage actor named Dustin Hoffman in the title role, came as close as any film can to being universally loved and admired. Stanley Kauffmann at *The New Republic* adored it. So did Bosley Crowther, the venerable film reviewer at *The New York Times*. College students cherished it, returning to theaters over and over again. Even radicals occupying the President's office at Columbia University to protest the Vietnam War took turns sneaking out to see it. *The Graduate* was briefly the third-highest-grossing movie of all time, bested only by the legendary *Gone with the Wind* (1939) and *The Sound of Music* (1964).

Not everyone liked the film and its director, however. Nichols and *The Graduate* were either savaged or, perhaps worse, dismissed by a backlash cadre of establishment critics, including the greatest names in the liveliest era of film criticism: Pauline Kael (dismissive); Andrew Sarris (initially positive but ultimately dismissive); John Simon (savage). Most notorious was a 33-page essay by Jacob Brackman in *The New Yorker*, which eventually accused Hoffman's character, Benjamin Braddock, and the film's *auteur*, Mike Nichols, of "complicity,"[1] for Brackman in his assumed role as counter-cultural apologist the dirtiest word he could conjure.

Nichols, ubiquitous in interviews and publicity appearances during 1968, had long since begun to show the strain of grinning so long in the public-relations glare. Sent out on a canny marketing tour of the nation's campuses by the film's financial sponsor, Embassy Pictures' Joseph E. Levine, Nichols had taken to looking earnest young undergraduates in the eye and telling them they'd misunderstood his film. The happy ending they were certain that they'd seen (some of them as many as a dozen times) was an illusion, a trick of cinematic point of view. It was Nichols's turn to reach for the dirtiest word he could imagine, as he attempted to describe his hero and heroine, and the word he came up with resonated through the generation gap: addressing the much-discussed ending of his film, Nichols would grimly intone that, within five years, Benjamin and Elaine would become their *parents*, those swamps of empty social striving and anxiety. In laboring on the preparation of his film, it had never occurred to Nichols to see Benjamin and Elaine as heroic, and it stunned him when he met with hero-worship from sea to shining sea. (This was a feeling shared by his team; Richard Sylbert, the production designer, predicts resignedly of the film's protagonists, "They're probably divorced six years later."[2]) If Nichols was impatient with populist garbling of the sounds of silence, he was also irritated by professional misinterpretation, and Brackman's essay was the phenomenal example in question. All his interviewers seemed to know Brackman's essay, and the subject inevitably came up during conversation. Of Brackman's verbose sincerity, Nichols was disingenuously cavalier, claiming that Brackman "was more interested in the picture than I am."[3]

There is, of course, overwhelming evidence that Nichols was single-mindedly invested in his cinematic project during the year of pre-production, the months of shooting, and the months of editing, previewing, and re-cutting his film. Nichols's comment thus comes across as the put-down rhetoric of a man who has despaired of being heard by a culture that had already made up its mind about him and his film. Rather than debate with Brackman and his other critics (or with the much larger populist waves who idolized *The Graduate*), Nichols reflects in his comment a desire simply to move on. By early 1969, he would be on location in Mexico shooting his third film, the chaotic and underrated adaptation of *Catch-22* (1970), and thence to *Carnal Knowledge* (1971). These four films, each characterized by a corrosively satiric vision of human society, constitute as remarkably varied and accomplished a five-year period, particularly at the inception of a career, as all but a very few directors working in Hollywood have been able to assemble.

Of the four, *The Graduate* is unquestionably the most enduring and evergreen. Yet few more beloved Hollywood films have been more persistently misunderstood than *The Graduate*. This is because, of the four, *The Graduate* features the most sophisticated complications of tone. Particularly in its second half, the film appears to be conventional, even at times cliché—easily palatable to a mass audience. Although a fixture on lists of America's greatest films, *The*

Graduate has been mysteriously ignored by film criticism in the four decades since it debuted. This critical silence may be attributed in part to the initial backlash by Kael et al., who rebutted the populist appetite for the film during its astonishing two-year run in theaters, but also in part to the quicksilver subsequent career of Nichols, who has not presented a unified auteur vision for easy packaging and consumption. Neither fans who thought the film spoke for the emergent counter-culture nor backlash critics who thought the film cynically meant to cash in on a new youth audience truly saw the film for what it was and remains: a negative satire of consumerist conformity presented with a complex juxtaposition of points of view. No character in the film is spared from *The Graduate*'s satirical eye, least of all Benjamin, its much-lionized protagonist.

When I include this film, as I often do, on a course syllabus in one of my classes, I know that part of my task will inevitably be to work with (as a way of overcoming) the initial, superficial responses my students have to the film. My course rosters are typically populated by students in Benjamin's general demographic: white, socio-economically privileged, profoundly inexperienced. These students are so acculturated to certain rituals of their own maturation, including the foregone conclusions of college and professional life, that many of them must be invited to ask the question that Benjamin's father provocatively asks his son in a variety of ways, beginning with abstract salvos like "What's wrong?" and culminating in direct demands like "Would you mind telling me what those four years of college were for, what was the point of all that hard work?"

To the first question, Hoffman admits under prodding that he wants his life to be "different." The implication, never explicitly stated by Benjamin, is that he wants to find some other model for his life besides the one provided by his parents and their circle. But to the second question, Benjamin can only reply, "You got me." My students laugh at this line; their laughter comes in recognition of their own blankness, of their having been steered to this spot, in a college classroom, by a succession of cultural authorities: their parents, teachers, counselors, clergy. Many of them are not yet ready to question their culture's assumptions. But that is an old story, and introduces one of the purposes of art: in dramatic narratives, we are invited to begin — or continue — our scrutiny of our selves and our world. Art, including cinematic art, invites us to look. And this is the irony of the history of cultural reception of *The Graduate*: both those who love and those who dismiss the film have often demonstrated an essential failure to see the film for what it is.

What emerging baby boomer audiences thought they recognized in this cinematic world of false-front marriages, neuroses, alcoholism, conspicuous consumption, and not-so-quiet desperation was confirmation of what they'd seen in their own suburban families' lives and aspired to circumvent in their own futures, what Robert Beuka calls "the superficial, self-destructive narcissism of the suburban dream."[4] In May 1964, addressing the graduating class of the University of Michigan, Lyndon Johnson had announced his ambitious plan for the Great Society, in which all might prosper and the privileged would not be "condemned to a soulless wealth."[5] Yet that condemnation persisted, even as southeast Asian villages and American ghettoes burned. Leonard Quart and Albert Auster, in *American Film and Society Since 1945*, label Nichols's film "the shrewdest [...] assault in a whole series of [Hollywood] attacks on the values of the affluent, upper-middle-class American."[6] *The Graduate* offered what felt like a reality check for middle-class children emerging from the shelter of their parents' charge accounts to assume their own place and responsibilities in the world.

Nothing so emphatically crystallized the sense of a new order overturning the old as did *The Graduate*'s stirring final quest, when Benjamin "saves" Elaine from a loveless, arranged wedding. The film ends with an ambiguously open-ended shot of the young couple aboard a municipal bus, their initial elation gone, settling in for the ride of their lives. My students, like the first audiences seeing the film in the late 1960s, laugh and cheer, vicariously jazzed by the stunning rescue—so much motion and purpose after an hour and a half of Benjamin's unaffected drifting. They barely register or else set aside the coda on the bus, with its mournful reprise of Simon and Garfunkel's "Sounds of Silence." They think Benjamin and Elaine have "won." This is a routine reaction, because it is the clichéd rhetoric the film offers us as a projection of Benjamin's point of view, and Benjamin wants to believe he's won, that he's beaten the forces of deadening conformity (as embodied by the monsters of his parents' generation), that he's finally moving—and in a positive direction.

But what have Benjamin Braddock and Elaine Robinson won by the final moments of this film? What have they figured out? Does *The Graduate* end happily for the counter-culture? Is it in fact possible to say in any respect that *The Graduate* is even *about* the counter-culture? This becomes the focus of discussion with my students after those brief final credits roll and the final note from Paul Simon's guitar fades, as surely as Benjamin's and Elaine's smiles fade in that extraordinary penultimate shot of the film. *The Graduate*'s narrative rhetoric, like that of nearly all Nichols's early films, is negative satire, a dissection of what is rotten in the culture, not advocacy for or even so much as a *depiction of* an alternative. Thus, taking their cue from audiences so besotted by what they understand to be the protagonists' positive movement at the end, the backlash critics decry the essential emptiness of that positive movement. Everyone assumes the story is as simple as Benjamin.

This garbled reception of the film has stunted critical dialogue. Although *The Graduate* routinely shows up on heritage lists (#17 in the most recent American Film Institute poll compiling a rank of America's greatest films), almost no commentary and debate has emerged. Despite its cultural enormity of influence and hold on the American imagination, there have been no book-length monographs on *The Graduate*; the longest response to the film, published in 1968 in the immediate wake of its blockbuster splash, remains that wandering polemical essay by Jacob Brackman in *The New Yorker*. Other than Brackman's essay, the most significant single discussion of *The Graduate* in print is in Mark Harris' excellent history, *Pictures at a Revolution: Five Movies and the Birth of the New Hollywood* (2008), about the five very distinct films nominated for the 1967 Best Picture Oscar. Harris's book is rich in fine reporting, though its focus is essentially on the production and reception of Hollywood films as the old system groped towards new models it wouldn't fully understand until well into the 1970s. In other words, Harris, though a perceptive cultural critic, is not primarily motivated by a desire to study and interpret the films themselves so much as to explore what their disparate legacies have meant for the art and business of American movies. In their respective surveys of the extraordinary, imaginative outpouring of the Hollywood Renaissance, Glenn Man and Elaine M. Bapis have devoted substantial chapters to discussion of the film, and Man's analysis in particular is sensitive to the sub-textual nuances of Nichols's tone (though he resists Nichols's dark interpretation of his own characters). Perhaps because its director's mercurial career has eluded an auteur's clearly defined and concerted preoccupations, *The Graduate* has not benefited from the book-length retrospective critical examination auteur careers encourage as a matter of course. Only one book has been published on Mike Nichols as filmmaker, and that was in 1978, at the end of the first (and most unified) phase of his career.

In sum, the story of Benjamin, Elaine, and Mrs. Robinson has become a canonical text that everyone knows but that most assume has nothing left to reveal. Deepening the viewer's experience of *The Graduate* is the primary objective of this book, first, in Part I, by revisiting its reception and the somewhat stunted critical discourse about the film, and then especially in Part II by undergoing an immersion in *The Graduate*'s cinematic languages — dramatic, visual, aural. Despite its much-discussed open ending, *The Graduate* seems to have remained an essentially closed text for most popular and critical audiences (although, as discussed in Part III, filmmakers have routinely unlocked and explored its contents). My hope is that this book will invite both cultural critics and non-academic enthusiasts to equally fruitful contemplation of a curiously familiar yet still largely unknown text.

Part I introduces the "problems" of the film's phenomenal box-office performance and the critical debate that resulted from a backlash against its popular reception. The film had such a high profile and was co-opted with such zest by a generation in need of manifestos that the film itself quickly became all but invisible. Voices as disparate in their opinion of *The Graduate* as David Thomson and Lee Hill have expressed a similar desire for increased dialogue about Nichols and his work. Hill, a Nichols apologist, believes that "a major shift in ambition and approach by Nichols did not endear him to critics, although his films continued to be successful with audiences," further noting that, "Outside of the usual film junket type publicity, there has been little serious commentary about Nichols's work (the only book length study on Nichols by H. Wayne Schuth came out in 1978, when many assumed [Nichols] had retired from film)."[7] Thomson dismisses Nichols as not a genuine film artist but merely a salesman with "a high reputation and a producer's instinct for what smart people might want to see."[8] Though Thomson believes *The Graduate* is "a cold, heartless entertainment," he nonetheless believes the film "cries out for thorough reconstruction and critical debate."[9] Linda Ruth Williams writes that study of *The Graduate*'s "significance for audiences and critics in the 1970s, 1980s and 1990s (especially as this cherished object of U.S. popular culture comes to be released on video and DVD) is a potentially rewarding area of enquiry."[10]

While I provide a representative sampling of what have essentially been the two camps in reception of *The Graduate* (the admirers of its perceived counter-cultural pieties and the critics of its perceived glib, audience-pleasing phoniness), I give particular attention to Brackman's essay, not only because of the sizable scale of his response but also because his positions serve as a time-capsule of 1968 polemics and because his arguments regularly surface in subsequent backlash dismissals. Part I ends by returning to a study of authorial intention — not only that of Nichols the director, but also that of the other young men who helped to create Benjamin Braddock, "the Graduate," whose point of view functions for long sections as the mind of the film. In addition to Nichols, they include Charles Webb, whose novel first introduced Benjamin into the culture; Lawrence Turman, who saw in Webb's character a person both sympathetic and exasperating; Buck Henry, whose screenplay adaptation focused Benjamin's point of view for a cinematic audience; and Dustin Hoffman, who embodied Benjamin's assumptions and frequent misassumptions (both faithfully recorded by the camera) about all he sees. Turman has written his own memoir of nearly a half-century in the film business, and all have sat for numerous interviews over the years that have given essential insights into their intentions for the film (as well as their consternation about the garbled popular and critical reception).

My thesis is that the film's complicated point of view has posed difficulty for mass audiences and critics alike, and so, in Part II, I return to Nichols's text for a close reading of point of view as essential to understanding the film's satiric intention. American culture, verging on revolution, was anxious for rallying points, and in 1967, they found a variety of those shared frames of reference on theater screens: Sidney Poitier's answering slap of a rich white Southern plantation owner in Norman Jewison's *In the Heat of the Night*; Warren Beatty and a Dust Bowl farmer forced off his farm, shooting holes in the bank's foreclosure sign in Arthur Penn's *Bonnie and Clyde*; and, as the year ended, Benjamin Braddock telling his father he wants his life to be "different" than that of his elders. The nuanced points of view in these films, particularly of Penn's and Nichols's complicated ironic narratives, were simplified by the majority's will. Beyond their distrust of *The Graduate*'s mass appeal, many of the film's critics also complained about the film's tonal shift from comedy of manners to romance in its second half, assuming the shift to be accidental and thus citing Nichols's failure of nerve to complete his black comedy about the childish behavior of consumerist conformity. It is true that, in its first half, the film looks through Benjamin's eyes (sometimes literally, as in the poolside, scuba-diving scene) at a blighted landscape of Beverly Hills social striving and arrested development; in its second half, as Benjamin breaks out of the affair and the hermetic boxes (pool, childhood bedroom, hotel room) that have held him, the narrative shifts his point of view toward something that *feels like* conventional romance: boy-wins-girl back. Yet this shift is deliberate and directly related to point of view. It does indeed depict conventional cinematic clichés of romance, as Benjamin might in his callowness imagine them. Far from a failure of nerve, however, Nichols's ambition is nothing less than to sacrifice his own protagonist — and at the risk of alienating his audience. In *Radical Visions*, Glenn Man writes, "It is not enough for Nichols's satiric bent that Ben and Elaine thumb their noses at the establishment; they must be gestured at as well."[11] Benjamin's point of view in the first half of the film depicts a series of social grotesques; as he becomes convinced that Elaine can save him, he views her and her world in an equally distorted way, only this time employing a young man's cliché of infatuation. The emphasis in the first half is on looking through Benjamin's eyes at how ridiculous the world appears; the emphasis in the second half is on looking at how ridiculous (and hypocritical) Benjamin *himself also* appears. His behavior is at its most outrageous regarding the social institution of marriage. Despite his horror at and eventual rebellion against Elaine being sacrificed by her parents to exactly the same sort of cynically arranged marriage the Robinsons once were made to endure, he and Elaine spend much of the film's final act cynically plotting their own marriage as what passes for a strategic counter-insurgency. Whatever else marriage is, it ought not to be a chess move.

Narrative point of view — particularly as a character himself is changing, evolving, and wrenching reality to suit his own emotional needs — can prove a very difficult and elusive quality for audiences to receive. When Benjamin becomes in his own mind the knight errant who must rescue the princess from the locked fortress of her captivity, the film's ironic distance from its protagonist's cliché-ridden imagination may collapse under the collective weight of the audience's own desire for happily-ever-after. Part II asks audiences and critics alike to set aside our various cultural paraphrases of this story and return to the actual text of this much-beloved film, to reclaim it (from decades of not only Benjamin's but also the audience's misassumptions) for the prophetic document it has turned out to be. Counter-cultural critics like Brackman (whose essay exudes equal parts earnestness and smugness) derided *The Graduate* for portraying bright young things like Benjamin and Elaine who, as Bob Dylan put it, don't seem to "know which way the wind blows." Yet historical hindsight tells us that far more Benjamins and Elaines in the culture came to retrace the steps of their parents (*à la* Nichols's prediction while on his barnstorming tour of college campuses): these self-styled revolutionaries, the Baby Boomers, yielded to the temptation of LBJ's dread apparition of "soulless wealth" instead of pursuing his dream of the "Great Society" or the even more radical route of "dropping out" and truly abetting a revolution. The title of Nichols's film, like the narra-

Just after the titles sequence, Benjamin Braddock (Dustin Hoffman) mopes in his childhood bedroom. Downstairs, a college graduation party in his honor awaits, attended exclusively by his parents' friends. He's to be the prize object, paraded by his parents in their game of social brinksmanship with their Beverly Hills neighbors. The aquarium, whose symbolism of pre-natal womb-water dominates the first half of the film, features a plastic scuba-diver. At his 21st birthday party, another affair populated by his parents' friends, Benjamin will become the diver, compelled towards objecthood in the plastic world of his parents and their associates, the Robinsons.

tive that accompanies it, is a challenge to audiences to see what Benjamin has seen but then potentially to advance beyond where Benjamin has advanced.

A practical note: in Part II, I have organized my analysis of the film into smaller episodic units, denoted by sub-title as well as by time elapsed. For instance, my discussion of the final five minutes of this 106-minute film is labeled, "More 'Sounds of Silence': The Finishing Kick (1:41:00–1:46:00)." The times provided in each sub-section are always rounded to the half-minute in correspondence to where my discussion of a scene or sequence from the film begins or ends.

The final, brief section of my study, Part III, looks at how *The Graduate* has perpetuated itself in some subsequent narratives, especially among Nichols's own and succeeding generations of filmmakers, from Hal Ashby and Robert Altman to Sam Mendes and Wes Anderson to Lone Scherfig and Marc Webb. When I took my first film studies course in 1979 as an undergraduate, *The Graduate* was one of a dozen films on the syllabus (alongside usual suspects like Hitchcock and Bergman); our course text, Louis Giannetti's *Understanding Movies*, was in its third edition and used *The Graduate* half a dozen times to illustrate film aesthetics (the first edition, published in 1972, made even more allusions to the film within a significantly shorter text). Thirty years later, the eleventh edition of Giannetti's much-expanded text mentions the film only twice. Part of the strategy in such revisionism is simply to keep current — new films are released each year that will seem more relevant by temporal proximity to a beginning film student.

Yet the reduction also feels like a critical judgment, considering that *The Graduate* remains evergreen in the cultural consciousness; a box-office bang this big will still be felt in cinematic galaxies far, far away. In 1997, when the American Film Institute announced its Top 100 American Films, *The Graduate* placed 7th overall; ten years later, it was still in the top 20, at number 17. *The Graduate* has been parodied by Garry Shandling and *The Simpsons*, by *Wayne's World 2* (1993) and *American Pie* (1999); it has been mounted as (and some would argue self-parodied by) a Broadway stage production, and *Home School*, a sequel written by the source novel's creator, Charles Webb, appeared in 2007. It has nourished the imaginations of succeeding generations of filmmakers,[12] serving as a direct artistic precedent for an Oscar-winning film, *American Beauty* (1999), whose director, Sam Mendes, was, like Mike Nichols, a force of nature in the theatrical world before being lured into straddling the worlds of stage and screen. Another highly regarded and influential indie film of the same era, Wes Anderson's *Rushmore* (1998), is an inspired variation on its themes — at least as important a second-generation response to *The Graduate* as even *American Beauty*, despite all the latter's awards. In 2009, *(500)*

Days of Summer starts from a premise that its protagonist formed as a young boy: true love will prevail. The seminal document for his belief is "a total misreading of the movie, *The Graduate*." Marc Webb, the writer-director of the film, goes to great pains to argue in the narrative that subsequently unfolds that this is *not* in fact a misreading (which, as we shall see, constitutes ... a total misreading of *The Graduate*). Mike Nichols's film remains an *idée fixe* of popular culture, and Part III serves as a selective review of some of the texts that owe their genesis in part to Nichols's foundational text.

The Graduate was a film worth understanding when it was released; now in its fifth decade, the film continues to say true things about how we fail, in a peculiarly American way, to avoid living lives of materialist conformity at various decibel-levels of desperation. I have believed, ever since that first undergraduate film course, that *The Graduate* was a sophisticated satirical masterpiece that rewards close, careful study. Perhaps because I was too young to be swept away in the initial cultural wave of the film and therefore uninterested in, as Buffalo Springfield put it, mostly saying hooray for our side, I was able to see all that Benjamin saw around him — all the anxious greed and pettiness and spiritual squalor — while also seeing Benjamin for what he himself was, in all his initial innocence, initiation into venal adulthood, and eventual failures of imagination and nerve.

Of course it occurred to me to think of Dustin Hoffman as an iconic Hollywood anti-hero, and I sought out subsequent screenings and revivals of other Hoffman films — *Midnight Cowboy* (John Schlesinger, 1969), *Lenny* (Bob Fosse, 1974) — wherever I could find them. By 1976, as "Woodstein" in Alan J. Pakula's *All the President's Men*, the two men who would be Benjamin Braddock — Hoffman, the Hollywood antitype who got the part on Nichols's intuition, and Robert Redford, the conventional prototype that everyone, including Hoffman, assumed was born to play the part — had become twin icons of cinematic presence. The counter-culture had swiftly become the culture. Hoffman's powerful presence in *The Graduate* is the anti-charismatic charisma of the 1970s ascendancy of the character actor, what made screens safe and even lucrative for actors as different as Woody Allen and Gene Hackman. (Hackman very nearly was a supporting player in the two best of the five films nominated for the 1967 Best Picture Oscar: both Arthur Penn's *Bonnie and Clyde*, in which he plays Buck Barrow, and *The Graduate*, in which he was the first actor cast to play Mr. Robinson. However, Hackman failed to make it past rehearsals on Nichols's film, either because he was finally judged to be too young or because he couldn't play his lines as written, depending on whom one asks.) Watching Benjamin mope and shuffle his way through *The Graduate*, I was dazzled by the wit and verve with which Hoffman presented such a witless, non-dynamic character. Unlike the cultural reception of many 1968 audiences, who reported their adoration of Benjamin's perceived iconoclasm, I didn't find myself wanting to be Benjamin Braddock; seeing my own passivity and compromise exposed, I wanted to *stop* being Benjamin Braddock. The artistic objective of Mike Nichols and his filmmaking team in *The Graduate* was and remains to provoke in me as in the rest of the audience a mingled sympathy for but horror of becoming Benjamin Braddock, plaything of his culture, reified conformist on the road to nowhere. For all of its bright comedy and girl-meets-boy wistfulness, the satiric heart of *The Graduate* is the black comedy of Mike Nichols's epitaph on Benjamin and Elaine's lives: *They will become their parents.* Coming from a comedian like Nichols, that's no joke.

PART I
Introduction

I was an object. No one knew my name. I wasn't a human being to them. I was the Graduate.
—Dustin Hoffman, to Mark Harris,
in *Pictures at a Revolution*

It really belongs to no one now. It certainly doesn't belong to Charles Webb. I don't think it served to unbalance him, but it served to age and confound him. It was whipped away from him. We didn't do it. We just made the movie! But then again, I think everybody feels it was whipped away from them.
—Mike Nichols, to Sam Kashner, in *Vanity Fair*

1
"Plastics"

As the Studio System crumbled toward collapse in the 1960s,[1] an unlikely film starring an unknown lead actor and based on an obscure first novel about a kid who dates both a mother and her daughter in the same summer emerged from the scruffiest of independent production companies on the Hollywood periphery. On paper, the phenomenon of *The Graduate* never should have happened. In fact, on paper it already hadn't: Charles Webb's 1963 first novel passed quietly enough through the literary world and had been forgotten. *The Graduate*'s cinematic production and release history is one of those legendary stories that sustain the mysterious allure of the "sleeper," the unpredictable box-office smash that defies the ultra-conventional wisdom of Hollywood's business model du jour.

The Graduate was to have been Mike Nichols's debut as a film director after unqualified successes in his consecutive careers as a stand-up comedian and as a Broadway director. The funding for *The Graduate* came so slowly, however, that Nichols wound up making his name in Hollywood by directing Richard Burton and Elizabeth Taylor in *Who's Afraid of Virginia Woolf?* (1966) before the way was finally clear for him to make the film he would conclude, during production, was about him. Released in late December 1967 in time for the 1968 Academy Award nominations, *The Graduate* would win him his only Oscar to date, as Best Director.

The Graduate was supposed to star Robert Redford, one of the most glamorous new lead actors in Hollywood, as Benjamin Braddock, the protagonist who would appear in every scene of the film; instead, the production wound up with an obscure Off-Broadway stage actor, Dustin Hoffman, who had one miniscule role as a Hollywood bit-player under his belt and who was nobody's choice but Nichols's. (Richard Corliss was still calling the casting a "mistake" in 1974, more than half a decade after the film had become a cultural juggernaut.[2]) *The Graduate* would garner Hoffman an Oscar nomination and change not only his own professional journey but also the casting of Hollywood films for the next decade and beyond.³ Steven Soderbergh has called Nichols's decision to subvert conventional Hollywood practice and cast Hoffman "the seminal event in the defining of motion picture leading men in the last fifty years."⁴

The cast member with the most accomplished résumé, Anne Bancroft, freely admitted she had no feel for the part well into the production. For her portrayal of the Machiavellian Mrs. Robinson, Bancroft also would be nominated by the Academy, for an award she'd already won, playing the saintly Annie Sullivan in *The Miracle Worker* (Arthur Penn, 1962); she would live with the notoriety of being Mrs. Robinson for the rest of her long, distinguished career: "'I've made other films, you know!'"⁵ was her standard exasperated reply to being asked yet another question about leopard-skin lingerie or cosmetic tan lines or extramarital etiquette.

Charles Webb, author of the seemingly cinema-friendly source novel, and three other men each attempted to shape the screenplay adaptation before a fourth, Buck Henry (a fast friend of Nichols once the comic-turned-stage-director arrived in Hollywood⁶), took the book in hand, humbly saved all its strengths virtually verbatim, and removed its inessentials without leaving a trace of scar. Richard Corliss refers to Henry's contribution as "less rewriting than retyping," though he acknowledges "Henry's perspicacity in knowing a good thing when he read it"⁷).

Nichols, the still-neophyte director, battled daily with his crew, which included veteran cinematographer Robert Surtees and talented younger technicians like editor Sam O'Steen and production designer Richard Sylbert; Nichols commanded Sylbert, for instance, to build a painstakingly detailed, full-scale set of the Robinson house (which made it terribly inflexible for actually filming in), and goaded Hoffman to maintain a Method-edge on the character's near-paralyzing angst. Surtees famously claimed that he employed more of his cinematographer's toolbox on *The Graduate* than on any other film in his career, which included three Oscars and work with legends like Vicente Minelli, William Wyler, and John Ford.

The money for the production didn't come from any of the major studios, all of which turned producer Lawrence Turman down not once but twice — before and after he had a shooting script. Instead the $3 million budget came from Joseph E. Levine, the unsavory producer of Embassy Pictures' low-budget genre flicks and distributor of sexually provocative foreign films. Levine looked at *The Graduate* as a way to lend what Sidney Lumet calls "'class with a capital K!'"⁸ to Embassy's operation, but Levine felt betrayed by the first rough cut of *The Graduate* when it didn't show enough female skin.⁹

1. "Plastics" 17

In other words, a typical Hollywood success story: Hollywood succeeding in spite of itself.

Before there was such a thing as People's Choice Awards, *The Graduate* was among the handful of films "chosen" by the general public and recognized with that most treasured of all industry honors: big box-office. Robert L. Carringer cites a *Variety* report that, three decades after its initial release, *The Graduate*'s inflation-adjusted earnings placed it among the top 25 in the history of Hollywood — "quite simply, a phenomenon, almost of the magnitude of the *Star Wars* cycle."[10] By the time 1968 was over, still a decade before Hollywood would routinely begin to schedule event-movies for summer openings calculated to crack the All-Time Box-Office records, three films loomed above all others in financial earnings,[11] and of those three, only one could be called a surprise. The first, 1939's *Gone with the Wind* (Victor Fleming) was all but assured of its stature by a pedigree (Margaret Mitchell's perennially best-selling novel) and David O. Selznick's publicity machine. The second, the 1964 film version of the Broadway smash *The Sound of Music* (Robert Wise), also carried a pedigree (Maria von Trapp's true-life account of escaping the Nazis, in addition to Broadway) and the publicity angle of a road-show extravaganza that reached every segment of the film-going public. Both these films were epic in length, production design, and expense. They were meant to capitalize, in the most literal ways, on the spectacle uniquely afforded by cinema. They had large casts placed on two of the great stages of recent human history: the American Civil War and the Second World War. They were as nearly review-proof as films can ever be. No one was terribly surprised when the paying film audience had a nearly inexhaustible appetite for their extravagant charms.

To call *The Graduate* the scruffy, non-pedigreed cousin of these two crowd-pleasers is an understatement. While the source material on which the film is based, written by Charles Webb, sold modestly, it could hardly be called a People's Choice — most of the book's total sales were driven in reverse, by the wild popularity of the film. (*The Graduate* is the only one of Webb's novels to return, periodically, to print.) Yet the cultural difference between 1963, when Webb's novel was published, and the last week of 1967, when the film was initially released, is seismic. The baby boomers who would continue to watch and talk about the film in subsequent decades were "exactly Benjamin's age at the time of the film's release."[12]

While film historians generally discuss the film in the context of the anti-establishment, counter-cultural film documents of the era,[13] *The Graduate* provides almost no period detail, let alone political or cultural reference points. Linda Williams writes that *The Graduate* "is an interesting text for historical reception analysis, because on its original release it was squarely aimed at a youth audience looking for plots and images appropriate to their experience in 1960s protest movements (anti–Vietnam, student revolts, the civil rights movement and the women's movement)."[14] Yet Aaron Cooley rejects what he calls much of what has passed for public discourse on the film as so much "ahistorical nostalgia"[15]; *The Graduate* is less a slice of late–Sixties life than a critique of late-modern consumer culture without a particular epochal reference point. Late in the film, in Berkeley, Dustin Hoffman as Benjamin Braddock emerges from a jewelry store where he has presumably bought Elaine Robinson's engagement ring, and meets a vaguely counter-cultural couple headed into the store, appearing to be unlikely customers. Such visual evidence of the changin' times is kept to a minimum, however. No one in the film talks about the culture. One would have no idea, watching the film, that a war involving young men Benjamin's age was escalating in Southeast Asia, that the Space Race had re-focused the Cold War, that America's ghettoes were burning. That Benjamin — and the freak-flag couple — are doing business in a retail jeweler's shop is the point: opting out of the system and all of its myriad trappings is much harder than it looks.

The lack of period-specific references on screen and in the dialogue would be a cynical stratagem if its only object were to keep the narrative from instant anachronism. Rather, the lack of cultural hot-spots is a revealing glimpse at the function of narrative point of view in the film: Benjamin's "anomie"[16] in the face of the seismic upheavals of the Sixties is evidence of his alienation and passivity. The reason we don't see what's happening in the larger culture is because Benjamin doesn't see it, or is too self-absorbed and socio-economically insulated to pay it heed. The most overt topical reference in the film to a Sixties hot-button issue is a subtle series of insertions made by Paul Simon in an otherwise faithful performance by Simon and Garfunkel of a traditional English folk song, "Scarborough Fair." Even here, the interpolated reference to soldiers preparing for undesired, meaningless battle makes no direct allusions to Vietnam, and the song's appearance in the film was in any case a distant afterthought of its original recording; only one song by Simon, "Mrs. Robinson," was written expressly for inclusion in the soundtrack. (And that song's cultural references are to icons of another time — the Joe DiMaggios of Mrs. Robinson's era, rather than the contemporary era of Benjamin, the 21-year-old protagonist; the song fragment's original working title when Nichols first met with Simon was "Mrs. Roosevelt.")

The lack of contemporary cultural reference points has served to keep *The Graduate*'s narrative evergreen through succeeding decades. For a film whose characters (especially the protagonist) are so preoccupied with the future, the future has been very kind. Via hindsight, the cultural revolution of the Sixties emergent in 1968 was, at best, ambiguous, and so the problems with plastic values and conformity have never truly gone away. What Nichols referred to as "'the Los Angelization of the world in which *things* take over a person's life'"[17] has become a cultural default since the film's initial run. Robert Carringer identifies the version of the city depicted in *The Graduate* as a "commodified Arcadia" and "a rarified world in which anything and everything can be had for a price."[18]

The Sixties hardly made materialism obsolete. In Oliver Stone's *Wall Street* (1987), Gordon Gekko is in his mid–40s — just a couple years older than Benjamin would have been 20 years after *The Graduate* was released. In *Risky Business* (Paul Brickman, 1983), Joel Goodsen (played by Tom Cruise in an early defining role) is about the right age to be Gekko's son — or Benjamin and Elaine's first child. When Joel wants to project an image of adult sophistication, he assumes precisely the uniform accoutrements once donned by Benjamin when aping adulthood: the dangling cigarette, the dark shades (behind which he cowers, hoping not to be found out for the craven blank slate that he is). Joel's happy ending in *Risky Business*, however, is the nightmare of anti-materialist rhetoricians of the Sixties: as unlikely as it seems, Joel manages to seduce a high-priced call girl, outsmart Ivy League recruiters, and out-maneuver the underworld gangsters. He's a capitalist cyborg living the dream and taking his style points, at least early on, from Benjamin Braddock. His "success," unlike Benjamin's, is irony-free.

The archetypal story *The Graduate* tells, of coming of age and coming to terms with one's familial and cultural inheritance (however empty), transcends a particular time and place. Its satire, directed at all its characters, including eventually the protagonist and his pretty girlfriend, weighs material against spiritual values in ways that remain relevant to affluent societies, where great material resources tend to mask injustices both beyond and within their borders. Aaron Cooley identifies the rote process of cultural inheritance in which Benjamin finds himself at the film's onset as a "reification" of mainstream social values and goals, displaying "the anxiety of an individual enveloped in a culture that is dominated by conspicuously consumptive practices and reified relationships."[19] Cooley argues that the reification is so innate within Benjamin that the narrative dramatizes a capitulation seemingly against his conscious will: Benjamin first "rebels" by conducting an affair at a fancy hotel, then "drops out" by roaring away in a late-model sports car: "at once rejecting the world of his parents and [...] embracing its leisure and benefits."[20] Most tellingly, Benjamin (and Elaine) spend the third act of the film locked into the idea of a rebellion against their parents whose central gambit is the social cornerstone of the marriage rite. As a satiric film nonetheless intended for mass entertainment, *The Graduate* communicates its ideas, including the essential hypocrisy and failure of its protagonist, without speechmaking or sanctimony (and this may in part be the source of its chronic misinterpretation through the years). Such philosophical resonances are not primarily the reason for the film's immediate and continuing impact on film audiences, however. While the film's social substance is a value-added feature, the essential source of the film as phenomenon is the ensemble perfection of its production: a smart, funny script; a talented cast well-fitted to their roles; a beautiful design expertly shot and cut.

The Graduate was an art-house film for the masses: "In its gentle, box-office-friendly deployment of soft *avant garde* techniques, it bears out a certain Hollywood Renaissance 'look' and attitude to counter-cultural subjects."[21] It continues to make audiences laugh with delight, squirm with discomfort, and, by the climax, cheer with satisfaction (even though Benjamin does NOT get to the church on time). It also refuses to leave audiences with that sense of satisfaction intact; the final minute of the film denies closure, reopening the narrative simply by inviting us to pause and reflect on the potential futures of two newly minted adults. We ruminate not only about Benjamin and Elaine's future but also, because of the film's insistence on vicarious identification with this couple, about our own.

A particular moment early in the film has become emblematic of the way Mike Nichols and his filmmaking team present *The Graduate*. It is a scene that plays as comedy, albeit with a critical eye on the direction of a society more and more concerned with easy and immediate satisfactions than with what is more difficult but also potentially more enduring. It is the "Plastics" moment.

This scene in *The Graduate* has become one of the touchstones of baby boomer culture, a kind of cultural bookend to Peter Fonda's final campfire epiphany as Wyatt in *Easy Rider* ("We blew it"): burly Mr. McGuire, solemn as a medieval scribe, puts a paternal arm around Benjamin and leads him away from the flirtatious flock of dowagers who have penned Benjamin into the vestibule of his own home. Benjamin, played by a diminutive 31-year-old Hoffman as a nervous, sexually naïve 20-year-old college graduate, appears to lose even more years in Mr. McGuire's bear-like embrace. They walk away from the camera into soft focus, while the foregrounded dowagers exchange knowing looks: *Man talk*. And for Ben, who in the preceding moments of the film has already expressed to his father the anxiety of youth's transition into future adulthood, the moment might reasonably seem to promise the confidential, perhaps even prurient interest of a veil lifted. Benjamin, respectful

1. "Plastics"

pup, waits for what ought to be wisdom. Mr. McGuire appears ready to unburden himself of a secret.

And so he does. Locked together by Mr. McGuire's grasp, they've paced their way out to the big backyard pool that figures so large in the symbolic, womb-stuck identity of Benjamin Braddock as he struggles to be born into adult autonomy. Fifteen minutes into *The Graduate*, Mr. McGuire reveals the anticlimactic central mystery of adulthood for the Beverly Hills milieu of the Braddocks, Robinsons, and McGuires—the men who sold the world. "'Just one word,'" Mr. McGuire promises. "'Are you listening?'" A worldly audience chortles at Benjamin's deadpan patience as he awaits the revelation of this central mystery. "'Plastics,'" Mr. McGuire breathily imparts. It is a moment of archly ironic full disclosure by the dyspeptic adults of Benjamin's world, all of whom—the Robinsons most of all—appear to be mystically drawn to Benjamin's dwindling youth and obvious hunger for experience. Later that same night, Benjamin will be fed two different tumblers of booze, each Robinsons' drink of choice, without regard for his own preference. He will receive both the Robinsons' confessions. Mrs. Robinson will proposition him, and Mr. Robinson will, with a wink and a nod, encourage Benjamin to "have a few flings." Despite all of this seeming intimacy, Benjamin will never call any of them by their first names, on this or any subsequent meeting.

"Plastics." The mod, modular, and ultimately empty promise of this word at the dawn of postmodernity must have given packed houses of knowing 1967 and 1968 movie-goers a thrill of the initiated, those who understood instantly the fatuity of wanting a future focused on so artificial a substance in so inauthentic a social reality. Carringer lingers over the word in exploring Nichols's depiction of Los Angeles, citing Roland Barthes' classic essay, "Plastic," as a prophecy of the usurping of all substances by one substitute, so that one day, the only reality may be, ironically, artificial.[22] Benjamin's blank stare is the residual politeness of a bitterly disappointed young man at his first private audience with the naked emperor. As usual, the film is less simple than this surface impression; *The Graduate* also demonstrates Benjamin's default gravitation to the plastic trappings of a culture reified for youthful tastes. Elaine M. Bapis writes, "Ben throughout the film floats on the plastic raft, wears stylish plastic sunglasses, listens to plastic records, and eats at hamburger stands that use plastic-ware."[23] Yet the point of all this petroleum-based material is more about spiritual than physical reality. Carringer references Jeffrey L. Meikle's *American Plastic: A Cultural History*, which observes of *The Graduate*'s set designs for the Robinson and Braddock homes that "Furniture, lamps, draperies—all indicated a high standard of upper-middle-class taste and nothing revealed origins in a chemical refinery. The epithet 'plastics' could only refer to Ben's parents, their friends, and the pseudo-reality of suburban life."[24]

"'Exactly how do you mean?'" Benjamin asks Mr. McGuire, unnecessarily. Benjamin's reaction is a hedged bet by the filmmakers, a moment of lost faith in their scenario's satire and in their audience's savvy. In Benjamin's dead-pan pause (as if timed for the canned laughter of television), the filmmakers wink at the audience, worried we won't intuit in one well-delivered word the credo of a generation and the battle cry from the generation gap. The film condescends to help us "get it." (Ironically, as the next chapter will show, such overt thematic orientation of the audience renders less overt ironies of narration, particularly in the film's second half, even more subtle by comparison, contributing to audiences' tendency to miss the increasing distance the film establishes between Benjamin's and the film's distinct points of view.) "Shh," says Mr. McGuire, less as if he's afraid someone will learn and co-opt his trade secret than as if he's afraid he'll be found out for a fraud. He puts a stagy finger to his lips: "'Enough said.'"

In forty years, *The Graduate* has continued to provide audiences of white, upper middle-class privilege with the opportunity to see and laugh at the alienating influence of affluence. Mr. McGuire, after all, was right: "'There's a great future in plastics.'" Or as Mr. Bernstein puts it in *Citizen Kane* (Orson Welles, 1941), remembering his late boss and hero, the man he works beside for half a century and never stops calling Mr. Kane: "'It's not hard to make a lot of money, if all you want to do is make a lot of money.'" In May 1964, U.S. President Lyndon Johnson delivered the commencement address at the University of Michigan, a speech that would define The Great Society and pose a pitched conflict between social altruism and profit-principle individualism. "Your imagination," Johnson said, "your initiative, and your indignation will determine whether we build a society where progress is the servant of our needs, or a society where old values and new visions are buried under unbridled growth. For in your time we have the opportunity to move not only toward the rich society and the powerful society, but upward to the Great Society."[25] Near his conclusion, he observes, "There are those timid souls who say this battle cannot be won; that we are condemned to a soulless wealth."[26] But Johnson expressed optimism to the promising next generation (as represented by the graduating Michigan seniors) that together, he and they could overcome what seemed to be society's default setting of disillusioned self-interest. This is precisely the condemned state in which the suburban sophisticates and matrons find themselves in *The Graduate*, boozing and cheating in ostensible effort to forget their dissatisfactions with the life they've chosen.

Neither *Citizen Kane* nor *The Graduate*, however, is particularly eager to pose an antidote to materialism, though each explores (and ultimately finds lacking) the potential of love to conquer greed. In the summer of '68, the box-office juggernaut of *The Graduate* continued to ring registers as the 1967 Summer of Love dissolved into the succeeding summer's fear (about what progressive leader might be the next assassin's target) and loathing (particularly in Chicago in August, about the paucity of desirable political leaders to represent the platform of the left). Cinematic audiences have worked hard to ignore the ambiguity of *The Graduate*'s second half, happily settling on the image of the rescued damsel by the young squire as their desired impression of the whole. This is, to a large degree, precisely what they did in 1967 and 1968 and what they have continued to do in subsequently returning to the film. There is no overtly articulated statement in *The Graduate* like Peter Fonda's character Wyatt makes in *Easy Rider*, about settling for the big score instead of dropping out; Lee Hill, in his study of that film, writes that the "makers of *Easy Rider* seemed to have known instinctively that the notion of the 60s as a decade of idealism, progress and hope for the future was as fragile and delicate as a strip of celluloid. Billy and Wyatt discover that the decade's optimism is akin to a brief, promising mirage like oil shimmering on the road's horizon."[27]

If the perfunctory realism with which Billy and Wyatt meet their deaths at the conclusion of *Easy Rider* has left little doubt in audiences' minds about the filmmakers' aesthetic motive, the ending of *The Graduate*, with its apparent triumph at the church undercut by the solemnity of that final long take of Benjamin and Elaine settling in for the ride of the rest of their lives, conversely has been a source of wide-spread misinterpretation. Charles Webb was angry about how the ending made a mockery of his idealization of marriage; Mike Nichols was consternated by the widespread assumption (both by fans and foes) that Benjamin Braddock was the filmmakers' idea of a counter-cultural hero.[28] The film's fans look at the ending and see two young people who have escaped from the black-and-white fortress of social conformity with nothing but the (ridiculously mismatched) clothes on their backs, ready to ride off into the romanticism of the Aquarian Age. This is an imaginative leap not only beyond the end of the film but beyond the particulars of the text Nichols and his filmmaking team have assembled. Those who have dismissed the film, including eloquent critics like Pauline Kael and David Thomson, or simply ignore it (as film criticism has largely done since the end of the Sixties) similarly misread the filmmakers' intent as commercial rather than aesthetic at its core — a failure of nerve on Nichols's part to forego what might be mistaken as easy or even careless ambiguity and make clear either that the film is nothing but a traditional fairy-tale rescue of the princess from the locked castle or else that the film is genuinely a counter-cultural document. Each of the two typical responses to the film has a central problem: a failure to see the film as a document not of what the mass audience wants nor of what the revolutionary rhetoricians want, but of how a social satirist sees a world where people are "drowning" in materialism.[29]

Nichols could certainly sympathize with Webb's consternation at seeing his personal vision transformed by a culture seemingly lying in wait to possess it for its own purposes, regardless of the formal design of the text itself. "'It really belongs to no one now,'" Nichols told Sam Kashner in a retrospective essay on the occasion of the film's 40th anniversary in 2007. "'It certainly doesn't belong to Charles Webb. I don't think it served to unbalance him, but it served to age and confound him. It was whipped away from him. We didn't do it. We just made the movie! But then again, I think everybody feels it was whipped away from them.'"[30] It has subsequently "become something of an American national treasure,"[31] but this enthusiastic cultural reception has served to burnish the legend while diminishing the actual film's legacy.

Benjamin and Elaine at the end of *The Graduate* are on the bus with "a cross-section of the American public," as Charlie Kane used to call his plain-Jane second-wife Susan Alexander, and that bus seems to be carrying Benjamin and Elaine toward ... nowhere in particular, only aimlessly away from where they've been. Benjamin begins the film as a passive being, conveyed by mechanized forces toward his future; in our last glimpse of him, he has ended in a similar state. *The Graduate*'s narrative is not about affirmation; it's about refutation. Robert Coles writes, "*The Graduate* is ... called a shiny, glossy film, clever and amusing but 'basically' (the word of words, the judgment of judgments) dishonest — when in fact the whole point of the film is to portray the thinness of a certain kind of rich, sensual world."[32] *Plastics* may be the film's wise glimpse of what Mr. McGuire calls the "'future,'" but the vacuum of positive goals or ideals at the core of *The Graduate* indicates why, although audiences chortled then and continue to chortle now at the gap widening between Mr. McGuire and Benjamin during their brief, hushed *tête-à-tête*, the culture continues to default to conspicuous consumption. "It's a comment on life," says Richard Sylbert, Nichols's production designer. "Plastics. The truth of it is if that guy came down the stairs today and somebody said, 'plastics,' he'd say, 'How can I get into them?'"[33]

At a certain point during the long siege of *The Graduate*'s colossal first-run success, Mike Nichols the social satirist found it necessary to bite the hand that was feeding him: he began making a point of stating to outraged groups of bright-eyed students who had reverently returned again and again to his film that, post-narrative, Ben and Elaine will become their parents.[34]

Linda Ruth Williams concurs with Nichols: "The final tableau on the bus suggests that the couple will inevitably take their place in the same old family structure and will probably turn out just like their parents."[35] Benjamin and Elaine may have tuned in; a little further down the road, they may even begin to turn on and drop out. But we can't help but wonder, in this film of cyclical recurrence and the failed imagination of its protagonists, how long will it be before they come crawling back?

2

Post-*Graduate*

It would be difficult to identify a more beloved and perennially popular movie that has been as systematically, categorically misunderstood by both fans and foes as Mike Nichols's *The Graduate*, the second film in what has eventually resulted in a long, illustrious, but elusive career. For its fans, *The Graduate* is a feel-good movie, an unconventional variation on boy-meets-girl, boy-loses-girl, boy-wins-girl-back; more important, it has assumed a place as an apotheosis of the cultural shift we have come to call "The Sixties." On the occasion of a career retrospective of Nichols's films in Spring 2009 at New York's Museum of Modern Art, Charles McGrath called *The Graduate* a "cultural landmark."[1]

Watching the film several decades after its initial release, *New York Times* writer Rick Lyman and film director Ron Howard share an uncertainty about what, specifically, made the film such a touchstone of its times, but Howard posits, in accents redolent of Holden Caulfield, "It has something to do with the view of the world of adult hypocrisy. [...] It's about the generation that had been through the Great Depression and the Second World War and who had come out on top — people who were living very comfortably, had everything they wanted — and yet there was something phony and hollow about their world. They didn't notice it, but their children did."[2] Howard and Lyman's impressions echo a mainstream assessment of *The Graduate* as a dissection of what was popularly called the "generation gap" between Baby Boomers and their parents. But it isn't that simple: Howard's distinction between what the children "notice" and their parents do not is only hazily addressed by Benjamin Braddock (Dustin Hoffman) and Elaine Robinson (Katharine Ross) — when it is addressed at all. In fact, Benjamin and Elaine are as lost as their parents.

In one of the first reviews after *The Graduate*'s release, the crusty and embattled *New York Times* movie critic Bosley Crowther praised the film as "one of the best seriocomic social satires we've had from Hollywood since Preston Sturges,"[3] and a week later, in the final column of his long career with the *Times*, he clarified his claims about the object of the satire, citing the film's "funny and sharp satiric thrust at [...] the piteous immaturity and anti-intellectualism of a large proportion of the supposedly educated and cultivated affluent middle-class."[4] The emphasis in Crowther's reviews is less on what one generation, the younger, seems to "get" that the older generation chronically misses and more upon a sense that, regardless of chronological age or generation, all the people in *The Graduate* generally fail at the project of understanding their own lives.

Despite the professional haste with which Crowther's deadline conclusions about the film had to appear, his reading of *The Graduate* particularly in his second take on the film is an incisive refusal to be swayed by any evidence other than that of the text itself. Such a claim — that to assess a film, one must pay close and careful attention to the film's text — would seem hardly worth noting if not for the persistence with which *The Graduate*, like many a cultural talisman, has been deliberately misread along ideological lines. Crowther's reviews appeared while the film remained in very limited release only in Manhattan; shortly after *The Graduate*'s general release, Andrew M. Greeley touted the film as "a devastatingly accurate portrayal of how upper middle-class young Americans view the society that their parents have created."[5] Such a response, while appropriate to at least part of the spirit of the film, implies that *The Graduate* privileges the perspective of the younger generation. "The sense of dissatisfaction over buying into the American dream was felt by *all* the characters, regardless of their ages," writes Barry Monush,[6] though it's essential to remember that no one in the film — older or younger generation alike — acts in a meaningfully productive way to counter that dissatisfaction.

For his own part, Nichols was surprised when the audience received the film as an ideological statement about the "generation gap": "[I]t seems to me a mistake to generalize people. They've been generalized so much — 'the middle class,' 'the kids'— that a very odd thing has happened: they actually think of themselves as instances of a generality. Which I don't think is a possible way to live. I think that there are gaps between people. But I find often as large a gap between me and somebody my own age as I do between myself and somebody nineteen."[7] A close and careful study of the film reveals that, as Lee Hill has written, "*The Graduate* remains a powerful fable about the difficulties of rebellion in a consumer culture where choice is rampant and yet illusory."[8] All ages are equally subject to the soul-ravaging cultural dangers *The Graduate* depicts. Benjamin and Elaine appear to be good candidates to break free of the conformist trap, but in the end, they are the most poignant examples of what Ron Howard labels "phony" and "hollow." They have seen the possibility of rebellion but not a practical way to make it work.

Those who love *The Graduate* because its young and appealing protagonists speak for a cultural revolution have misread the film's uniformly satiric tone, from which no character, not even Benjamin himself, is spared. However, they are not alone in misapprehending Nichols's text. For the film's detractors, *The Graduate* was, as John Simon called it in a devastatingly negative review, "a piece of calculated pseudo-innocence" that made some generally sympathetic noises toward the 18–30-year-olds who could be understood to reside demographically within the vanguard of the cultural revolution, all the while the film's narrative remained in a commercially secure, even anachronistic location on the side of cultural conformity. Simon identified the "principal weaknesses" of the film as "oversimplification, overelaboration, inconsistency, eclecticism, obviousness, pretentiousness, and, especially in the penultimate section, sketchiness."[9] Tom S. Reck, writing in *Commonweal*, denounced the film as "a hoax and something of a threat."[10] Writing in *Film Quarterly*, Stephen Farber and Estelle Changas echoed Reck, calling the film "an evasive gimmicky hoax" and, despite the sensational buzz, "only the most cleverly fashionable and confused movie of the year."[11] "*The Graduate*," pronounced Pauline Kael in *The New Yorker* two years after the film's initial release, "only wants to succeed and that's fundamentally what's the matter with it."[12] In his legendary *Biographical Dictionary of Film*, David Thomson has condescendingly characterized *The Graduate* as "the cutest package" of a director who "makes movies from really neat, cute, smart ideas that can be grasped in twenty minutes."[13]

The mainstream critics screamed their outrage with such vigor precisely because audiences were speaking so loudly in the film's favor with their cold hard cash. When it opened in December of 1967, just under the wire to qualify for Academy Award nominations (of which it garnered seven and eventually won Nichols the Best Director Oscar), *The Graduate* immediately attracted a repeat, word-of-mouth clientele that created serpentine lines around city blocks at the two theaters where it was playing in Manhattan during its initial run. In the history of Hollywood before the Blockbuster era of coordinated, wide openings on thousands of screens amid concentrated first-weekend buzz, *The Graduate* was the little film that could. By the time the film was generally distributed across the country, weeks later in the coldest months of the winter of 1968, it was still attracting lines around the block at those two original theaters. But now *The Graduate* was breaking "house records for attendance in nearly 90 percent of the movie theaters where it played"[14] and was well on its way to box-office history, at that point in time the highest-grossing film not only of its year but of its kind. The film ran for nearly two full years in theaters[15] and grossed $86 million in the U.S., in addition to significant, multi-million-dollar success in foreign markets; Embassy quickly re-released the film with significant additional box-office returns in 1972.[16]

Only a few other films had inflation-adjusted, box-office track records in the same league — legendary productions like *Gone with the Wind* and *The Sound of Music*. While those films adopted a vision of cinema as spectacle, an epic canvas upon which to present lavish, costumed dramas on the largest historical stages, *The Graduate* was by contrast intimate, nearly hermetic. The film is a chamber drama in which the first act unfolds in a total of three settings — two houses and a hotel — all of them carefully selected and designed to project the smallness and stillness of the film's protagonist. There was no reason for its producer, Lawrence Turman, to expect that this small movie (based on a minor novel so little regarded by Hollywood that a marginal player like Turman, just embarked on a producing career, could afford the rights) would change lives, starting with his own.

Nor, as noted, would *The Graduate*'s unlikely success be driven by anything like critical consensus. Although some of the first mainstream reviews like Crowther's were positive, and while the mainstream media eventually lavished dutiful attention on the film as the cultural phenomenon it had become, the film's initial critical reception can only be characterized as mixed, and the nucleus of America's most eloquent film critics — Kael and Simon, but also Andrew Sarris, Richard Corliss, Richard Schickel, et al. — were or became frankly dismissive of the film. No two of their objections were exactly identical, either. Some of these backlash critics argued that the film is dishonest because it promotes its protagonist as a counter-cultural hero when he is really nothing but a sullen loser; others railed that the film is as misogynistic in its demonizing of Mrs. Robinson as in its desexualizing of Elaine; most critics also faulted the film's young director for quoting his foreign cinematic influences too heavily in his own mise-en-scène. As the popularity of the film continued to grow, these and other objections multiplied with parallel rapidity. Hill writes, "As is often the case with social satire, Nichols was accused of superficiality, misogyny, ripping off Fellini, and various other cinematic war crimes by critics who resented the film's broad appeal."[17]

And then, soon after its release, an interesting phenomenon was visited upon *The Graduate*: people stopped talking about it. Although Kael would include it as a put-down example of Hollywood glibness in a hand-wringing feature about "Trash, Art, and the Movies" in 1969 in *The New Yorker*, the critical "last word" on *The Graduate* was delivered during the height of *The Graduate*'s box-office ubiquity in the summer of 1968, when the film had been playing in theaters for more than half a year: *The New Yorker* ran one of its characteristically long, searching essays hoping to locate the key to the film's unpredictable, unsinkable success. The writer, Jacob Brackman, an earnest, self-appointed spokesman for the counter-culture, concluded that the film was a cynical piece of Hollywood product calculated to please crowds while refusing to tell the truth about a new generation. It was manifestly a backlash article, *the* backlash article — fueled by disappointment that a film that had so little positive to say *about* the emergent counter-culture could be such an audience-favorite *of* the counter-culture. In the wake of its appearance, Nichols got into the habit of joking that Brackman "had thought more about his film than he had."[18]

Brackman starts out his essay optimistically, noting the film's enormous financial success, good reviews from established critics like Stanley Kauffmann in *The New Republic*, and multitudes of awards. Soon his apparent ardor brims; *The Graduate*, Brackman enthuses, is "a nearly mandatory movie experience, which can be discussed in gatherings that cross the boundaries of age and class. It also seems to be one of those propitious works of art which support the theory that we are no longer necessarily two publics — the undiscerning and the demanding — for whom separate kinds of entertainment must be provided."[19] This would seem to be a cause for celebration, the kind of claim subsequent decades would make for films as distinct as *The Godfather* (Francis Ford Coppola, 1972), *E.T.* (Steven Spielberg, 1982), *The Silence of the Lambs* (Jonathan Demme, 1991), and *The Matrix* (Andy and Larry Wachowski, 1999), renewing the argument that the popular audience not only does not recoil from well-made cinema but craves it, particularly when imaginatively packaged in familiar genre forms. By the time his essay's preamble is over, Brackman has analogized to Andy Warhol's Brillo boxes and made the kind of bold claims for *The Graduate* that would have tempted *The Graduate*'s notoriously disreputable but "class"-starved producer, Joseph E. Levine, into printing new movie posters, coaxing people back into theaters for yet one more viewing. *The Graduate*, Brackman declares near the climax of his introductory remarks, "is clearly the biggest success in the history of the movies."[20]

The praise turns to hyperbole so fast that one can't help scanning ahead for the caveat, which inevitably comes, a few pages later: Brackman regretfully reports that the film, "although it is terrific fun to watch, begins to fall apart under reflection."[21] Brackman's dissection has soon uncovered all sorts of problems. Why is Benjamin so inarticulate and passive when he's supposed to be such a bright and talented go-getter? Why the cartoonish rendering of all the adults? Why the happy ending? An essential revelation about Brackman's agenda comes when he unburdens himself of his exasperation with "most of the critics," who "have steadfastly ignored the evidence of the text and insisted that Benjamin's long search for himself arrives at its payoff. The Philadelphia *Evening Bulletin*, typically, informed us that 'The Graduate' is 'rooted in the affirmative premise that the young can escape the traps of a society created by their parents.' And *Glamour* explained Benjamin's barely controlled hysteria at the wedding by saying, 'He doesn't care what other people think because [now] he knows who he is. That's growing up.'"[22]

Brackman resists this popular misinterpretation of the main characters in *The Graduate*, and he is right to point to the text as the basis for his objection. *The Graduate* creates the illusion of character development, of effective action undertaken by a protagonist after several months (his May graduation through Elaine's fall semester up at Berkeley) of personal disintegration. The "film proceeds awkwardly, deceptively,"[23] says Brackman, and he's right again: the film's narration is deceptive — but if read as the film's increasing tonal distance from the point of view of the protagonist, one man's deception is another's irony. The appearance of positive change at the end of *The Graduate* is essentially a question of ironic point of view.

Through a satiric send-up of several kinds of cinematic climax, from the Western showdown to the epic quest to the screwball comedy, the film's last ten minutes provides a witty but devastating commentary on our appetite for resolution. We get what looks like a happy ending — but isn't. An audience cued by years of movie-going to the genre conventions of happy ending must sift through all these generic signifiers to find the film's true point of view. Brackman in his frustration quotes the conclusion to the august Stanley Kauffmann's review: "For once, [...] a happy ending makes *us* feel happy."[24] But Brackman, right to be suspicious of Kauffmann's simplistic reading of the film's ending, adds up the film's argument to this climactic point and, reading it just as literally as the throngs of audiences and enthusiastic critics that have frustrated him, dismisses the moment and, by extension, the film. The problem is that, while Kauffmann represents a popular but simplistic reading of the film's ending as a triumph of the counter-culture, Brackman represents an equally simplistic dismissal of the film's ending as a failure of aesthetic nerve, a pandering to the least sophisticated desires of the mass audience, part of a shared belief by many critics that Nichols's first desire is always to please rather than challenge his viewers. Farber and Changas acknowledge Nichols's "talent and ambition" but conclude, "He's adored because he's hip and safe at the same time; his audiences know that he won't go too far."[25] Decades later, David Thomson, pronouncing for the ages in his *New Biographical Dictionary of Film*, writes condescendingly that Nichols is "a proven success" who makes "movies that are smart, funny, 'adult,' 'on the pulse,' and 'of their moment.'"

Thomson dismisses such success as the product of a "producer's instinct" for what sells and finds it "hard to grasp a him in there, a movie director."[26] Many of the critics and audiences who have loved *The Graduate* since 1967 have loved it superficially, without acknowledging the darker sub-textual ironies of the film's point of view; yet critics like Brackman do a similar disservice to the film if they assume that so many viewers can't possibly be mistaken, that audiences and enthusiastic critics are simply following Nichols's lead in sweeping away the "darkness" and "silence" of the first 100 minutes of his film's narrative in the bright, colorful swirl of noise and motion at its conclusion. The film in fact never stops being a satire, and everybody — even the protagonist — is a target.

Brackman oddly turns to a passage in Charles Webb's novel to explore what he believes to be Nichols's thematic objective; during their long dithering debate in and around Berkeley about whether their relationship could ever be expected to work, Elaine tells Benjamin in the novel that he's wasting his time sitting in his rented room waiting for her to decide, just like he'd be wasting his time trapped in a room and a marriage with her. (Brackman leaves out what Webb takes pains to include: that Elaine believes this is because she is not Benjamin's intellectual equal.) Brackman writes, "Nichols could not have included Elaine's keen remark; it is fundamental to his upbeat resolution of the movie that we do not stop to reconsider Elaine's relation to Benjamin's anguish about his life. Nichols cannot let us leave the theatre feeling that nothing has changed, so he gives us what he thinks we want by packing the last thirty minutes with [...] the horror of confronting brute, implacable stupidity — *wrongheadedness* — in others. With the over-obvious exception of Benjamin, people all appear to see the world so wackily that, like Benjamin, we have no idea what would be involved in getting them to see it straight."[27]

What Brackman discounts is the possibility that Benjamin sees things "wackily" too. An insular kid who spends far too much time alone in his room (Peace Corps, anyone?), Benjamin Braddock is well-positioned to begin distorting his world as a matter of course, to dismissing adults as bugbears and bogeymen intent upon consuming him, and, by contrast, to embracing Elaine (before he can possibly be expected to know who she is or even whether she likes the same music and movies) as his overwhelmingly cinematic true love.

Brackman comes closest to recognizing Nichols's ironic intent when objecting to Benjamin's infatuation with Elaine: "Benjamin's precipitate and (one wants to say 'therefore') consuming love for Elaine makes very little sense. We find ourselves sucked in by a cinematic convention: That's how people fall in love in the movies; it doesn't *have* to make sense. Katharine Ross's scrumptiousness becomes a more than sufficient cause. Yet [...] the romance has now grown crucial to the scheme of Benjamin's life, because we are encouraged to imagine Elaine as the light at the end of his darkness."[28] Brackman's crucial phrase is the "scheme of Benjamin's life": the "scheme" is Benjamin's, the delirium of a 21-year-old drunk from the carnal but uncommitted Mrs. Robinson's seduction and in need of a chaser of something sweeter and more idealized. He gets it into his head that Elaine can save him, because she seems to be pushed around by the adults as much as he himself is (why are they out on their first date, after all?— only because it's a business deal transacted by the patriarchs). Elaine can verify Benjamin's own understanding of the world. Plus she's scrumptious.

Yet somehow Brackman can't quite untangle Benjamin Braddock from Mike Nichols, so that the "scheme" that Benjamin concocts (get to the church, get Elaine, get away, and live happily ever after, which Brackman appropriately calls "deeply illogical"[29]) becomes in Brackman's interpretative logic Nichols's scheme to dissect human social predation and despair with careful and creative precision until the climax, when it's suddenly time to sell out his own film and send us away happy: "All that remains when the bus drives Benjamin and Elaine off into a presumably roseate adulthood is the bare convention of young love triumphant. The trials that Benjamin seemed to forget once he had fixed upon getting the girl, we, too, are encouraged to forget."[30] This is an extraordinary statement from a writer who has thought as specifically about the film as Brackman clearly has. Through the use of exceptionally long-take close-ups both in the church and on the bus, Nichols actually goes to great cinematic pains to *remind* us of what Benjamin and Elaine can't get out of their heads. Brackman claims that "the elation of the [final] scene is almost untainted by any residue of Benjamin's confusion" and predicts, most mystifyingly, and without evidence, that "they will have a proper wedding night."[31] While *The Graduate*'s narrative remains open-ended, optimism for Benjamin and Elaine's smooth and ghost-free sexual consummation requires less interpretation than imagination.

In the second half of his essay, Brackman moves past these sorts of problematic assertions about the film to the larger subtext of his argument, which he has promised since the first page, when he asserts, "Whatever is authentic or meretricious in 'The Graduate' must reflect what is authentic or meretricious in our sentiment about its themes, and perhaps even in America's current conceptions of itself. [... A] uniquely celebrated movie may be worth a pretty close look."[32] In other words, what feels for its first half like a referendum on Mike Nichols's failure of nerve and desire to please the crowd becomes in the essay's second half a grander statement about the tenuous possibilities for social revolution. "Should the 'optimism' of the ending be undercut by what we have already glimpsed of society?" asks Brackman. He concludes that the answer is, of course, yes — and Nichols and his filmmaking team are the ones who have undercut it. Benjamin's confection of a happy ending is demonstrated (by Nichols and his filmmaking team) to be just that: a sweet and disengaged fantasy. But Brackman objects to Benjamin's "slipping away" at the ending without having to reconstitute himself as a model of counter-cultural resistance; Nichols "is forever reintegrating his material into protective conventions" that comfort and reward unadventurous audiences.[33] Brackman enters at this point upon his sociological thesis: that characters like Benjamin Braddock are an anachronism, "Eisenhower youths" who "were forever finding poignant contradictions in the lives of their parents" and who "rejected a number of life styles within the system but never deeply questioned the necessity of the system itself."[34]

Brackman's essay at this point stops being an interpretative essay about the film at hand; it becomes a treatment for a rewrite of the film. His thesis is that "Johnson youths" have moved beyond Benjamin's anguish about conformity, "driven by the need to change the system or to take revenge upon it."[35] Brackman understands Nichols's film, but isn't satisfied with the film Nichols successfully made: "I suggested earlier," he writes, "that the principal reason Benjamin couldn't look forward to becoming an adult was that his environment had offered him no viable ideal of adulthood. He had to imagine for himself what a creditable grown-up life might look like, and he failed to come up with much of a picture."[36]

Nichols would absolutely agree with such an interpretation of the film — it's a characterization of the film as a negative satire. But Brackman presses his ideological agenda, citing Benjamin's ideal situations at a prestigious eastern college and at home in Southern California as parlays to Benjamin's becoming part of the vanguard of the new social revolutions taking place in sexuality, politics, the arts, the media. "The Graduate," Brackman writes, "obfuscates the truth about Johnson America, which is that hardly *any* of its most interesting young men look forward to 'making it' in our present society."[37] Brackman believes *The Graduate* ought to reflect his version of "contemporary reality,"[38] one in which the Benjamins of the Johnson era have turned a social corner on the Eisenhower era's quiet desperations: *The Graduate* should depict the enlightened path Brackman and his peers ("There are now a million such Benjamins, with visions of a healthier culture"[39]) have already trod; Nichols's film, he argues, should provide both the problem and the solution, the culture to be avoided and the counter-culture to be embraced. Mark Harris writes that "some members of the young left" thought of the film "as a failed newsreel, a dishonest portrait of their lives that reflected only passivity,"[40] yet in spring 1968 SDS radicals who'd taken over the President's office at Columbia University took turns sneaking out to see the film.[41] *The Graduate*— in particular, its famously ambiguous conclusion — challenges the audience to find a solution that its protagonists can't themselves envision. Historical hindsight tells us that the tentative progress Brackman's "Johnson youths" had made by July 1968 toward alternative paths to adulthood began to bog down the very next month at the Democratic National Convention in Chicago, and subsequent decades would reveal a wearying pattern of Aquarian Age addictions, in-fighting, and (that most dreaded of all Sixties endings) conformity.

Richard Corliss summarizes Brackman's long-winded argument so succinctly that one may imagine he must have encountered it in *The New Yorker* and allowed its digested thesis to become his own: Benjamin's "revolution," writes Corliss, "is pure fifties: like the best minds of the Eisenhower-McCarthy era, he simply withdraws." Summarizing more radical sentiments expressed by Brackman and Reck, Corliss believes that the film's confection of a traditional happy ending is a sell-out by the film rather than a sell-out by its protagonist. Corliss permits Webb, writing in the early 1960s, an Eisenhower-era perspective, but feels the sea change of the Sixties had already been mainstreamed to the point that, "In 1967, Ben was less an apotheosis than an anachronism."[42] Why all this enthusiasm, critics like Brackman and Corliss wonder, for a nostalgic look back on a poor soul like Benjamin who never quite sees the light? Brackman and Corliss share the assumption that cultural transformation had, by 1968, become a done deal, that everyone had already dropped out of the deadly culture of conformity bequeathed by the parents of the Baby Boom. Brackman ends his essay with the claim that neither Webb in his novel nor Nichols in his film has significantly advanced an argument already made by J. D. Salinger in *The Catcher in the Rye* more than a decade earlier. Ron Howard, watching the film from the historical remove of several decades, consistently and revealingly retains Holden Caulfield's preferred diction when he says, "I don't think there is a single character in *The Graduate* that is not a phony, to one degree or another, except Benjamin and Elaine, and only in the scenes when they are alone together."[43]

Salinger's insight (and Webb's, and Nichols's) is that there will always be phonies. Yet Howard betrays the conventional romantic misapprehension of the film when he identifies Benjamin and Elaine, once they have found each other, as exceptions. Now that the dust has settled on the revolution of the Sixties, are conformity and phoniness the exception or the rule of our culture? Brackman suggests that "most of the audience" at his screening began to gather coats and move toward the aisles when Benjamin and Elaine are boarding the bus, as if "anticipating" some aesthetic compromise of or challenge to the triumphant happy ending they'd just been made to witness.[44] In a largely appreciative cultural report on the phenomenon of *The Graduate* published the same month as Brackman's essay in *The New Yorker*, Hollis Alpert concludes with a striking series of observations, including an acknowledgment that Nichols has shrewdly "lined up old Hollywood with avant-garde Hollywood. He has contrived a truly real ending, and a most positive one at that. Honesty wins the day. Sex without love has been put in its place. Ancient taboos have been struck down. Material values have been shown to be hollow. As uninhibited and refreshing as *The Graduate* is, we are still left in a fantasy land. 'Most of us,' a friend of mine ruefully commented, 'still miss the bus.'"[45]

It's a gloomy prognostication on the counter-cultural project: the implication made by Alpert's friend is that the "bus" is not the dreary cross-section of social drones we actually see on the Santa Barbara bus with Benjamin and Elaine at the end of the film but yet another fantasy, conjured by the mass audience and not depicted in the film, of a counter-cultural magic bus that most quietly desperate people never summon the nerve to board. Brackman condemns *The Graduate* in his essay because he believes that most people, especially those with the demographics of Benjamin and Elaine, know where the magic bus stops and are boarding it to ride right out of the old, dead system; Alpert's friend seems to think somehow that Benjamin and Elaine are, in fact, on that magic bus as the film ends. Neither Alpert's friend nor Brackman has seen the film for what it is. And Alpert's friend, despite his failure to see the film, may nonetheless have the longer perspective on what has eventually become of the counter-culture of the Sixties.

That *The Graduate* has very little to say about the counter-culture — either positive or negative — is a matter of aesthetic choice, not aesthetic failure. The film Lawrence Turman and Mike Nichols created isn't about the counter-culture at all; it's about the majority culture. It's a negative satire, and its target is the affluent, materialist bankruptcy of post–World War II American culture and the manufacture of the next generation of hollow men. Most specifically, it's about one young hollow man in training, without ideas for how to conduct a meaningful life, drowning in a culture similarly without ideas. Nichols summarizes his narrative as "the story of a not particularly bright, not particularly remarkable but worthy kid drowning among objects and things, committing moral suicide by allowing himself to be used finally like an object or a thing."[46] The backlash in the mainstream and underground media may have been directed at Nichols and his film as instigators, but what fueled the critics' fury was disgust with the lemmings of the mass audience.

The backlash, with few exceptions, came from the film's astonishing success — its box-office numbers suggested that both kids and their parents were seeing the film, laughing and cheering side by side to Nichols's well-choreographed rising action and crises. (Actually, more careful market research subsequently revealed that audiences over 30 were mostly staying away.[47]) Audiences — particularly the youth culture — spoke adoringly of the protagonist as a spokesman for their own emergent rebellion, and the critical backlash condemned such devotion as blindness: how could Benjamin Braddock be a spokesman for anyone else when he can't even speak for himself?

The question is a reasonable one. The young people who paid their way into theaters a dozen or more times could be regarded with skepticism when they claimed that Benjamin spoke for them. The irony couldn't have been more piquant: through most of the narrative, Benjamin is sullen, inarticulate, and a champion conformist despite himself. For such a precocious student (graduated with honors and awards, presumably from an Ivy, before his 21st birthday), he's a painfully slow learner, except as a social mimic of the adults he ostensibly desires to be "different" than. He is, most certainly, NOT a *spokesman*. He's profoundly inarticulate. No moment in the film better encapsulates this essential verbal emptiness in his character than the poolside scene when Mr. Braddock, exasperated by his son's newly acquired indolence, demands to know "what those four years of college were for, what was the point of all that hard work." "You got me," says Benjamin, with a defiant but misplaced sense of triumph.

This moment comes across as a condemnation of Mr. Braddock's vainglorious aspirations for his son, but if we fail to see that the film has simultaneously presented us with a protagonist who has absconded from responsibility for his own life, we miss an important point and are in the awkward position of potentially misreading everything that follows. Audiences may have received Benjamin's put-down line to his father in the same sneering spirit as Marlon Brando's Johnny Strabler in *The Wild One* (Laslo Benedek, 1953), made 15 years earlier; when asked, "What're you rebelling against, Johnny?" Brando's character famously shoots back, "Whaddya got?" Yet the two scenes are worlds apart. The vision of Brando's brute of a biker in *The Wild One* is the sociology of the disadvantaged. Johnny Strabler can't see anything but blind alleys and dead ends down which to drive his bike, because that's all there is to see. The film is in sympathy with him even as it exploits him; poor Johnny can't think his way out of his cage. On the other hand, Benjamin Braddock has been given ample opportunities, one presumes with Brackman, to "tune in" at his prestigious eastern university — his film can't provide the same alibis for him that *The Wild One* provides for Johnny Strabler — nor does it try. If lying on a raft, drinking beer bought with his father's money is the best he can come up with, Benjamin *ought* to be a little worried about his future.

The backlash critics dismissed the film because its enthusiastic 1968 audiences cheered the ending and burst from the theater into the streets bearing the banner of Benjamin Braddock, counter-cultural hero, mostly saying hooray for our side. The critics were right to be alarmed at audience response, right to be gadflies attempting to inject genuine counter-cultural perspective into a "debate" that had devolved to mono-vision, to a failure on both sides finally to see Benjamin in all his failure and compromise. The backlash critics were shortsighted, however, to dismiss the film simply because audiences were simplistic in their embrace of it. Taking their cue from the audiences they meant to confront, the backlash critics also settled for a simplistic interpretation of the film. Wayne Schuth writes, "That [Benjamin] cannot free himself makes *The Graduate* a true tragedy"[48]; yet the character's failure does not necessitate that the film must be a failure, too.

On frequent campus stops designed by Joseph E. Levine's Embassy Pictures publicity machine, Nichols was notorious for dashing the illusions of fresh-faced rebels-in-waiting by making the pronouncement upon his protagonists that Benjamin and Elaine will become their parents in five years. The line represents a director's frustrated interest in rekindling debate about a film whose mass popularity had swept the narrative away from his control. Brackman can't ignore Nichols's observation and duly alludes to it, only to immediately dismiss it as disingenuous: Nichols's prophecy "remains unsaid in the film — young audiences would find it unbearably offensive."[49] While he is right that college students received Nichols's statement with dismay, no one finds Nichols's statement (interpreted as a pronouncement upon "a million such Benjamins" like Brackman) more offensive than Brackman himself: "'The Graduate' offers youth a subversive message: You cannot sustain an opposition to America; find someone to submit with, if you can. It seems unaware that history has upped the price of submission. In the fifties, 'conformity' was the dragon against which valedictorians tilted their earnest lances. The trap of the sixties is complicity."[50]

But why does Brackman claim that Nichols's jejune prophecy "remains unsaid in the film"? Back to the text: Is there any evidence, particularly in the scenes in Berkeley, to suggest Benjamin (or Elaine) has a "different" vision of adult life than the one their parents are so anxious for them to embrace, thus legitimizing the lives of the older generation? The backlash critics assume — alongside the audiences they scold for failure to see Benjamin as a pawn of the mainstream, conformist culture — that Benjamin Braddock's point of view is *The Graduate*'s point of view. If Benjamin fails to grasp a positive vision of the counter-culture, then so must Mike Nichols's film. But the problem of point of view in a well-made narrative is always more complicated, always more open to interpretation than a simple equation of protagonist and film. The backlash critics have dismissed (and continue to dismiss) *The Graduate* as crowd-pleasing rather than truth-telling based on an assumption that the film posits Benjamin Braddock as a counter-cultural hero. Certainly, this is how most mainstream film audiences have received him.

Yet taken solely on the aesthetic terms of the film itself, Benjamin is an even less-likely candidate for counter-cultural hero-worship than those two hard-times cultural conformists, Clyde Barrow and Bonnie Parker, stars of the other mega-hit embraced by youth culture in 1967 carrying over into 1968. Bonnie and Clyde proceed on the familiar capitalist assumption that money will buy them happiness and a ticket out of their small-town blues. Even their short run through the mid-western United States to the banjo accompaniment of Flatt and Scruggs provides ample time for Bonnie in particular to determine they have miscalculated their own solution. They haven't only doomed themselves by breaking the law and thus bringing down on their own heads the consequences of defying establishment order; like Wyatt and Billy in *Easy Rider*, they have doomed themselves even if by some miracle they should happen to escape the wrath of the law, precisely because they have accepted the terms of the culture: that material wealth is the easy answer to a deeper, spiritual need. Bonnie and Clyde, Wyatt and Billy, Benjamin and Elaine: none of these counter-cultural couples ever manages to articulate the source of spiritual fulfillment. What they all articulate is dissatisfaction. Benjamin and Elaine, like Bonnie and Clyde, commit outrages against their culture and voluntarily exile themselves from what is familiar, their "inheritance"— in Bonnie and Clyde's case, a hard life in a Dust Bowl town; in Benjamin and Elaine's, a soft life in Beverly Hills. But Benjamin and Elaine have no clue about genuine alternatives to their culture.

The Graduate is a satire of cultural conformity, of human beings drowning in a sea of affluence, but far from exempting Benjamin, Mike Nichols's film ultimately satirizes its own protagonist as the very center of the problem: here is a bright, talented young man with all the cultural advantages of education (hence the ironic title) but without the imagination to see another way. Perhaps this makes him a dullard and thus beneath our notice, but such a sweeping generalization also dismisses many ordinary people in compelling kitchen-sink dramas (and many ordinary people sitting in theaters watching them). David Thomson claims that Benjamin's "acquiescence is so passive as to absolve him from responsibility,"[51] but passivity is no excuse in Benjamin's privileged case, nor does the film ask us to absolve him.

I. Introduction

Four decades later, from a vantage where the obituaries for 1960s counter-cultural idealism have become a verdict, it may be possible to return to *The Graduate* and see the film for what it actually is, rather than what it has been misunderstood to be. In his mini-essay on *The Graduate* as one of the several-hundred films designated so far by the National Film Registry for historic preservation, Daniel Eagan might be expected to have a longer perspective, but he concludes that the film "never challenges the status quo — it ultimately accepts it."[52] The film's bright, glossy surfaces continue to prove impenetrable, both for the characters and for many viewers. *The Graduate* is not what its first-run, ticket-buying audience (and subsequent legions of fans of the numerous video releases) largely thought it was: the promotion of a protagonist as spokesman for the emergent counter-culture. Nor is *The Graduate* what its backlash critics (and the resulting critical consensus) accused it of, mistaking its protagonist for the film itself: a safe, conformist fairy tale of boy-gets-girl, lives happily-ever-after. Mike Nichols's film skewers everything in sight, including its protagonist and his rescued princess. Mrs. Robinson is not ultimately Nichols's most painful poster-child of lost opportunity. That distinction must belong to Benjamin Braddock. Especially in its third act, *The Graduate* prophesies the lamentations that have accompanied Death-of-the-Sixties rhetoric ever since the 1970s. The mostly young audiences who stormed from movie theaters in 1968, grinning triumphantly, missed the fact that what they'd witnessed was a deconstruction rather than a construction of their counter-cultural happy ending. To fail to see Benjamin as the perfect embodiment of his culture, incapable of imagining his way out of a bankrupt social and philosophical labyrinth, is ultimately a failure to see the film. It's a demand to see a film that Mike Nichols and his filmmaking team didn't make, never intended to make.

Mike Nichols's post–*Graduate* directorial career is instructive for understanding the rhetorical strategy of his satirical film-making. The two films he made immediately after *The Graduate* were *Catch-22* (1970) and *Carnal Knowledge* (1971). Like his first film, *Who's Afraid of Virginia Woolf?* (1966), these films are negative satires. Their characters, with the exception of Yossarian (Alan Arkin) in *Catch-22*, are simultaneously victims, products, and exemplars of a sick culture — nothing more, nothing less. They, like the cultural environments that have produced them, are indelibly objects of Nichols's satire, and while the films allow us access to their points of view (and even sympathy with their predicaments), this should not insinuate blind loyalties in us that leave us incapable of seeing the inherent rot in characters like George

(Richard Burton) and Martha (Elizabeth Taylor) in *Who's Afraid of Virginia Woolf?* or Jonathan (Jack Nicholson) and Sandy (Art Garfunkel) in *Carnal Knowledge*. Yossarian, Joseph Heller's iconic anti-hero played by Alan Arkin with nebbish verve in Nichols's film version of *Catch-22*, is in this sense an anomaly in Nichols's oeuvre: a character who, although stuck in a sick culture and thus subject through much of the narrative to its whims and vagaries, nonetheless can see and clearly articulate the culture's malaise. According to Schuth, an over-arching theme of Nichols's cinematic vision is the man "trapped by his past culture. He cannot break out; he can only achieve understanding and be true to his own values."[53] Benjamin Braddock understands that he's stuck; Yossarian presents an exception, a genuine anti-hero who refuses to be trapped.

In the second act of Nichols's career, following a cinematic silence of eight years (spanning from the critical and box-office disappointment of *The Fortune* in 1975 to the critical and box-office success of *Silkwood* in 1983), such anti-heroic characters, in the moral right and at odds with the sick culture around them, shine through the familiar satirical darkness of his narratives: Meryl Streep as Karen Silkwood, Melanie Griffith as Tess McGill in *Working Girl* (1988), even Tom Hanks in *Charlie Wilson's War* (2007). (In a similar revolution of his formal aesthetic, perhaps stung by those early charges of wearing his stylistic influences on his sleeve, Nichols would evolve from an obsessively formalist visual stylist to a practitioner of the Invisible Style characteristic of Hollywood's Golden Age. Lee Hill quotes Nichols on his change of aesthetic: "'[Y]ou use the technical things to make people completely unaware of technical things.' Nichols the expressionist ha[s] become Nichols the seamless craftsman."[54]) These are later developments in Nichols's rhetorical strategy, however, and his depiction of positive philosophical movement in anti-heroic characters remains exceptional in a vision that has always been, in the larger satirical tradition, essentially negative. The product of satire, a satirist hopes, is ultimately positive, but the immediate argument of satire is to direct a fun-house mirror at human madness in hopes that the audience will see a sick culture for what it is. The young audiences that recessed from theaters, beaming in non-ironic delight at Benjamin Braddock's "triumph," could not have been very reflective about the narrative's trajectory. Benjamin Braddock is no Yossarian.

Nichols speculated that the first post-narrative crisis of his characters in *The Graduate* would have come several blocks later, still on the bus, when Elaine would have exclaimed that she didn't have anything to wear. Nichols says, "My feelings about, for instance, the ending, what it means, who Elaine really is, what happens between her and Benjamin, are, at this point, just my

In a Beverly Hills backyard, Benjamin Braddock (Dustin Hoffman) drifts. The montage sequence built by director Mike Nichols (in dark windbreaker next to the diving board, with three unidentified crew members) became one of the most memorable stylistic flourishes of the film. With Simon and Garfunkel's "The Sounds of Silence" reprised from the titles, Nichols assembled a mesmerizing visual essay on Benjamin's alienation: he drifts through the summer, and the climactic image of the montage equates the plastic raft with Mrs. Robinson. Nichols told Joseph Gelmis shortly after the film's release that *The Graduate* is about a "kid drowning among objects and things, committing moral suicide by allowing himself to be used finally like an object or thing."

feelings, and my opinion really doesn't have much more validity than anybody else's. Who's to say I'm right and somebody else is wrong? I have certain very specific thoughts about it. I've expressed them to kids and they've been stunned and enraged. In my mind, it's always been that in five miles she's going to say, 'My God, I haven't got any clothes.'"⁵⁵

This is hardly the vision of a filmmaker who has over-romanticized the transcendent, anti-heroic qualities of his protagonists. Nichols has always talked about Benjamin and Elaine as not terribly strong or perceptive dupes of their culture, and a close, careful look at *The Graduate* only underscores this reading of the film's main characters. The immediate and longer-term backlash-dismissal of *The Graduate* by film criticism continues to perpetuate the misapprehension of Benjamin and Elaine and of the film's rhetoric. No, *The Graduate* does not provide a positive vision of counter-cultural philosophy. (Ultimately, how many films of this era did?) *The Graduate*'s argument posits that capitulation to the known enemy is inevitably simpler than rugged, individualistic invention of a viable alternative. Nichols says, "A lot of us have the fantasy of breaking out, of dropping everything, of disappearing with that one girl, and extending a certain feeling forever, [... a]nd the fantasy of breaking through everything and living for that is a very powerful one. I think it can't be done. I think a lot of people, myself included, wish to God it could be done. And that's what the end means to me. That I'm moved by somebody who wants to try and do it and I'm pulling for them. But I don't know if they can make it."[56]

The other great sleeper success-story of that cinematic era, *Easy Rider* (1969), an even more unlikely, shaggier dog than *The Graduate* as a box-office smash, drew similarly doom-saying conclusions for sustained counter-cultural growth. Like Benjamin and Elaine, *Easy Rider*'s protagonists present no viable alternatives to the sick culture around them. Sitting by a campfire near the end of the film, Wyatt (Peter Fonda) is struck by the epiphany that, in much the same way as Bonnie and Clyde, they "blew it" by getting their hands (and fuel tanks) dirty with the dream of the big drug score, of money as panacea for culture-sickness (rather than seeing it for a root cause). In Robert Altman's *M*A*S*H** (1970), Hawkeye and Trapper John stand within, yet beyond, the madness of "Korea's" Catch-22 and seem to embody a vision of anti-heroic, life-affirming efficiency and effectiveness; yet they are capable of remorseless cruelty and deception that make them, at best, ambiguous saviors—and Altman would retreat into wholly negative satire in ensembles from *Nashville* (1975) to *Short Cuts* (1993) to *Gosford Park* (2001), full of monsters and well-meaning but ineffectual by-standers. Robert Kolker, in his massive study of New Hollywood iconoclasm, *A Cinema of Loneliness*, likens *The Graduate* to *M*A*S*H** as "hymn[s] to the passive side of the rebellion of the sixties,"[57] negative satires that say more about what is wrong than about what could be right. Glenn Man chastises Nichols's default "predilection for satire," which "ignores the significance of Ben's rescue of Elaine and makes both the butt of the joke along with everyone else in the film, rather than its preferred standard of measure."[58] Yet Nichols has offered audiences at a crucial moment in cultural history an opportunity to see the danger of aimlessness in a life built on negative recoil rather than on a positive vision.

As if to cap the era's counter-cultural argument with a rhetorical flourish,

I. Introduction

Martin Scorsese posed Travis Bickle in *Taxi Driver* (1976) as the antidote to the illusion of the anti-hero. Travis has no problem with taking action to effect positive change — and while he is celebrated in the press and in a letter from the grateful Pittsburgh parents of the waif (played by Jodie Foster) whom he has "saved," the bloodbath Scorsese draws for us at the end of his film leaves scant room for interpreting Travis' actions as exemplary. In a sense, *Taxi Driver* closed an era, and what emerged was a new, non-ironic age of heroes, typically in some fantastic, melodramatic guise: Luke Skywalker and Han Solo in *Star Wars* (George Lucas, 1977), *Superman* (Richard Donner, 1978), the Indiana Jones serials, the Rambo franchise, and the Dirty Harry films (in which Clint Eastwood plays Travis Bickle with a badge and without the mohawk). The filmmakers who created these characters envisioned a pure, unambiguous relationship between protagonist, narrative, and audience — the purest, most surefire formula for box-office success. Their protagonists' actions were intended as the will of the film itself, as well as the will of the audience: a perfect simpatico. These are profoundly sincere, anti-ironic narratives of protagonist as hero, champion of the majority culture. If these protagonists depict negative forces in human culture, they do so with the conviction that their protagonists can right wrongs and promote positive action, even if only a few are on the pro-social side of a culture — even if only a lone hero with a Millennium Falcon, a long-barreled automatic weapon, or at least a long whip remains standing to assert his principled conviction. They are all variations on the fantasy of the Western, on the rule of civilized order.

The iconic films of the 1960s, during the era that stretches roughly from *The Graduate* and *Bonnie and Clyde* in 1967 to *Taxi Driver* in 1976, are as typically characterized by irony and negative, satirical rhetoric as the iconic films from *Star Wars* until the opening of the Sundance era of independent filmmaking in the late 1980s are not. *The Graduate*'s idiom is the ironic idiom of the New Hollywood, sometimes called the Hollywood Renaissance, when filmmakers' default narrative strategy might separate a character's point of view from the film's point of view as often as it made the two consonant (seeing character, film, and audience bonded by an un-nuanced, shared vision). The problem of audience reception in *The Godfather* films is a case in point. Francis Ford Coppola sought to make powerful genre narratives about a sick culture (a politically corrupt, racist, class-bound America beginning at the turn of the 20th century, during the great waves of European emigration, and reaching across three generations to the era of the multi-national corporation) and an immigrant family that believes it can operate parallel to but separate from the sick culture. The Corleones find themselves assimilated in ways that obliterate all that was once supposedly superior in them to American conformity and injustice. Despite the fact that Coppola loads on all sorts of evidence that the Corleones and their Sicilian obsession with *vendetta* (not to mention patriarchy) have never held a moral high-card to their American counterparts, audiences thrilled to the Corleones' old-world traditionalism and palpable family-feeling. In an essay on genre ideology in Coppola's Godfather Trilogy, Glenn Man writes, "The tension that arises from the competing four myths — the Mafia as evil, society as evil, the romanticized individual, the romanticized family — [...] surfaces and becomes palpable again at the end, beginning with the baptism sequence which Coppola purportedly intended to be ironic — revealing the hypocrisy of Michael, the family, and religion." Yet Man argues that the audience's perceptive apparatus has been tampered with by the skillful use of vicarious identification, with the result that, by this point late in the narrative of the first film in the trilogy, "the audience has bought into Michael's fight for power to the extent that the reaction can only be mixed and complicated."[59] Something similar is at work in *The Graduate*: a filmmaker underestimates the audience's genuine hunger for non-ironic narrative resolution at his peril.

The Corleones' power (as personalities, not as ruthless underworld thugs) is seductive — so seductive that it's easy to overlook (as the Corleones themselves studiously do) that this power is both destructive and, ultimately, self-destructive. In the ironic sepia tones of Coppola's rhetoric, audiences can overlook (as Coppola and his film-making team do not) the very unsentimental operations of the Family's business. It's the old story of the charismatic power of cinema: it's hard not to love a star. *The Godfather* (1972) and *The Godfather, Part II* (1974) made or re-made some of the most compelling icons of a cinematic age (Marlon Brando, Al Pacino, Robert DeNiro), and audiences were and continue to be seduced by that star-power into an almost involuntary swoon of acceptance of the Corleones' ruthless predation.

In *The Graduate*, Dustin Hoffman became Hollywood's most unlikely star of all, not only because of his unconventional appearance but also because of his character's moping, uncharismatic ... charisma. Nichols alludes to the mysticism of stardom in an interview with Mark Harris: "That's what a great movie actor does. They don't know how they do it, and I don't know how they do it, but the difference is unimaginable, shocking. This feeling that they have such a connection with the camera that they can do what they want because they own the audience."[60] Beyond the power of the star, the cinema's rhetoric also commands a bond (through Benjamin's ubiquity scene-by-scene and frame-by-frame, through close-ups, through subjective camera set-ups) between audience and character that further intensifies the cinema's mystical tradition of audience identification and compelled sympathy; as a result, we gain ironic distance on Benjamin Braddock only by paying the very closest attention to what transpires on screen, as well as to the style in which it is depicted.

In writing about *The Graduate*, a common criticism of the backlash critics is a perceived tonal shift in the second half of the film. The first half, these critics say, is all enclosed spaces and broad, almost burlesque comedy; the second half opens up the landscape and turns the narrative into a conventional love story, in which, as Richard Schickel puts it, Benjamin "suddenly starts to emerge as a romantic hero of the unhyphenated variety. [... T]he emotional distance from which we previously viewed him — a distance absolutely essential for satire — suddenly disappears."[61] The implication is that the first half of the film, with its lampoonish humor, is unmistakably the arena of satire, while the shift to the generic characteristics of romance in the second half signals the end of satire and the introduction, mid-film, of non-ironic, even sentimental story-telling. Such a conclusion is symptomatic of a failure to see that the film, which has largely used Benjamin as our lens for viewing the sick culture throughout the film's first half, continues to offer us Benjamin's distorted, hyper-romantic subjectivity (Mrs. Robinson as witch; Mr. Robinson as cruel, patriarchal despot; Elaine as tragically beautiful damsel in distress) while beginning to direct more and more of its satirical gaze *at* Benjamin, rather than merely at the madness all around him.

Richard Corliss, for instance, dismisses the film's narrative grotesqueries as a strategy to "force a sympathetic identification onto the viewer in the simplest way possible: by turning all the other characters (except Ben's eventual true love, Elaine) into easily recognizable villains."[62] This is, of course, a strategy that could be adopted by a character himself— as Benjamin in fact does with all the adults around him, dutifully revealed to us as his point of view (and not necessarily the film's). David Denby senses Nichols's intention when he describes Mrs. Robinson as "a fairy-tale monster"[63] after the affair sours, but he misattributes this vision to Nichols rather than Nichols's protagonist, Benjamin. Stephen Farber and Estelle Changas note correctly that we first see Mrs. Robinson as Ben initially sees her: "a young man's deliciously provocative sexual fantasy come to life"— only later is she transformed into "a hideous witch."[64] Yet Farber and Changas are puzzled when, in the film's second half, Benjamin and Elaine are not depicted as erudite, fascinating exemplars of the best of the counter-culture, but rather as vapid and insipid, "surrounded by modish out-of-focus shots of flowers and foliage."[65] Mark Cousins recognizes in these romance clichés a conscious design choice by Nichols, the "ironic pastels" depicting a faded sense of the American dream.[66] Nichols told Gelmis in 1968 that the critics' complaint about "structural slippage" in the film's second half was a misunderstanding of ironic intention: "[I]t was deliberate on our parts. The picture changes in every way. The whole section with Mrs. Robinson is hard and glossy and Beverly Hills and cold and sexy in that way that things can be sexy when you get laid without a great deal of feeling. And with Elaine and his fantasy of Elaine, everything changes into a kind of fantasy prettiness."[67]

We've assumed from his early alienation that Benjamin is onto the secret that the prevailing adult culture around him is bankrupt and that he will, as the sharp kid just returned from his college success, provide thoughtful alternatives to the culture depicted so negatively everywhere he looks. Indeed, Brackman claims that "the movie's importance rests upon our assumption that Benjamin represents the best, the vanguard, of his generation."[68] But Benjamin isn't a part of the solution; he's simply more of the problem. The second half of the film represents, despite what seems to be a positive flurry of motion on Benjamin's part, a retreat into the safety of fantasy and the familiar, not the hard work of re-imagining one's life and possibilities. Glenn Man writes, "From the perspective of more than two decades, the contemporaneous complaint of its lack of unity strikes one as more significant for what it reveals about its detractors' classical sensibilities than about any structural flaw the movie may possess."[69] To paraphrase Brackman, then: *The Graduate*'s importance rests upon our understanding Benjamin as a cautionary reflection of our own failures of nerve in resisting capitulation and conformity.

A satire's faith in its rhetoric and its audience is that, having established the problem for the audience's consideration, the audience will emerge from the theater's darkness into an illuminated sense of direction, *away* from the negative depiction and (presumably) towards a positive alternative (which is how Brackman determines a film's "importance"). *The Graduate* presents in its second half the *illusion* of solved problems: love lost but then found, escape from various forms of entrapment. But all along, the narrative's ambiguity has questioned whether Benjamin and Elaine ever genuinely envision an exit route from their sick culture toward a positive alternative. During the second half of the film, its "romance" iteration, *The Graduate* does not stop its satirical humor, much of which has consistently been at Benjamin's expense. In the scenes during the first half of the film (those with the Taft Hotel desk clerk played by Buck Henry and particularly those scenes of his gradual seduction by Mrs. Robinson), Benjamin is overwhelmed by the enormity of the contemplated affair. Nichols has Hoffman play these scenes as a long string of humiliations, like the ones perpetrated at the hands of Benjamin's parents but more painful because Benjamin has sought out and abets these new indignities. Despite the overwhelming evidence of moral conscience and social manners, he keeps himself in the line of fire. He's an awkward, ill-at-ease, but ultimately still lovable child (thanks to the ironic animation with which Hoffman renders Benjamin's passivity), and our sympathy for him in his predicament grows.

In the second half of the film, Benjamin is still awkward, still ill-at-ease, and his childishness is still played for laughs, as in the scene in the college library where Benjamin's increasingly aggressive, anti-social behavior culminates in the question-tantrum, designed to humiliate the woman he supposedly loves: "It wasn't in his car, was it?" (The question, as we will see, is especially cruel given what he has learned in confidence about the Robinsons' family history—concealed Robinson intelligence that he may have passed along to Elaine.) Once Elaine begins to entertain Benjamin's attentions in Berkeley, they are like tedious schoolchildren playing "house," and *The Graduate* makes no effort to present either of them as noble, principled, or exemplary of anything but the paucity of choices their culture (and their own "counter-cultural" imaginations) may afford. Man and Bapis both make a point of citing the impassioned words of Miriam Weiss, a Stony Brook co-ed quoted in *The New York Times* at the height of *The Graduate*'s 1968 popularity: "I identified with Ben [...] He was confused about his future and his place in the world, as I am. He was chasing an ideal in spite of all the obstacles that society put in his path in the attempt to co-opt or eliminate him."[70] Yet the example Weiss gives to illustrate her point is Elaine's late rejoinder to her mother, "Not for me!"—which in its rhetoric is an eloquent example of Elaine's *repudiation* of the values in which the elder generation has drowned, not an articulation of what the "ideal" might be. Benjamin and Elaine's solution to the dilemma of their families' understandable objections to their continued contact, for instance, is to use marriage the same way older generations had: to get married as soon as possible as a means of solving social problems—the very "solution" once offered, at the end of a symbolic shotgun, to the Robinsons themselves. "Ben's is to be, after all is said and done, a conventional, even a bourgeois, future," writes Murray Pomerance; the film's style promises a "break from convention," but its romantic-genre plot line "spells a heteronormative love triumphing over every obstacle to achieve blissful harmony and nothing more. Was it really this and only this, we must wonder, that Ben's important education was preparing him for?"[71] Mark Cousins writes that *The Graduate*'s "ending was as open as closed romantic realism is closed."[72] In other words, there's no happy ending to *The Graduate*, only a wistful, heavily ironic fantasy.

The continued infantilism of Benjamin and Elaine in *The Graduate* should not "play cute" to audiences willing to sort through tone and distinguish Benjamin's impoverished perspective from the richer ambiguity of the film's point of view. Naturally for audiences who do not absorb the tonal ironies of the film's second half, the famous long take of Benjamin and Elaine on the bus at the end of the film seems to be grafted uncomfortably onto a conventional romance with a "happy ending." But for audiences who have been left increasingly ill-at-ease and at ironic remove from their beloved protagonist throughout the unfolding of the second half of the film, this final scene delivers a confirming verdict upon Benjamin and Elaine's failure to imagine alternative futures. If the backlash critics wanted to express disappointment with audiences who left the movie theater thinking Benjamin Braddock was their hero, so be it. But Mike Nichols's film is very aware from beginning to end — and especially in the Benjamin-inspired subjectivity of the romance conventions of *The Graduate*'s second half — that Benjamin is no hero. He's just another lost soul on the bus.

3

The Graduates

One of the most compelling qualities of *The Graduate*'s enormous cultural appeal is located in the curiously fecund blankness of Benjamin Braddock, the novel's and then later the film's central character. If Gustave Flaubert famously observed, "*Madame Bovary, c'est moi,*" to demonstrate how invested he was in his most vivid and enduring character, the production history of *The Graduate* reveals how many personalities believed, "Benjamin Braddock, that's me." Would the effect of Benjamin's character be as universal if he were more outspoken, more idiosyncratic? Or is it precisely his undeveloped inner life that makes him so adaptable to the mass audience, and even before that, to the various men who signed on to realize him aesthetically, first in print and then in celluloid? Mike Nichols has said, "Benjamin was Charles Webb [...] first. Then he was Buck Henry [...]. Then he was me. And then he was Dustin Hoffman. [...] Certainly in my mind, through the whole picture, he's both literally me and metaphorically me."[1]

Charles Webb was the first Benjamin Braddock, giving the protagonist of his novel his own tall, blond, well-educated characteristics. In *Pictures at a Revolution*, his excellent study of the five Oscar-nominated films from 1967, Mark Harris describes Webb's novel as "cool-temperatured, deadpan prose."[2] Harris relates an episode from Webb's own life, in which his pregnant girlfriend's parents removed the coed from school and subjected her to an abortion. Although Webb eventually reunited with the young woman and married her, the trauma of the incident fed the inception of the novel,[3] in which the hyperbolic intervention of the Robinsons in their daughter's life drives a similar, temporary wedge between Benjamin and Elaine. Webb's depiction of Benjamin's quest to get to the church on time is forever tinged by his sense of the moral upper hand. One of the most notorious alterations made by the filmmakers to Webb's original story is the timing of Benjamin's climactic arrival at the church. It was vital to Webb that Benjamin stop the ceremony before its official conclusion. In a letter to the editor of *The New Republic* expressing his outrage at the film's tampering with his novel's ending (as well as with Stanley Kauffmann's laudatory praise of the cinematic ending), Webb wrote: "In the book the strength of the climax is that [Benjamin's] moral attitudes make it necessary for him to reach the girl before she becomes the wife of someone else [...] In the film version it makes little difference whether he gets there in time or not. As such, there is little difference between his relationship to Mrs. Robinson and his relationship to Elaine, both of them being essentially immoral."[4] What Webb failed to acknowledge at the time (and what the film's alteration highlighted) was that not even the sacred institution of marriage was immune from social manipulation; however deeply Webb himself regarded the sacramental properties of the wedding vow, the narrative he had created envisioned a world of cynical opportunism, where marriage is a cage, and where his young protagonists see their own marriage more as an escape from their own cages than as their overwhelming sense of belonging to one another. Looking back, Webb acknowledges a "cringe" as he reconsiders the strident claims of his self-righteous youth, admitting to Harris how "tightly" he'd been "locked [...] into that world at the time."[5] No doubt his 1968 attitudes must be understood as residing at least in part in that still-fresh sense of having been denied fatherhood.

Webb's novel performed predictably as a first book by an unknown author[6]: it disappeared. Its reviews were mixed but respectful. If not for the film, the book would almost certainly be forgotten. In his *New York Times* review of *The Graduate*, Orville Prescott expressed his frustration that *The Graduate* "raises questions about the psychological motivation of its hero and makes no effort to answer them."[7] Although the review's overall response was mildly enthusiastic, such an indictment of characterization begins to suggest how a literary problem became a cinematic opportunity. Webb's novel is composed as a juxtaposition of unaffected, deadpan prose and long, dispassionate scenes of dialogue, in which inflection is often blanched from the words and phrases, such that questions even occasionally appear without question marks. During the Berkeley section of the novel, for instance, Benjamin responds to Elaine's repeated queries about where he intends to go next with his life, "Elaine, [...] what business is it of yours what I do."[8] There is passion implicit in the words, yet a reader comes to the end of the question only to find the familiar signifier of inflection (and thus animation) missing. Surely some of what David Thomson terms Dustin Hoffman's "intricate, self-serving flatness"[9] originates in the seemingly emotionless treatment by Webb of even what would seem to be scenes of high emotion in Webb's novel.

Comparative allusions to J. D. Salinger's archetypal *The Catcher in the*

Rye are apt. The numerous conversations in Webb's novel directing Benjamin to think about or speak to his future remain intact, if often radically condensed, on the screen. Most of them are variations on the conversation Holden Caulfield has with "old Spencer," one of his teachers at Pencey, whom he briefly visits early in the novel, after his expulsion:

> "Do you feel absolutely no concern for your future, boy?"
> "Oh, I feel some concern for my future, all right. Sure. Sure, I do." I thought about it for a minute. "But not too much, I guess. Not too much, I guess."
> "You *will*," old Spencer said. "You will, boy. You will when it's too late."
> I didn't like hearing him say that. It made me sound dead or something. It was very depressing. "I guess I will," I said.[10]

This exchange is most closely paralleled by the one Benjamin has with Mr. Robinson just after Mrs. Robinson's first proposition: asked if anything is wrong, Benjamin says, "No. I'm just—I'm just—I'm just a little worried about my future. I'm a little upset about my future." The cadences, with their repeated phrases suggestive of immediate and long-term anxiety, wind their way towards Mr. Robinson's eventual conclusion that "You'll never be young again."[11] Webb recaptures Salinger's palpable tone of elegiac defeat, of resignation to the social fates.

Richard Corliss credits Webb for much of the film's dramatic interest[12]—this despite this infection of resigned inertia that Webb introduces. Film adaptations sometimes lose the texture of incident that a novel affords its readers; it may be an indication of the novel's essential thinness that not a single incident lost in the cinematic compression of Webb's book to a feature-length but modest 106 minutes is ultimately missed. Rather, the compression tightens causation. Relatively early in the novel, Webb actually introduces us to a side of Benjamin we never glimpse in the film when, in the middle of Chapter 2, he sends Benjamin away on one of those quintessentially 1960s pilgrimages "on the road,"[13] alluding to the Kerouacian quest for authenticity. "I am going out to spend the rest of my life with the real people of this world," Benjamin tells his parents. He distinguishes this cohort by a series of fanciful characteristics: "I want simple honest people that can't even read or write their own name. [...] Ordinary people who don't have big houses. Who don't have swimming pools."[14] The reference to pools as a climactic summation no doubt captured Nichols and Henry's imaginations as they sought the visual shorthand of cinema. This scene concludes Chapter 2, and tellingly, Chapter 3 begins back at his parents' house, with a dismissive opening sentence: "The trip lasted just less than three weeks."[15] Benjamin's great experiment in action takes place entirely off-stage, and while a long, expository dialogue between Benjamin and his father unfolds the disillusioning particulars of the trip, the overall effect is to maintain the narrative's "claustrophobic" grip on Benjamin, which Sylbert acknowledges is one of the ways in which the filmmakers distinguished the first half of the film from the second.[16] Thus, when the film's first half renders Benjamin in a series of tight, airless spaces controlled by adults (until Elaine enters the film more than halfway through the film's running time), *The Graduate* reflects the filmmakers' essential faithfulness to Webb's novel, despite the excision of all reference to Benjamin's romantic quest (albeit in his late-model foreign sports car) to find the "simple people" of America. "I'm leaving home,"[17] Benjamin announces in the novel, but the narration does *not* leave home. At some level, Webb recognized traveling beside Benjamin on his road trip to be, in the formal terms he had envisaged, a dead end. The film takes that recognition literally and removes the trip altogether.

As for the problems with motivation that Prescott raises in his review of the novel, Mike Nichols's film works to clarify them in useful cinematic ways, underscored by montage. In the film, for instance, a sequence of scenes (Mrs. Robinson's first offer to Benjamin the night of his graduation party, the birthday party by the swimming pool, and the consummation of Benjamin and Mrs. Robinson's affair at the Taft Hotel) is knitted together in a tidy causal logic by voice overlaps between scenes. "[T]he thing which you are seeing now leads to the one you are hearing," Nichols has said of the montage sequencing. "This boy in this diving suit at the bottom of this pool has been caused by this moment to call Mrs. Robinson."[18] This improves upon the novel's more aimless drift, in which Webb presents Benjamin's decisions as narrative non sequiturs: "Two days after he got home from the trip Benjamin decided to begin his affair with Mrs. Robinson"[19] or "Then after he had been home for nearly a month and Christmas had passed and the new year had started he decided to marry Elaine."[20] No wonder Prescott in his otherwise respectful *Times* review found himself groping to locate motivational momentum in Webb's novel.

Despite its mixed judgment of Webb's book, that review by Prescott captured the attention of Lawrence Turman, a first-generation UCLA graduate in literature whose father had hoped in vain that Larry would follow in his own garment-industry footsteps. On the lookout for an inexpensive property to pursue as his first foray into the volatile world of film production, Turman saw possibilities in what Prescott's review described. A considerable factor would have been that the author of a first novel would be in no position to command an enormous option price; Turman writes that "it was against my religion to put up my own money," and Webb's book marked his one-time, but relatively low-risk, exception.[21] A one-year option cost Turman $1,000, and he simultaneously began courting Mike Nichols, "another industry outsider,"[22] while also beginning to cast about for a financial backer at one of the major studios. Nichols came easier than the studio money; with no screenplay or studio deal in Turman's pocket, Nichols nonetheless signed on to split the profit on the eventual film straight down the middle, because he was sold on the story embedded in Webb's pages.[23]

It was a deal that would eventually change both men's lives, once they finally found a script they could use and someone to write the checks. This was easier said than done, despite what Turman thought to be Nichols's outstanding reputation. Turman painstakingly reminds us, "But three years (note: repeat, three years) elapsed between the time I made the deal with him and when we filmed *The Graduate*."[24] When Turman recruited Nichols, the director was exclusively a stage director, albeit the hottest stage director in the history of Broadway, with numerous long-run, critical and box-office hits running simultaneously (he'd won the Tony for Best Director in 1964 *and* 1965). But Broadway was not Hollywood, and studios couldn't become enthusiastic about a project whose story they didn't find compelling. The studios didn't like Webb's novel. By the time principal photography finally began on *The Graduate* in early 1967 on Paramount Studio's venerable Stage 18 (home in 1950 to an even darker satire of Los Angeles, *Sunset Boulevard*), Nichols had already made his first film and, confirming Turman's instincts, had immediately become recognized as one of the hottest directors in Hollywood, having created an indelible cinematic version of Edward Albee's *Who's Afraid of Virginia Woolf?*, starring Richard Burton and Elizabeth Taylor.

There were three equally prominent reasons for the delay in *The Graduate*'s production. The first, most pressing problem was money. With a certain amount of residual acidity, Turman likes to recount this long fallow period in the production's history: "No studio liked the book. At all. They didn't get it. Or rather, the readers who covered the material at each studio didn't get it. I submitted *The Graduate* to every single studio. They all said no."[25] Without money to move forward, Turman encountered his second problem. Nichols, much in demand, found himself inevitably enticed into other projects, including more Broadway hits and then, in what must have been the most painful blow of all for Turman, a smashing cinematic debut with Burton and Taylor that included 13 Oscar nominations and five awards. As wary as the studios might have been about taking on Albee's scabrous and profane play, they had Burton and Taylor to take to the bank.

Finally, Turman encountered a problem that, because of the nature of Webb's eminently adaptable novel (virtually a screenplay already, with its minimal narrative lyricism and iconic dialogue), seems particularly surprising: four writers would take a pass at making a film out of the book before Turman and Nichols had a script they believed in. William Hanley's and Peter Nelson's drafts have slipped away into the foggy recesses of the production's history. Hanley recalls to Harris that "Charles Webb's dialogue couldn't be improved on — it was pointless to try. All the script needed was structure."[26] Calder Willingham's draft remains more prominent because of the writing credit (and subsequent Oscar nomination for best adapted screenplay) he shared with Buck Henry. Willingham was an unlikely choice to adapt the book, although to that point, as Stanley Kubrick's "go-to screenwriter,"[27] he had the strongest Hollywood pedigree of anyone Turman had recruited. By all accounts, the script Willingham turned in was impossibly tone-deaf to the ironic possibilities of the book: he goosed the sex-comedy particulars of the affair between Benjamin and Mrs. Robinson into something unsuitably "vulgar,"[28] in both Turman and Nichols's estimation. Willingham and his script were out. (Harris reports that, in the self-parodic machinations of Hollywood, Willingham knew he had retained enough of Webb's original scenes and dialogue in his version — subsequently also incorporated by Henry in his own draft — to demand a Writers Guild arbitration hearing on co-credit, which was duly awarded. Peter Nelson, a less commanding Hollywood identity than Willingham, requested a hearing and was denied; William Hanley did not even press the issue. Henry has always categorically asserted that he never saw a single page of Willingham's draft, though their names will be forever linked in film history.[29]) While in Hollywood working on *Who's Afraid of Virginia Woolf?*, Nichols had become friends with Henry, and he passed along his new friend's name to Turman.

A former comic who'd become a comedy writer and successful producer (with comic filmmaker Mel Brooks) of the popular television spy-spoof, *Get Smart*, Henry became the next man associated with *The Graduate* to understand Benjamin Braddock as an extension of self-identity. Mike Nichols and Buck Henry's first meeting was suitably momentous: at an epic Independence Day party thrown by Jane Fonda and her fiancé, director Roger Vadim, mustering Old Hollywood for cocktails with Henry Fonda in the great house and New Hollywood for hash pipes on the beach below. Purportedly a sarcastic Nichols ad-lib on Southern Californian mellow-speak caused each to recognize a kindred soul, though it wasn't until later the same summer that George Segal, playing Nick in Nichols's version of *Who's Afraid of Virginia Woolf?*, regularly brought his buddy Henry to the set, and Nichols and Henry began to talk in earnest about the troubled script for *The Graduate*.[30] Henry was immediately hooked. "Nichols, Turman, and I all thought we were Benjamin," he says. "That's how the book affected us. Nichols and Turman saw the behavior and events in the film as reflecting what they felt at Benjamin's age. So did I."[31]

I. Introduction

Henry sensed the impossibility of Benjamin's rectitude as it had originated in Webb's autobiographical mistreatment at the hands of his eventual in-laws. Turman had first put his finger on this tonal issue: "In the novel, Benjamin Braddock is a whiny pain in the ass."[32] Henry went further still: "I had a feeling that in real life, Benjamin Braddock was not a person you'd want to know now [... H]e doesn't give anybody much of a chance."[33] Henry summarily removed from consideration for the cinematic Benjamin any trace of the naively fanciful rhetoric about "simple people" that Webb had used to posit a more sensitive, politically aware Benjamin. Far from sensitive, let alone aware, the cinematic Benjamin is numb. Until we get a greater understanding of the film's satiric point of view during the two party scenes (in which all the adults are cartoon caricatures of Benjamin's alienated perspective), he seems unaccountably sullen and rude. After we see and connect to point of view, we should still see his behavior as rude — but this time we may be better prepared to understand why: he thinks everyone around him is a buffoon. The "simple people" speech focuses on Benjamin's desire to leave home and find ... himself? America? Authenticity? Sensing Webb's discomfort with the entire road-trip enterprise in the fact that the narrative does not venture out on the road with Benjamin, Henry was the one who removed the entire incident's existence from his screenplay. It allows him to focus on the insularity and solipsism that perpetuate Benjamin's unreflective hypocrisy right from the opening moments of the film: Benjamin wants his life to be "different," but the only difference we can discern is that he is less active than anyone around him.

Removing the road-trip would prove to be perhaps the single biggest plot change from the novel, though the aforementioned change in timing of Benjamin's arrival at the church is surely the most significant change, followed closely by the final disposition of Benjamin's car. In the novel, Benjamin arrives in Berkeley and, almost instantly, sells the car to meet his living expenses. Almost everyone who has fallen under the spell of Benjamin Braddock's story has been bewitched by the cinematic rather than the literary version, in which the enormous symbolic weight of the car, roaring up and down the lower half of California and eventually sputtering into uselessness, looms impressively large. Therefore it is stunning, with a full third of the novel still to be encountered, to come upon Webb's description of Benjamin's first full day in Berkeley: "In the morning Benjamin found a rooming house several blocks from Elaine's dormitory and moved into a room on the second floor. Then he sold his car. A used car lot in town paid him twenty-nine hundred dollars in cash for it. He carried the money back to his room, put it in a drawer of his desk, then lay down on his bed and spent the rest of the afternoon

3. The Graduates

on his back staring up at the ceiling."[34] The money is a novelist's solution to how Benjamin manages to live in Berkeley; the experience of the film barely gives us time to consider where all his money is coming from during the Berkeley idyll, but if challenged to think about it, viewers may well have to conclude that it is only another in the long line of Benjamin's hypocrisies: the money is undoubtedly from his father. The car serves as another illusion of Benjamin's fanciful transformation. It's such a persistently visible symbol of his moral compromises that, when he discards it, we may think he has sloughed the last of this materialist skin that has confined him, only to find that the film's final ironies still await us.

Typically, Henry's revision of the narrative adds by subtraction. Long, sometimes-repetitive gusts of dialogue from the novel disappear without a trace, including conversations between the Braddocks and their son and particularly between Benjamin and Elaine once Benjamin is in Berkeley. This is fundamentally appropriate in a film narrative so intent upon reproducing "the sounds of silence." Henry instead allows a few short conversations to stand in for all this talk, yielding equal or even superior insights into the characters involved. In the cinematic version, there are two short conversations between father and son, one in Benjamin's room, the other poolside, as well as one short conversation between mother and son, in the steamy intimacy of the bathroom. The film depicts most of the ongoing dialogue between Benjamin and Elaine in the most allusive way, in montage snippets for dramatic and sometimes comic effect; the two longest conversations between Benjamin and Elaine that the film allows us to witness are both about Benjamin's affair with her mother. One of these, the night of their first date, falls short of full confession because Benjamin's nerve falters and he dissembles; the other, when Elaine comes to his room in Berkeley, falls short of full confession because of Elaine's hysterical scream. The great exception to Henry's "rule" of oblique conversation and pervasive silence is the doomed experiment undertaken by Benjamin with Mrs. Robinson in their Taft Hotel room. All these conversations are ones originated by Webb; Henry's excisions give them their proper formal weight. Henry's is the topically satirical voice of the "Plastics" conversation between Benjamin and Mr. McGuire, but such topicality is wisely reduced to a minimum to make Benjamin's dissatisfaction productively archetypal. Harris observes, "By favoring Benjamin's bumbling attempts at moral rigor over his cold, sour narcissism, Henry and Nichols located *The Graduate*'s comic center in his complete failure to live up to his own standards."[35] While Webb saw Benjamin in his novel as an emerging moral force, Henry simultaneously demands in his screenplay that we laugh *with* Benjamin as he regards the fun-house grotesqueries of his affluent milieu and *at* Benjamin as he keeps defaulting to the subjugating influence of that milieu. The sophistication of this irony would make the film's reception problematic.

Nichols should have been next in line after Webb, Turman, and Henry to identify with Benjamin. He liked the novel; he liked Henry's screenplay. He'd told Henry his satirical vision of the film, about Benjamin "drowning among objects and things,"[36] and Henry had run with it: "I understood what he was getting at. So I tried to put in as many water things as I could. When Benjamin goes underwater, that's sort of a central idea for the movie. Most of us have gone through that in our lives at one time or another, that remove that one feels between one's self and everyone or almost everyone around us."[37] Ironically, all this symbolic distancing of the protagonist in the film's visual motifs — through glass, through water, through doorways — may have contributed to keeping Nichols himself at a remove from fully understanding the personal resonances of Benjamin's character. "My unconscious was making this movie," he told Harris. "It took me years before I got what I had been doing all along — that I was turning Benjamin into a Jew. I didn't get it until I saw this hilarious issue of *MAD* magazine after the movie came out, in which the caricature of Dustin says to the caricature of Elizabeth Wilson, "Mom, how come I'm Jewish and you and Dad aren't?" And I asked myself the same question, and the answer was fairly embarrassing and fairly obvious: Who was the Jew among the goyim? And who was forever a visitor in a strange land?"[38]

Nichols's remarkable biography has been recounted many times: born Michael Igor Peschkowky in Berlin in 1931 to a White Russian Jew who'd fled the country after the Revolution, Nichols was a sickly member of an ailing family in a stricken social milieu. Two years after Nichols's birth, Hitler ascended to the chancellorship of Germany, and by 1938, his physician father had emigrated to the U.S. and changed his name to Paul Nichols; he began a profitable medical practice in Manhattan. His two sons followed the next year, his ailing wife only in 1941. The image of Nichols the pitiful immigrant child is equal to any drama he has created in his stage and cinematic career: Nichols was permanently hairless from early childhood (as a result of a reaction to an immunization) and master of just two English phrases: "I do not speak English" and "Please, do not kiss me."[39] By 1944, Paul Nichols was dead of leukemia, but by then he'd settled his family in a comfortable life on Central Park West and at elite private schools.[40] With so much upheaval and loss (including extended family murdered by the Nazis[41]), Nichols discovered early "the ruthless detachment of great comedians."[42] At the University of Chicago, he was an undistinguished student but in 1954 met Elaine May; the duo ascended to national stardom with their edgy, improvisational comedy act skewering every sort of cultural inanity and social hypocrisy. When May wrote and directed a play with Nichols as the lead actor, however, the edginess of the dynamic slipped over into acrimony, and each pursued a new direction. For Nichols, this soon meant a shift from performance to directing the performances of others.

One of Nichols's great joys of the theater is in the preparation of a play — the revisions with the playwright, the rehearsals with the cast.[43] In important ways, *The Graduate* came together the way one of Nichols's Broadway productions was assembled: over time. "It's painful and hard to remember now how long and how carefully we worked," he says, contrasting the painstaking production of *The Graduate* with the speed and lack of care with which contemporary productions are, in relative terms, slapped together to maximize profit. "We prepared that film for about a year [... W]e rented some space out at Paramount and went to our bungalows every day. I remember one day the art director came and said that when Mrs. Robinson got undressed maybe we should see the marks from the straps of her bathing suit. That was a day's work — time just spent soaking yourself in a subject."[44] The production designer, Richard Sylbert, recalls that "Sam O'Steen, the editor, called it 'the perfect movie' and he stayed with Mike for the next twenty years."[45]

Eventually the production shot for nearly 100 days,[46] a remarkably inefficient total by contemporary standards, especially for a film whose formally hermetic first half was located almost exclusively at a grand total of three locations: the Braddocks, 'the Robinsons,' and the Taft Hotel. This was hardly *Lawrence of Arabia*. What made all this production time possible was that Turman had located the money. The major studios had made it all too clear they did not believe in *The Graduate*'s chances, but Joseph E. Levine and Embassy Pictures needed Turman's production as much as Turman needed Levine. Nichols, by then signed on as Turman's partner and the director of the film, offered "something Joe Levine lacked — class."[47] Turman describes Levine as "king of the schlockmeisters. He was a larger-than-life character, a throwback to old Hollywood, an uneducated, great salesman — but a salesman of schlock."[48] Levine had made his reputation (for better or worse) importing foreign B-movies like the Italian *Hercules* films and the occasional European art film — but only if there were a way to sell its unexpurgated sensuality in the last days of the Hollywood production code, which censored everything from skin to obscene language to endings that might suggest crime or infidelity could go unpunished. As Turman stresses, Levine's commercial genius was not in recognizing art when he saw it but in selling product when he owned it.

When Turman first approached Levine, he asked for one million dollars, to which Levine agreed (though they nearly broke the deal over an executive producer credit, which Turman refused to grant Levine).[49] But by then Nichols had been made an offer he couldn't refuse by Ernest Lehman, Elizabeth Taylor, and Richard Burton. In March 1967, a month before principal photography on *The Graduate* finally was to commence, the budget had swelled to $3.1 million.[50] Now, however, there was a working script, and Anne Bancroft, who'd won a Tony and an Oscar, was on board. Nichols had been lionized by Broadway but now, more important, also by Hollywood. Never had the prestige of the production been greater. When Levine appeared unable to raise the necessary funds, Turman thought optimistically that he might have a deal-breaker and quietly re-shopped his property to every one of the major studios. Again, the studio heads unanimously turned him away, still unable to see what Turman and company saw in Webb's source material. Levine found the money; Turman and Embassy were stuck with each other until the bitter end (which came long after the film had become a blockbuster, when Turman sued Levine and Embassy for misrepresentation of profits).[51]

Nichols was in a peculiar position when making *The Graduate*: he was still a neophyte cineaste who barely knew which way to look through a lens, and yet he was already one-for-one in Oscar nominations as a director. He simply proceeded under the assumption that *The Graduate* would be made as one of his plays had been made, by assembling an excellent team and demanding their very best work. Robert Surtees was a good example of this phenomenon. "I needed everything I learned in the past thirty years to shoot *The Graduate*," he would say.[52] Sometimes this was because Nichols had come up with a brilliant but technically complicated idea; other times it was because he simply didn't have a clue, technically: "'I asked for such peculiar things,' [Nichols] recalls. In the scene in which Elaine confronts Benjamin in the tiny apartment he has rented in Berkeley, Nichols wanted to use a long lens. 'Surtees didn't say to me, "But that has no meaning." He would figure out a way to do it. He took out the entire wall of the apartment and we shot the scene from all the way across the stage.'"[53]

The stage set itself posed unnecessary difficulties. Rather than working within the two- or (at most) three-walled illusions of a house's various rooms on a typical soundstage, Nichols had demanded that Sylbert, the production designer, oversee the fully three-dimensional construction of the Robinsons' entire house. Dustin Hoffman recalls, "[T]here was a full bathroom even though it wasn't in the script, because you didn't know what Mike might want."[54] (Ironically, Hoffman was the one who eventually recognized the necessity of the bathroom, in the beautifully conceived conversation between Benjamin and his mother as he's shaving.[55]) Despite all the intense pressure Nichols brought to bear on cast and crew, the oral histories of the production (as recorded in Harris' detailed book or in the video documentaries included with various DVD versions of *The Graduate*) testify to a spirit of collaboration, in which the ideas of writers, producers, technicians, and cast all contribute. Nichols insisted upon "an almost unheard-of luxury for a small film: three weeks of rehearsal, during which the actors would have a chance to explore their characters, improvise scenes, and feel their way into relationships while Nichols shaped them into an ensemble."[56] Hoffman remembers this period as "the greatest experience I've ever had in terms of film, bar none."[57] Sylbert recalls, "We rehearsed that script for three weeks. That script and those rehearsals and that movie were identical. You know how pictures change. They change constantly. It never changed. Once it was cast and once it was rehearsed it never changed. Every idea, every shot was exactly what we had planned at the beginning and that's very satisfying."[58]

Among the iconic moments in the film that exist precisely because of those rehearsals is the terrible experience Benjamin has when, in a fit of high anxiety in the hotel room the first night with Mrs. Robinson, he tentatively, awkwardly gropes her breast. The effect suggests a horrific parody of the maternal dynamic lingering between them, and the horror is that his naïve need is met with such indifference that Mrs. Robinson's full attention remains fixed by a stain on her blouse. The grope had been an improvisation concocted by Nichols and Hoffman to goose the scene; Dustin Hoffman, surprised by Bancroft's cool returning improvisation, turned away to hide his admiring laughter and walked to the far wall, where he banged his head in self-mocking frustration. Nichols loved it; her non-reaction was in, as was Hoffman's further improvised reaction *to* her improvised non-reaction.[59] The rehearsals were filled with such discoveries. Early in the mounting seduction, Hoffman took to making whimpering noises in his throat to externalize his nerves. Nichols claims to be the source of the mannerism: "[T]hat whimper he does? He got that sound from me. I was told that I used to do that in meetings with Jack Warner [during the production of *Who's Afraid of Virginia Woolf?*]. Somebody said, 'When Mr. Warner is telling his jokes, you must stop whimpering.'"[60]

The final and ultimately the foremost Benjamin Braddock of all the men who made *The Graduate* must be Dustin Hoffman — the least likely of Benjamins. Hoffman had begun to establish himself off–Broadway; he envisioned for himself a long and semi-anonymous career as a character actor, inhabiting the skins of fictional figments. Hoffman told Kashner, "So when the part came along, I read the book, I talked to Mike Nichols on the phone, and I said, "I'm not right for this part, sir. This is a Gentile. This is a Wasp. This is Robert Redford." In fact, I remember there was a *Time* magazine on the coffee table in my apartment, and it had the "Man of the Year" on the cover, which was "Youth Under 25," with a kind of sketch of a young guy who looked like

Matt Damon. So I said, "Did you see this week's *Time* magazine? *That's* Benjamin Braddock! Nichols replied, "*You mean he's not Jewish?* Yes, this guy is a super–Wasp. Boston Brahmin." And Mike said, "Maybe he's Jewish *inside*. Why don't you come out and audition for us?"[61]

All who were there have adopted the uniform memory of Hoffman's ensuing audition (with Katharine Ross, his eventual co-star) as epically disastrous. While it could scarcely have been as bad as their comic stories insist, it must certainly have left room for doubt about the casting of the title role. A fun-house image from the end of the twelve-hour day of screen testing crystallizes the bad vibrations. Hoffman gave Nichols a parting handshake and was mortified by the nervous dampness of his own hands, which he hurriedly thrust into his pants pockets. The next time he took them out, several New York subway tokens flew out at the same time, which a crew member returned with a rhetorical flourish: "Here kid, [... y]ou're gonna need these."[62] Despite all the evidence (and professional advice) to the contrary, and despite endless casting calls and screen tests of other actors, Nichols never saw somebody he was more convinced could inhabit the callow skin of the Benjamin Braddock that Nichols envisioned. Certainly Hoffman's own nomination of Robert Redford, who does in fact fit the novel's physical description and campaigned for the part, fell on deaf ears. Nichols was adamant that Benjamin was a "loser," and he doubted that Redford could adequately defuse his cool dignity on screen to become a schlemiel.

Benjamin is actually on the precociously young side when he graduates from college, but Nichols also quickly gave up on the idea of having an actor of a commensurate age play the part. Turman had advertised a national search for a twenty-two-year-old, perhaps attempting to ride the publicity wave of what had become an *idée fixe* of the culture, as evidenced by *Time*'s "Man of the Year." For Nichols, however, what was at stake in the casting was the film's perspective: "I discovered that boys who really were that age couldn't get the distance to get rid of the self-pity and ... have an *attitude* toward that point in one's life," Nichols told *Films and Filming* in November 1968.[63] Such a point cannot be overemphasized, given the systematic misinterpretation of the film over the years. Even at the casting stage of the film's pre-production, Nichols always simultaneously intended the film's subjective gaze through Benjamin's point of view as well as a distinct, ironic distance from its protagonist. *The Graduate* would not be an apologia for Benjamin Braddock, and the man who eventually played Benjamin would have to see not just the problems beyond but within his character.

For his part, Nichols knew he had his man not from directing the seemingly miserable all-day screen-test, but by watching the print of the test: "He had that thrilling thing that I'd only seen in Elizabeth Taylor," Nichols told Harris. "That secret, where they do something while you're shooting, and you think it's *okay*, and then you see it on screen and it's five times better than when you shot it. [...] Elizabeth had it, and by God, so did Dustin."[64] Kashner points out that Hoffman was able to see the part once he caught Nichols and Henry's vision of Benjamin as the ultimate outsider — not a part of the culture, but not a part of the counter-culture either. Nichols and Henry envisioned Benjamin as a "genetic throwback" among these "walking surfboards"[65] of angular, blond vigor — the American WASP mainstream. In a very real sense, this had been at the root of Hoffman's casting ordeal: Nichols wanted Hoffman to project an estrangement that began in the blood. Renata Adler, writing in *The New York Times*, was the first to state the reality of Benjamin's Jewish identity; readers immediately pilloried her for stereotyping. But J. Hoberman affirms Adler's observation, identifying Benjamin as, at the very least, a "crypto–Jew" and *The Graduate* as "an example of an ascendant Jewishness" in the Hollywood Renaissance.[66] (Ironically, the enormous popularity of *The Graduate* and Hoffman's anti-heroic character made the Jewish outsider for a "brief period [...] the ethnic Jewish matinee idol and youth icon in the forms of George Segal, Elliott Gould, Richard Benjamin, Charles Grodin, and Gene Wilder."[67])

In the context of the diegetic world of *The Graduate*, however, Jewishness was yet another strategic source for depicting the character's alienation. Nichols worked hard to maintain Hoffman's alienated edge: although he was capable of lavish praise for work done well by his cast and crew, Nichols often intentionally avoided any implication of reassurance for his lead actor; he made disparaging remarks in makeup about Hoffman's large features; in essence, he wore Hoffman down as Hoffman's character Benjamin has been worn down by the prevailing adult culture around him. For his part, Hoffman still believes that Nichols's bullying behavior was not solely about method-preparation of his actor but was also rooted in an essential fear that he'd hired the wrong man to be the fulcrum of his film.[68] When Hoffman walked away at the end of the shoot, returning to New York and what he hoped would be a resumption of the modest life on the boards he'd imagined for himself, he was about to become more like Benjamin than he could have known: a young man pushed along on a cultural tide much larger and more powerful than himself.

To illustrate the "Benjamania" that engulfed him during the next year, Hoffman likes to tell the story of attending a sneak preview with his fiancée late in 1967. He'd previously appeared for all of about 30 seconds in one film, *The Tiger Makes Out* (Arthur Hiller, 1968), which had yet to be released when *The Graduate* premiered, but now "the picture starts, and the first shot is a close-up of me," says Hoffman. "I literally shook through the entire movie. [... M]ainly I'm looking at scenes and thinking, "I should have done that better." And then it gets to the church, and what got me out of my self-flagellation is that I looked down, over the edge of the balcony, and these kids were on their feet, cheering for me to get away. They had gone wild."[69] After the film, Hoffman and his fiancée waited for the crowd to thin before exiting the theater, but a slow-moving older woman with a cane stopped him. Hoffman recognized Radie Harris, a Hollywood gossip columnist. She recognized Hoffman, too. Pointing her cane at him, she declared, "You're Dustin Hoffman, aren't you? You're the Graduate. [...] Life is never going to be the same for you from this moment on."[70] Nichols remembers a preview around the same time, at which he was running the sound, since the film had not yet been dubbed. At a certain point, he stopped fretting about the sound, he says, because of the noise the audience was making: "It sort of sounded like a prize fight. I have never heard an audience make that noise before. Laugh like that. Shout like that. Yell like that. And for the last five minutes of the picture they began to cheer and they didn't stop. And I was very taken aback, and in my own bizarre way, pleased. And then I ran the hell out of the theater."[71]

Both Hoffman and Nichols were surprised to find the audience so exuberant in their joy; naturally, their first reaction would have been relief and pleasure at having pleased the crowd. Indeed, they delighted crowds of all kinds in record numbers. Carringer summarizes a 1968 analysis in *Variety* as declaring a box-office triumph for *The Graduate* that transcended traditional demographical barriers of age and culture.[72] Upon reflection, however, especially as the first previews were followed by opening night and the box-office snowball through the winter and spring into summer, the audience reaction began to pall. "'I was an object,' [Hoffman] says. 'No one knew my name. I wasn't a human being to them. I was the Graduate.'"[73] That was around the time that Nichols began reminding people that Benjamin and Elaine become their parents — that his film was about the void of counter-cultural momentum that has Benjamin and Elaine grimly, passively riding the bus at film's end. It had been "whipped away"[74] from all of them, and all of Nichols's ironic cinematic rhetoric couldn't take it back.

Nichols would work with Sam O'Steen, the talented editor he'd first met and with whom he'd established such a simpatico during the production of *Who's Afraid of Virginia Woolf?*, to complete the film for a holiday release, just under the wire to qualify for the 1968 award season. O'Steen had served as an invaluable on-set advisor to Nichols throughout the production, but Nichols brimmed with the confidence of artistic vision. Surtees, who'd worked with some of the iconic directors in Hollywood, was obviously impressed by

Nichols's quickly assumed cinematic authority: "Mike was the boss. Nobody was going to come onto the set and question what he did. They wouldn't dare; he wouldn't stand for it. Which was nice for me. The only man I had to please was Mike Nichols."[75]

During post-production, no one was certain what they had but Nichols: "I saw the whole thing—I knew what the movie was." In a rented house in the Hollywood Hills, Nichols would wake every morning during the production and play Simon and Garfunkel albums like *Sounds of Silence* and *Parsley, Sage, Rosemary and Thyme*. Over time during the editing process, he and O'Steen became convinced that the music they had used for their rough cutting of montages like the swimming-pool sequence, "The Sound of Silence" and "April Come She Will," were "what was happening in Benjamin's head," says Nichols.[76] There could be little doubt that, however distant he might have been from an emotional connection to Benjamin as the years had elapsed since he'd first read the novel, these were now the sounds inside Mike Nichols's head: *Benjamin Braddock, that's me*. Over the next couple months in New York, working with O'Steen at the editing table, he was ready to believe that these would be the sounds in the head of the typical audience member. The noises he heard at the previews only confirmed his sense of the audience's accord with "what was happening in Benjamin's head." Of his cinematic vocation, Nichols claims, "What the director is saying to his audience is, 'This happened to me; did it happen to you too?'"[77] Somehow, between them, the various men who were Benjamin Braddock—Webb first, then Turman, Henry, Nichols, Hoffman—had invested the character with enough of the authenticity of their own experience with failure and alienation that Benjamin was ready to be embraced—and misunderstood—by millions.

PART II
Seeing The Graduate

"Hello, darkness, my old friend..." was what was happening in Benjamin's head.

—Mike Nichols, to Mark Harris,
in *Pictures at a Revolution*

4

"The Sounds of Silence": Of Human Baggage (00:00—03:00)

The Graduate as conceived by Charles Webb in his novel begins at the graduation party; the film as created by Mike Nichols begins somewhat earlier, in a plane nearing the end of its journey west across the nation. Buck Henry's vision of where the cinematic story of Benjamin Braddock should open, however, travels backwards beyond the trip home — back onto Benjamin's undergraduate campus, into the dark heart of the traditional graduation ceremony. The film, after all, is about a graduate; Henry's vision commences, fittingly, with that college commencement. Benjamin is the valedictorian at his prestigious east-coast school, presumably one of the Ivies. He is young and full of a sense of the vast solemnity of the occasion. As Henry's script begins, Benjamin has reached that point in his address at which he is about to impart the "purpose" of collegiate education. He echoes his own father's interrogative words to him weeks later, during the summer, when Mr. Braddock finds him drifting in the family's swimming pool: "What is the purpose of these years, the purpose of all this demanding work, the purpose for the sacrifices made [by] those who love us? Were there NOT a purpose, then all of these past years of struggle, of fierce competition and of uncompromising ambition would be meaningless. But, of course, there is a purpose and I must tell it to you. I ask you to remember this purpose always and I pledge that I shall endeavor to carry it with me forever."[1]

But a wind has been threatening the fragile order of his notes on the podium. Distracted by trying to hold down his papers, he verbally stumbles, failing to retrieve that purpose that he claims has brought them together. Henry's script envisions a series of comic cuts from an increasingly anxious

Benjamin to the clinically impassive audience, watching his spectacular flame out. The rising wind becomes the roar of the jet's engine, and we enter into the scene that now opens the film. While the commencement scene has its own logical consistency as the opening of a social satire called *The Graduate*, it is unnecessary to the film's narrative; Mark Harris deems it "overexplicit" of the film's themes.[2] Benjamin's father asks a question that Benjamin himself can rejoin, simply, by the disillusioned, "You got me." The scene at the pool is more organic and more fraught with generational tension than the generic commencement scene.

Most important, starting the narrative in the plane starts Benjamin in a series of spatial and aural boxes that will entrap and contain him throughout the first half of the film. Nichols told Harris that he decided to lead with the scene on the plane, cutting the graduation scene, because it offered the opportunity to begin with a vision of entrapment and a disembodied, mechanically distorted voice talking about a literal and metaphorical "descent": "It's a statement of theme that you don't really hear, even though it's perfectly loud and clear."[3] In fact, the opening shot of *The Graduate* presents that most basic of cinematic boxes, the close-up—a focus on the non-traditionally handsome head of Dustin Hoffman, against what appears to be an uninflected white background. Hoffman was anything but a household face in America in 1967. He'd spent a decade scratching for work in New York theaters; when Mike Nichols and Hollywood came calling, Hoffman had only just begun to feel his feet under him off–Broadway. Taking the Hollywood job meant starting over, again. Nichols notoriously used Hoffman's nervousness during the production to accentuate the protagonist's unease, but Nichols and his cinematographer, Robert Surtees, also used the camera. In this first image of the film, Benjamin is shot slightly off-center; we note, in these opening seconds, a vague discomfiture. Linda Ruth Williams writes, "Nichols makes liberal use of decentered compositions and asymmetrical framing, losing human figures in a wider canvas and refusing to prioritize their identities by fixing them centerstage."[4]

An off-screen, diegetic voice begins speaking over a public amplification system; we hear the ambient sounds of a pressurized airline cabin, in flight. The voice portentously tells the passengers (and the audience), "We have begun our descent into Los Angeles." Henry shared with Nichols a sense that this film could be a satire of Southern California life, of its sunny narcissism as depicted in novels as different as Webb's book and Thomas Pynchon's *The Crying of Lot 49*, published within three years of each other. Pynchon has his heroine, Oedipa Maas, driving down through Southern California to the richly allusive San Narciso, "less an identifiable city than a grouping of concepts—

census tracts, special purpose bond-issue districts, shopping nuclei, all overlaid with access roads to its own freeway. [...] Oedipa resolved to pull in at the next motel she saw, however ugly, stillness and four walls having at some point become preferable to this illusion of speed, freedom, wind in your hair, unreeling landscape — it wasn't. What the road really was, she fancied, was this hypodermic needle, inserted somewhere ahead into the vein of a freeway, a vein nourishing the mainliner L.A., keeping it happy, coherent, protected from pain."[5]

What Pynchon's meditation on Los Angeles implies is a kind of urban plan for the narcotic submission of its citizens. We encounter a less hallucinatory but no less dystopian vision of the relationship between civilians and civic space in *The Graduate*, where the "descent" line (which belongs to Henry and Nichols, not Webb) typifies a briefing for a descent into a well-heeled hell. Nichols told *Films and Filming* in November 1968 that Los Angeles represented for him "a parody of everything that's most dangerous to us."[6] On his college lecture-circuit tour in promotion of the film during 1968, Nichols liked to refer to the film's vision of "the Los Angelization of the world in which *things* take over a person's life."[7] In the film's opening shot, the camera zooms out from the close-up on Benjamin to reveal that, far from a solitary figure against a blank background, the young man on whom our automatic audience instinct for identification has imprinted is not alone but one of dozens of equally impassive heads nestled against white headrests in the main cabin of an airliner. The amplified voice speaks to everyone with warm impersonality, hoping to "see you again in the near future." The owner of the voice, self-identified as captain of the flight, hasn't seen any of them. It is a mockery of polite social convention whose only sincerity is commercial: it is in the captain's economic interests to invite his guests to "join" him on some future journey, the sooner the better.

The first shot of the film ends abruptly with a cut to the cinematically audacious multi-tasking second shot, a minute-and-a-half take of Hoffman, nearly motionless, riding a moving walkway through Los Angeles International Airport. Choosing another blank, white background, doubly perfect for serving as projection space for his film's titles and as a projection of the blankness at the center of his protagonist, Nichols takes care of cinematic business while giving us a visual *koan* on movement/stasis. Wayne Schuth writes that the abundant use of white in the art design of *The Graduate* "connotes a sterile, cold environment,"[8] and the prologue involving air transportation magnifies this sense of alienation as the dominant mode of the film, one we'll re-encounter in the Braddock and Robinson houses, in the Taft Hotel, and at the climax, in the sterile ultra-modernism of what Robert Coles calls "that grotesque church in Santa Barbara."[9] Hoffman steps onto the moving walkway, still a fixture of "space-age" conveyance at airports. However, unlike many airport travelers, who hurtle onto these walkways and stride along the left side of the belt, Hoffman as Benjamin settles into a stationary, resigned attitude of passivity. Many go-getters in the culture have somewhere to go, something to get — though much of this film is designed to question the ultimate substance of their goals. In his paralysis, only Benjamin's eyes move: they furtively spy upon young women passing on the opposite belt.

In two shots, totaling well over two minutes of screen time, the only focus of *The Graduate* has barely moved. Except in its multi-layered, ironic point-of-view, which has proved particularly thorny for audiences and some critics, *The Graduate* is not a subtle film. It may strike a *nouvelle vague* pose in its youthful disaffection, but Nichols and his filmmaking team are actually more informed by the satiric distortions of expressionism (not to mention the broad comedy of the American mainstream dating back to vaudeville). These first two shots depict a young protagonist under the influence — not of the controlled substances fashionably propagated by the emerging counter-culture, but of his parents and their culture's success fantasy. Benjamin is passively conveyed, first by a plane, then by a moving belt, and each time with the diegetic voice of a machine — an artificial replica of a human voice — instructing him, expressing care for him, yet utterly unaware of him. Nichols again unbalances the composition, leaving Benjamin uncentered at the right edge of the frame, at the periphery of his own life, a lingering visual insight on Benjamin's psychology as the film begins. The profound simplicity of this dual-purpose shot under the titles also provides the audience with the opportunity to concentrate on a new element of film language introduced in this long-lingering second shot: non-diegetic musical soundtrack, underscoring Benjamin's point of view.[10] As Hoffman steps from the airplane onto this second mode of passive conveyance, Paul Simon's plaintive guitar plucks at the opening notes of "The Sounds of Silence." The duration of the shot — nearly the entire length of the song — allows us ample time to understand Simon and Garfunkel's presence as the sounds of Benjamin Braddock's silence. Paul Monaco writes that, while the adoption of popular folk-rock songs on the soundtrack was "new and different," their "essential purpose remained strongly narrative, precisely as in classic Hollywood scoring."[11] David R. Shumway notes that this film introduced the idea of fully replacing the commentary of an orchestral film score with a choric soundtrack of popular music.[12]

This song will play three times during the course of the film: here at the titles; again, just after Benjamin falls into the summer-long affair with Mrs. Robinson; and then, most arrestingly, a final time at the film's conclusion, countering the "happy ending" to the fairy-tale rescue of the maiden from the barred fortress and its assembled ogres. We're led to believe, through the surface progress of the narrative, that Benjamin has shattered the alienating silence of materialist self-absorption by finding — and rescuing — Elaine. Ultimately, the omnipresence of "The Sounds of Silence" from beginning to end posits an essential stasis ironically dissonant from all the frenetic movement and supposed purpose of the film's final 20 minutes. The more things change for Benjamin, the more they remain the same. Here at the film's opening, however, Benjamin's apprehensive demeanor suggests no dissonance between sound and vision. Over the titles, as the camera tracks left beside the moving walkway and watches Benjamin's numb stare in profile, the song reinforces the chilly alienation established in the film's first two shots. Benjamin, stony-faced, has been chatted up in both shots by disembodied, electronically altered voices that have zero awareness of him as an autonomous human being. They are the proverbial trees that fall in the forest whether we hear them or not; to them, Benjamin's presence is no more real or acknowledgeable.

The inflections of European art cinema seem immediately pronounced, potentially creating a predisposition in experienced critics to seek further allusions and to interpret them as slavish unoriginality on the part of the filmmakers. "Antonioni seems to be the most direct source for Nichols's depiction of bourgeois malaise," writes Glenn Man, specifically citing *L'Avventura* (1960). "*The Graduate*'s images of characters caught in the web of their environment have the look and feel of Antonioni's visual motifs of alienation as his own characters play out their listless or desperate actions in unaccommodating locales."[13] The formal qualities of these two shots — their undeniably Antonionian pace; their emphasis, in a motion picture, on lack of motion — serve up "The Sounds of Silence" on the soundtrack as a kind of epigraph to the film. Shumway describes the visuals as "intentionally 'boring'" in order to assert the centrality of the music and lyrics and "establish the theme of alienation."[14] *The Graduate* will be about communication breakdown and its effects on the human person. Nichols's belief that the mass audience "whipped away" the film's meaning is thus an ironic corroboration of the film's themes — people watching without truly seeing the film.

The role of Benjamin Braddock would make Dustin Hoffman a star, after a fashion. Although he would famously be photographed by *Life* collecting unemployment during the spring of 1968, as the box office boomed for *The Graduate*, Hoffman (and others, like his one-time New York roommates Gene Hackman and Robert Duvall) would form a new cluster in the Hollywood star system. The camera would love their characters more than their faces, and the audience would eventually adjust to loving a new kind of face, real rather than ideal. Hoffman's next big role, as crippled street-grifter Ratso

Rizzo in John Schlesinger's *Midnight Cowboy* (1969), could not on the surface have appeared more different from the spoiled Beverly Hills rich kid of *The Graduate*, yet Schlesinger's use of Nilsson's "Everybody's Talkin'" functions as "The Sounds of Silence" does, and for all the hop-along effort of Ratso, the two films end in precisely the same way, with the illusion of forward movement into the future: alienation and existential doom on a public bus. Like *Midnight Cowboy*, *The Graduate* spends much of its narrative in asserting that genuine, empathic connection with another human being is salvation, only to ironically undercut the certainty of such an assertion by narrative's conclusion. These are not happy endings, although both Nichols and Schlesinger offer the tantalizingly ambiguous promise of redemptive change.

The long, objectifying shot of Benjamin on the moving walkway finally signals its conclusion as the camera stops its track and allows Hoffman to be conveyed, still a statue of immobile gloom — screen-left. As he passes out of the frame, the film cuts to its third, associational shot, of another object on another conveyor belt: a suitcase, Benjamin's luggage. The shot's composition mirrors the one we've just watched: the suitcase is off-center, screen-right. Benjamin, like his luggage, is being carried passively in some unknown future direction. This shot of the suitcase also tracks beside the conveyor belt. Tellingly, in this film about alienation, we are encouraged to compare our protagonist in the opening moment of the film to an impassive piece of luggage. Aaron Cooley refers to Timothy Bewes's *Reification, or the Anxiety of Late Capitalism* to identify the process by which reifying culture commodifies relationships and individuals to objecthood.[15] Hoffman's depressive acting in the first half-hour, full of mopes and sighs, confirms the identification of Benjamin as valuable object rather than valued person; when Mr. Braddock, Mr. Loomis, Mr. McGuire, and Mr. Robinson in turn put a fatherly arm around Ben during the night of his graduation party, there is status in appearing intimately connected to Ben's worldly accomplishments in his eastern college, though they might as well be tugging at a piece of unwieldy but ultimately compliant baggage.

Before the shot of Benjamin's suitcase ends, Nichols the comic can't quite help himself from indulging a sight-gag: the suitcase briefly disappears behind an airport information sign instructing passengers on the proper use of baggage claim tickets. "Do They Match?" asks the sign, displaying iconography of an appropriate luggage tag and claim ticket. Given the associational cut between the similar shots of Benjamin and his bag, however, we sense Nichols exhorting the audience to acknowledge his film language: a visual elbow in the ribs. Benjamin *matches* the baggage, objectified by the wills of others who talk without listening. (Such elbow-in-the-ribs stunts may have been a further

4. "The Sounds of Silence"

goad to some critics to take Nichols to task for European cineaste pretension, though the impulse may actually have more to do with an improv comic's sticking with a gag a little longer than might be ideal.) The suitcase re-emerges, is dumped down a chute into the baggage carrousel, and is immediately and firmly claimed by Benjamin, his first energetically decisive movement in the film.

As the titles end, the song ends. Our last shot of this opening sequence, the fourth shot of the film, is through a set of glass airport doors (with another sign centered to warn Benjamin to "Use Other Door"), as Benjamin gives an ambiguous smile and wave and passes through, into the foreground of the frame. Presumably the acknowledgment he makes is of his parents, waiting to drive him home. It may register during a subsequent viewing that it is odd his parents were not with him at his commencement from undergraduate school — not sharing in the joy of his precocious achievement or at least basking in the reflected glory of his recognition as among the finest of the graduates. It's a small but telling detail: his parents reveal themselves to be too caught up in the press of their own lives to make this effort for their son. Their enthusiasm for his party thus becomes all the more about them and the social capital to be gained by showing him off. Are we to understand the ambiguity of his fading smile as he exits the airport (like the much remarked-upon fading smile at film's end) as relief to be through the ordeal of what it must have cost him to be an overachieving track star and honors student at the unnamed but clearly prestigious eastern college he attended? Is it merely the jet lag of a transcontinental flight? Or is it the resignation of being back in the place he started, no wiser for the past four years that the culture assures its youth will prepare them for adult life? It's a first glimpse of the cyclical vision that *The Graduate* projects for all of its characters, regardless of age or temperament. The film will end as it began, with a young man glumly being carried away into a future he cannot foresee.

5

The Graduation Party
(03:00—06:30)

Our first centered composition of *The Graduate* comes in the fifth shot of the film, the one that dissolves from the titles sequence into the opening night of the narrative: the welcome-home graduation party. This is where Webb's novel begins, and it's also where, for all intents and purposes, Nichols's narrative truly begins. *The Graduate*'s fifth shot is a close-up, and it reminds us of the intimacy of the first shot, that close-up that opened the film. We are again regarding Dustin Hoffman's glum face in tight, crown-to-chin framing. Yet here the resemblance of the two shots ends. That initial shot appears to be against a blank backdrop, belied as the camera soon zooms out to reveal his face among a fuselage of faces on the plane. In the first shot of the graduation party sequence, however, a rich, marine background creates a sense of genuine intimacy. Benjamin leans his head against a small aquarium, diffusing light to an ambient green. The lulling sound of the water filter burbles just off-screen. Yet Benjamin is not asleep. He remains dully conscious, eyes open but inactive, waiting. At the left of the screen, a plastic scuba diver aims a harpoon at Benjamin's head. Other than Benjamin's typical dourness, the implied violence of the diver is the only hint of unease in the overall mood of tranquility, and it is the harbinger of Benjamin's own scuba dive at the next party his parents throw for him, to celebrate his twenty-first birthday.

Water is central to this first act of *The Graduate*. It is womb-water, the "amniotic fluid of that summer of indecision between college and 'real life'"[1] in which Benjamin drifts, waiting for his adult life to start, both barred from and intimidated by entering his majority. We come to recognize this first shot after the titles, with Benjamin seemingly submerged in a child's aquarium, as his retreat from the adult world he has failed to enter, despite the supposed rites of passage available to him at college. Ironically, this suspended state of

5. The Graduation Party

adolescence gives him something in common with all the adults around him — all of them selfish, arrested adolescents intent only on super-acquisitive brinksmanship.

Again in the close-up of Benjamin backgrounded by the aquarium, Nichols shows great patience, allowing the shot to run without interruption and with no camera movement for more than a minute, well after Mr. Braddock has arrived, until Mrs. Braddock intervenes, commanding motion. (At this point actors *and camera* all move — an indication that the maternal base of power beneath the superficial appearance of affluent patriarchy must be reckoned with.) Despite the persistence of Benjamin's immobility in this fifth shot, the subsequent blocking of the scene suggests a cultural intolerance for stillness. As we will see, that intolerance conceals terror, never more apparent than in the misery of Mr. Braddock serving as ringmaster at the birthday party. In the first half of the film, no one in *The Graduate* is settled, centered, at peace, even when a composition visually suggests that illusion.

The fifth shot of the film waits in solidarity with Benjamin; then a door opens off-screen, and harsh white light from the hallway strikes Benjamin and the aquarium. Benjamin's eyes furtively shift, narrowing against the harshness of the light but also in response to the identity of the intruder: his father. As we felt the camera's psychological identification with Benjamin in the long tracking shot at the airport, we feel it again here. The camera, like Benjamin, does not budge from its fixed position; there is no adjusted relation to Mr. Braddock. Benjamin's father must carve out his own space in the intimacy between Ben and the camera. We do not always see subjectively through Benjamin's eyes in *The Graduate*, but with few exceptions in the first half of the film, the camera is his brain. When we watch his parents and other adults, we see Ben's psychological point of view: comic-book caricatures of adults, naked ids of competition, dissatisfaction, and not-so-quiet desperation. As Mr. Braddock looms into soft-focus foreground, Nichols and Surtees create the sensation that Mr. Braddock is intruding between Benjamin and us, and our own resentment is thus, like Benjamin's, piqued. Mr. Braddock will have to "get in Ben's face." From the camera's vantage, this means his profile is literally in Ben's face, as Mr. Braddock sits on the bed to have a brief pep talk with his son. In short, William Daniels as Mr. Braddock literally upstages Benjamin.

The effect is a partial- to full-eclipse of the son: Daniels' head, in profile, blocks our view of the original, centered composition. We glimpse Benjamin only when the enormous foregrounded head of his father accidentally allows. The psychological relationship of these two males is thus established in visual terms that remain consistent throughout the film's first half. Similar moments of visual dominance come in the famous shots of Mrs. Robinson's foregrounded legs, trapping Benjamin in a pyramid of illicit desire later on the night of the graduation party, and then again after their failed "conversation," serving as a barrier in their room at the Taft Hotel, as she resignedly pulls on her stockings. Late in the film, Mr. Robinson also gets in on this act of physically barring Benjamin, pinning him by a rain-streaked window in the noir-lit eaves of Ben's Berkeley boarding house room, where he has lived while stalking/courting Elaine.

A short conversation between father and son ensues. Mr. Braddock reminds Ben that all his guests are waiting downstairs — a guilt-inducing image that Benjamin accepts with the passivity to which we've already become accustomed. "What's the matter?" his father says, and then, more impatiently, "What is it?" He coaxes from Ben a vague concern about his "future." And then, with a bit more prodding, and while tellingly meeting his father's eyes as he says it, Benjamin admits that he wants his future to be "different." Despite the imprecision of the word, the moment contains no ambiguity: Ben wants to be *different* than his parents and their circle. To what does he object? The remainder of the film loads us down with evidence, but almost none of it takes the form of verbal condemnation by Benjamin.

Pauline Kael argues that the film's "small triumph" is not thematic but formal, keeping Benjamin from talking too much and becoming a bore or a prig, which would make it "absurdly evident that he has nothing to communicate — which is just what makes him an acceptable hero for the large movie audience. If he said anything or had any ideas, the audience would probably hate him."[2] Yet this infers commercial rather than aesthetic calculation on the part of the filmmakers, for whom, Kael believes, crowd-pleasing is more important than getting at the truth of a character's inner life.

Jacob Brackman, writing for the same magazine as Kael, believes that inarticulateness in a youthful protagonist is not merely Kael's cynical sense of what will play on a big screen for an easily distracted audience; it's also verisimilitude. A "Johnson youth," confronted by his parents and asked to explain his apparent disaffection for their world, "would say 'I don't know' right at the start because he wouldn't consider explanation pertinent, or even feasible. The very language given him by the adult world, he would feel, leads perniciously, inexorably back into that world. 'So you've got no *respect*!' a father accuses" (like Mr. Robinson will accuse Benjamin, much later up in Berkeley), "and as soon as the son tries to redefine the word his case is lost."[3]

But there is yet another possibility, beyond Kael's theory that Nichols and Henry won't allow their protagonist to speak or Brackman's theory that Benjamin would know better than to think his father could hear a reasoned argument. There remains the theory that Benjamin has nothing to say. In their *Film Quarterly* reflection on the film during the height of its popularity in 1968, Farber and Changas took umbrage at Benjamin's lost opportunity to tell off his father: "He's supposed to be a champion college debater, but he can hardly form a sentence. [...] All he knows is that he wants his future to be 'well ... different....' He really sweats to get that word out, but he doesn't seem capable of going further. [...] We soon learn that Ben, for all of his credentials and in spite of his vulnerable face, is clean-cut and stupid."[4] Fans of the film typically read into Benjamin greater depths than he in fact possesses; the film's detractors condemn the film because the protagonist has no depths.

Mrs. Braddock disturbs this motionless tableau to announce that "The Carlsons are here! They came all the way from Tarzana!" As played by Elizabeth Wilson, Mrs. Braddock is a bright, big presence, taller and much fairer than either of the Braddock men. She is Mr. Braddock's trophy-wife. As blocked in this shot, she is also a projection of Benjamin's womb-struck psychology. She immediately upstages Braddock *pere* and *fils*, stepping into the middle of the shot, her spangled dress so close to the camera that it envelops the entire frame in a soft-focus shimmer. Her brassy voice exhorts the Braddock men to "get cracking." Between Mrs. Braddock, Mrs. Robinson, and Elaine, the narrative always manages to find its next propulsive force: Mr. Braddock couldn't budge his son, but Mrs. Braddock kick-starts the graduation party; Mr. Braddock and Mr. Robinson beg and plead Benjamin to date Elaine, but Mrs. Braddock makes it happen by threatening a dinner party for the two families; Mrs. Robinson deflowers Benjamin, cuts off the relationship between Ben and Elaine by calling Ben's bluff, and nearly gets her daughter to the church on time; Elaine shifts the Berkeley sequence from stalking to courting by coming twice to Benjamin's room, and she approves her own "rescue" with her scream at the church. Even the conversation Benjamin tries so desperately to have with Mrs. Robinson is predicated upon a miserably failed conversation with his mother. All this feminine power serves to project Benjamin's continued infantilism.

The Braddock family descends the stairs (a second descent within the first ten minutes); just as we are about to enter Benjamin's maelstrom, however, the camera stops its track and pan and the trio of Braddocks continues on without us. We linger on a ghastly black-and-white painting of a gloomy clown. The pause is significant for its invitation to see the parallel to Benjamin, who will be dressed up against his will at two parties thrown by his parents to parade him like a best-in-show Airedale before their guests. Already established as Ben's psychological point of view, the camera's gaze here implies that Benjamin has noted the painting as his parents prod him down to the party and that he has made the internal comparison of the clown to his own predicament. In essence, the clown lingers on-screen because the image and all it signifies lingers in Benjamin's mind.

That the clown is monochromatic is the jolt that sticks with us: it reinforces the black-and-white motif that adorns his parents' living spaces and those of the Robinsons. The older generation has made its choices and now lives with what we increasingly come to see as the desperate consequences of conformity. Both the Braddocks and the Robinsons expect their children to excel at the finest schools and, inevitably, take the roads they themselves have taken. Mr. Braddock and Mr. Robinson are partners in a law firm (not stated in the film but in Webb's novel); their wives apparently do little else besides present themselves as fashionable matrons. Benjamin eventually learns more about the Robinsons' impoverished marital relationship than the film ever tells us about his own parents' marriage. Yet one has the sense that, at some level, the overachieving men and trophy wives are all drab and dour clowns performing as hard as they can for anyone who can be bothered to notice. The clearest of all Nichols-the-ex-stand-up-comic's demonstrations of this may be the poolside barker's banter of Mr. Braddock, trying to induce a reluctant Benjamin to perform while simultaneously keeping the assembled crowd warmed up with what amounts to a stale stand-up act, complete with heckling. Or there is Mrs. Braddock at the graduation party, announcing in velvet tones her intention to read out the data on Ben from his college yearbook, then blaring out an admonishing demand for quiet when his super-human résumé of activities fails to create the appropriately reverential hush. The black-and-white clown on the wall could as well be the Braddock coat of arms.

After the quiet contemplation of the clown painting, the straight cut to a handheld camera shot of Benjamin in close-up, negotiating the final few risers of the stairway into the noise of the well-wishers, has the impact of a jump cut. The feeling is claustrophobic, always at least two other heads crowded into the frame along with Benjamin's: hands reach out to touch him, ruffling his hair, stroking his cheek; a red-lipped woman his mother's age leaves a scarlet imprint of her mouth on Benjamin's face. The scene plays like the queasily erotic dream of a pubescent boy, in the soft, engulfing press of a harem of mothers. And there are the awkward, inter-generational stabs at conversation — the new car his parents have bought him as a graduation present ("the little red Wop job"), in which he'll have no trouble picking up "the chicks, the teenyboppers" (as indeed he proves himself to be agile: two generations of Robinson women will ride shotgun beside him in the shining red Alfa Romeo Spider). Infusing all this chatter is the poser the narrative circles

5. The Graduation Party

back to with obsessive frequency (his parents, Mr. Robinson, and Elaine are all equally devoted to learning his answer): what Benjamin intends to do with all the ability and potential he supposedly has, with "your life, your future." Only Mrs. Robinson never bothers to ask; this is because she's already intuited his blankness, the non-answer.

The reference to the Alfa Romeo provides a momentary possibility of escape — he gets away by claiming to need to "check something" on it. It's a brilliant stroke on Benjamin's part: these materialists bow to the urgency of maintaining conspicuous possessions; his father, beaming in reflected glory in the background, can hardly object, since the car is an accoutrement of the lifestyle to which he is apprenticing his son. But the house is lousy with the older generation. They lurk everywhere, pestilential. Benjamin opens the door to be instantly crowded by Mr. Loomis, leaning in like he's trying to sell Benjamin something: "How are you, track star?" The nickname objectifies Benjamin, and Mr. Loomis continues to garble the name of Benjamin's prestigious graduate scholarship, even after he's been corrected. Mr. Loomis claims to want to hear all about it, but he wants a drink first. (Alcohol is the obligatory preliminary of this social sub-set.) Only the plastic gravitas of Mr. McGuire can provide a buffer from the press of middle-aged, mostly female flesh in the scrums at the stairwell, and only sheer rudeness can extricate him from the next wave of his parents' friends after Mr. McGuire's brief prophetic huddle. Aaron Cooley sees Mr. McGuire's insider advice as an overt demonstration of the reification process: "For Ben, in this instance, plastics and reification become synonymous. Literally and metaphorically, the world Ben returns to inhabit is demonstrably covered with the spilled crude oil of reification; it follows that, if Ben pursues a future in plastics, his life, his relationships, and his existence will become increasingly plastic and reified."[5]

It's clear by now that not a single person Benjamin's age is in attendance at the party, despite his father's exhortation to him earlier that "All our good friends are here." Now, darting through the crowd like a sprinter, he passes a woman in black smoking a cigarette. Turned backwards in a chair, away from the party, in an unmistakable attitude of boredom, she insolently observes him. An attentive audience in 1968 would have recognized this woman as Anne Bancroft, thus lending a magnetic star-attraction to her otherwise diminished figure in the frame. It's our first glimpse of Mrs. Robinson. The camera doesn't quite linger on her as it did, for instance, on the clown. But it doesn't quite glance off her as it does off all the others in the room. Perhaps here *The Graduate* privileges us, through the camera's access to Benjamin's brain, with the glimmering awareness that, for Benjamin, Mrs. Robinson has always been "the most attractive of all my parents' friends." There is, in the slight hesitation of the camera lingering on Mrs. Robinson (ostensibly as Ben fights off yet one more well-wisher), a split-second exchange of pheromones. Ben's consciousness registers that neither he nor Mrs. Robinson is at home here in the hollow gaiety. Mrs. Robinson may in fact be the cougar in all that follows, but the camera, Benjamin's roving consciousness, has spotted her and made his callow curiosity known.

6

The Locked Womb
(06:30–16:30)

Mrs. Braddock's grating voice cuts off as Benjamin slams shut and leans against the bedroom door. He appears to be anticipating an assault. A dartboard behind his head underscores his feeling of being under assault. He gasps, surprisingly out of breath for a track star, then, perhaps sensing no imminent threat from the other side of the door, wanders to the window and notes more of the partygoers between him and the pool. Eventually he returns to the place we'd first found him in this house, the aquarium. Harris writes that "Nichols and Sylbert wanted Benjamin to be shot through or against clear but impenetrable surfaces as often as possible, as if he were trapped in a fishbowl."[1] Water, whether aquarium or pool, is thus an ambiguous symbol of refuge and entrapment. It is ultimately a "horrifying, self-contained cyst" from which he must be "rescued," writes Murray Pomerance, and in the dark ironies of *The Graduate*'s narrative, Benjamin receives an ambiguous savior.[2] Equipped with a transparent confection about not finding the bathroom (how many times must she, the partner's wife, have been in this house?), Mrs. Robinson barges into Benjamin's womb-space, another adult casting unwanted light into Ben's hiding place.

After this scene, nothing else of interest in *The Graduate* will happen in this bedroom: while Benjamin retreats here on occasion for refuge, the film is about his at least being smart enough to want to be born into adulthood, not stranded forever in the well-appointed cell of arrested adolescence his parents and their circle have to offer. From the obsequies of her own youth, Mrs. Robinson understands all too well Benjamin's ambivalence about belonging to his parents yet also desiring autonomy. She begins to nudge him from the nest, befouling it with cigarette ash; in this scene, we see him working hard to keep the room spotless, even vigorously scrubbing out a glowing bit of ash in the waste can. Later, after the falling out with both generations of Robinson women, we will see him indifferently chain-smoking in this room, pushing ash along furniture edges to drop off-camera, presumably into the waste can, though perhaps as likely onto the floor of a house he can no longer be bothered to maintain the pretense of respecting.

In a single, economical declaration, Mrs. Robinson simultaneously makes fun of Benjamin *and* his parents by observing that she recalls now "the track star doesn't smoke." This is Benjamin's — and our — first introduction to her cruel and manipulative wit. All his parents' friends know and objectify him as a walking résumé: the "track star," the "award-winning scholar." In the one moment of what appears on its face to be parental bragging by Mrs. Robinson — when she invites Benjamin up to Elaine's room later the same evening to see Elaine's oil portrait (oddly placed in Elaine's own room rather than where the family might be able to bask in its glow; the logic of where it is placed must be found in its function as yet another monument to the insular adulation of self) — we quickly understand that Elaine's portrait does not serve as an emblem of maternal pride but as a ruse in the next phase of a particularly delicate and arduous seduction. She makes Benjamin nervous, and thus the projected image of Mrs. Robinson in *The Graduate* demonstrates only one interest in parental dynamics: the exercise of power.

Her "track star" comment unveils an exhausted disgust with the Braddocks' triumphal display downstairs. In this Benjamin and Mrs. Robinson might find common ground; Aaron Cooley writes, "they have very similar perspectives on living in a reified world, but they are at different stages — Ben hates what he might become and Mrs. Robinson hates what she has become."[3] What makes it a multi-layered moment, though, is the imbalance of power: there is the potential that two human beings have found common ground in this unlikely setting, but in her condescension rather than sympathy, there is a transference of Benjamin's passive subservience from his parents to this parental surrogate. Mrs. Robinson has an interest in helping Benjamin break the bonds of servitude to his parents' self-image, because she has her own designs on him. During rehearsals, Bancroft was dissatisfied with the character she was creating and came to Nichols for help. He didn't like her character either, telling her she was being "too nice." Bancroft wanted to know what Nichols thought Mrs. Robinson might sound like; the line he read to her was her character's request for Benjamin to drive her home, delivered with "as much frosty, deadpan neutrality as he could muster." Bancroft recognized what she was hearing immediately: "I know what that is. That's *anger*."[4]

We know Benjamin has raced up here in outrage at what his parents are perpetrating downstairs; now a kindred soul has appeared, as aghast as he is.

6. The Locked Womb

The cinematic frame is heavy with doors, all of them closed save for the one Mrs. Robinson enters, stands in, and eventually coaxes Benjamin through. The next ten minutes will offer a series of doors for Benjamin to be pushed and prodded through, leading inexorably to his birth into adult misanthropy at the backyard birthday party. For now, in his childhood room, the most potent symbol remains the bubbling aquarium: "The aquarium motif itself underlines both the feeling of being separated from the world and the sense, in Nichols's words, of people 'drowning in their wealth.'"[5] Thus Nichols returns to this watery microcosm to get Benjamin and the narrative out of the room and into what passes for the adult world. Once more Benjamin dives back into the womb, though this time with the most overtly Freudian overtones we will encounter at any time in the narrative (save for the literally climactic moment of the musical montage that turns a rubber raft into Mrs. Robinson).

Mrs. Robinson claims not to know how to work a foreign shift and returns Benjamin's keys to the Alfa Romeo. Nothing so pedestrian as handing them over, however: with a sneer, Mrs. Robinson whips the keys past Benjamin's shoulder and into the aquarium. (Accentuating the intentionality of a Freudian implication in this gesture is the recognition that, given the angle and velocity to get the keychain past Benjamin but have it nonetheless land in rather than overshoot the tank, her throw is a virtual impossibility.) The phallic car key (already acknowledged downstairs as a sexual talisman, with which one is able to slay the "chicks, the teenyboppers") aggressively transgresses the womb-space of the Braddocks. It is the first of several symbolic sexual assaults on this callow boy over the next half hour of the film. Having already heard our first sample of Mrs. Robinson's verbal violence, we now witness a physically malicious, even violent act. (Could the keys have broken the glass of the tank? Struck and killed a fish? But even having done none of these, the act still stands out as wanton and unprovoked: a blow out of nowhere, one which the narrative's back story concerning Mrs. Robinson will have to fill in for us later.) The Keys have in fact felled the plastic diver.

Now Benjamin is obliged to roll up his shirtsleeve and dip his arm into the maternal vessel of childhood. A cut to a close-up of his hand extracting the keys under the wary gaze of the fallen scuba diver ends the scene: the keys extracted, the camera continues to roll, and we watch through the amniotic water as Benjamin recedes with Mrs. Robinson, heading through the room's one open door, back out into that harsh hallway light of another attempt at adulthood. The tableau of Benjamin retrieving the keys anticipates a notorious early painting by Eric Fischl. In *Bad Boy* (1981), a naked older woman writhes in frank erotic abandon on a bed while an adolescent boy reaches a stealthy hand into the dark slit of her purse. The louvered blinds on the windows, visual signifier of noir mise-en-scène, echo the shades Benjamin shuts, opens, shuts at the Taft Hotel the night of the affair's consummation. Fischl identifies the boy's age as twelve in the finished version of the painting, though he'd "started out as an infant lying next to the woman, then became a five-year-old sitting on the edge of the bed looking out the window. He literally grew up in that room."[6] Benjamin, like the young man in Fischl's painting, is at once on the brink of sexual maturity and taboo territory. Benjamin's gaze, as noted earlier, has already rested long enough on Mrs. Robinson's lithe, coiled form to succeed in summoning her upstairs. This is the gaze of mingled horror and desire, explored with greater frankness, that we see in the flash cuts of her naked body during the initial seduction scene in Elaine's bedroom. Benjamin, simultaneously terrified and yet desperate to grow up, embarks on what feels like the safest and yet most outré course to manhood: the sexualized return to the mother.

Fischl has commented that, in his own mind, the themes of *Bad Boy* connect to another notorious painting from the same era, *Birthday Boy* (1983), in which, in a room that could as easily be a midtown–Manhattan hotel room as an apartment bedroom, an older woman and post-adolescent boy lounge in an ambiguous relationship to one another on an enormous bed. The ambiguity comes not in their circumstances (they are both naked) but in their postures, which suggest at best that they are both lost in their own thoughts or, at worst, that neither is aware or interested in the slightest about the proximity of the other. "*Bad Boy* and *Birthday Boy* are sister paintings. Even though they were done apart, they're really the same event." Fischl recalls that both paintings had long gestations, with false starts and adjustments. "I remember at one point," he says of *Birthday Boy*, the viewer "was going to see the whole thing through a fish tank."[7] His interest was to project the sense of "a barrier" within the image — exactly the same instinct that led Nichols and his film-making team to so many images seen through water and glass. The sequencing swiftly moves the characters — and the viewer, via voyeuristic complicity — from danger into banality. It is precisely the nature of the route Benjamin will travel with Mrs. Robinson.

The Braddocks and the Robinsons have lived and worked side by side for so long that Mr. Robinson can claim of Benjamin, later this same night, "I feel as though you were my own son." The maternal refuge of the aquarium will transfer to the pool in the first half of *The Graduate*, and increasingly, we come to see this maternal water associated with Mrs. Robinson. Benjamin's transgression with Mrs. Robinson is far more than the act of adulterous sexual curiosity we assume it be on first viewing, aided by Hoffman's brilliant comic aping of pre-adolescent insecurity and monosyllabic inarticulateness. At various levels of sub-conscious desire, he is sticking it to the wife (and, by extension, to an entire way of life) of a man he doesn't respect but obviously fears, enacting a variation on the Oedipal myth.[8]

As the introductory-titles sequence to *The Graduate* dissolves into the graduation party sequence, so the graduation party sequence, using the aquarium once again as its centerpiece, overlaps the first seduction sequence, now using sound. The overlap-editing, which will continue to lace together sequences right up through the consummation of the seduction, winches tight the causation of Benjamin's behavior, demonstrating how a boy might come to climb into bed with a woman he's known all his life. At the curb before the Robinsons' "faux–Tudor mansion"[9] (found on Alpine Drive in Beverly Hills on a scouting expedition by Richard Sylbert), Benjamin's instruction as the dutiful son of a new mother-figure begins in earnest. Mrs. Robinson waits expectantly in the passenger seat for Benjamin to realize his responsibility to get out, walk around the car, open her door, and see her out onto the sidewalk. When he begins to walk back to the driver's seat, she must instruct him further on responsibility: to see her to the door; once there, to see her safely inside; eventually, to see to *all* her "needs." The irony is that we are watching a lesson in social etiquette conducted by a social predator: lulled into thinking that we are watching yet another adult from Benjamin's childhood treat him as if that childhood persists, we are as surprised as Benjamin is by the turn the conversation takes once they are inside. The protagonist's quest in *The Graduate* is twofold: for adulthood and for meaningful connection. By initially looking to Mrs. Robinson as his single-source solution, Benjamin fumbles both of these otherwise worthy goals.

The two pause at the door while Mrs. Robinson finds her key. The open door frames Benjamin against the white-lit interior of the house, while Mrs. Robinson pauses against the dark wood of the door. The symbiosis of light and dark creates a snapshot of innocence lured into its inevitable trap — yet this trap is hardly a typical scenario for innocence lost, and Benjamin's innocence will be a tenacious thing, lost only in stages, and finally and completely erased not by a sexual act but in a sustained perpetration of emotional violence upon another innocent, Elaine, at the strip club. Light and dark are echoed in the décor of the Robinson's house (as in the Braddocks', particularly in that awning out by the pool where Mr. Braddock and Benjamin will perform for the birthday party guests); the implication of all this black and white is of the cut-and-dried, of a world without the nuance (and vitality) of color. Mrs. Robinson's boldly sexualized aggression, as she leads him back through the house and into the sun porch — her den (or lair) — suggests the love/death mating rituals of the insect and animal worlds. Apprenticing himself to Mrs. Robinson's misanthropy kills something in Benjamin, but it is also the catalyst, at the strip club with Elaine, of a regeneration of his spirit.

As the broad-leaf fronds flood-lit beyond the glass doors of Mrs. Robinson's sun porch suggest, Benjamin is in the jungle now, a fleet but inexperienced creature beyond his own territory, in "a nighttime lair for predatory animals."[10] To accentuate this, Mrs. Robinson turns on a radio to music, composed for the film by Dave Grusin in order to stridently broadcast a style and sensibility from beyond the borders of "Benjamin's" Simon and Garfunkel soundtrack. She forces a glass of bourbon into Benjamin's hand, blows cigarette smoke in his face, makes embarrassingly personal confessions. If these are typically admissions that might be expected to cause vulnerability in the confessor, they have the opposite effect here: Benjamin accepts them as they are intended, as acts of aggression. Her truths are assumed to terrify and tame, not to share and connect.

Of all the many attempted conversations Benjamin has in *The Graduate*, only the ones with Elaine are predicated upon a mutual interest and exchange. This, too, is a reflection of Benjamin's psychological point of view, since, as he tells Elaine, "You're the first thing for so long that I've liked. The first person I could stand to be with." The camera, faithful in its first half almost without exception to Benjamin's sensibilities, offers us a world of boorish narcissism. Mrs. Robinson flirts, parts her legs, and drops the unambiguously transparent hint that her husband isn't due back "for several hours." Hoffman dutifully delivers Buck Henry's double entendre, swallowing hard as he takes in the panorama of Mrs. Robinson's thighs while accusing her of "opening up" her "private life," concluding, "Mrs. Robinson, you're trying to seduce me." It is the boldest statement Benjamin has made thus far in the film, almost miraculously glib, even playfully flirtatious in the Robinsonian manner, particularly considering Benjamin's by-now familiar tongue-tied, retiring sullenness. But Nichols has positioned the camera and the famously diminutive Hoffman so that Benjamin's new-found sense of urbanity never takes: Benjamin is dwarfed beneath the enormous arch of Mrs. Robinson's exposed leg, a mere baby boy — depicted in this frame as hardly progressed beyond umbilical length from the birth chamber. The monstrous mother-figure proceeds to laugh in sport at his discomfiture, and Benjamin instantly recognizes the horror that is the flip side of maternal titillation: "Mrs. Robinson, please forgive me. That's the sickest thing I've ever said." Ironically, this is one of the few times that Mrs. Robinson displays something other than the irritation of being tested by a disobedient child (as Benjamin will, sometimes infuriatingly, prove to be). Benjamin's repeated protestations of loathing for his having contemplated the taboo leave her apparently on the verge of similar conclusions: "Forget about it," she says. "Finish your drink": an articulation of the liquid solution to the nag of disappointment, disgust, or despair.

Mrs. Robinson suggests the party move upstairs, now with the social legitimization of Elaine as mutual object. Hoffman solves the problem of how to play an otherwise bright boy who must pretend to forget everything he's just realized, using a mixture of autonomic drone and breezy politeness. Asked if he'd like to see Elaine's portrait, he assents robotically: "Very much." Bound to her by the taboo he has given utterance, he will gratefully do anything she asks, though we suspect that, having been afforded a glimpse of the taboo, what Benjamin wants more than anything is "the sickest thing." Hoffman's ingenuous comic delivery in the scene in Elaine's room is heartbreaking. Mrs. Robinson undresses, but it's Benjamin who feels exposed. Nichols's *mise-en-scène* is used to solid effect here, where the two characters only rarely venture into two-shot proximity. With the bed as ambiguous boundary, Mrs. Robinson undoes a bracelet latch and casually drops the jewelry on the carefully made-up covers. Benjamin's eyes follow her motions like an obedient pet's. She just as casually asks him to come across the room to her. "Over there?" he asks, referencing the vast psychological terrain represented by those several steps that would bring him into physical proximity to a hyper-sexualized woman de-jewelling herself in an otherwise empty house. She makes him complicit by drawing him near and having him unzip her dress, which she then sheds like a snake's skin, without self-consciousness, to reveal leopard-print lingerie and dramatic tan lines that suggest her flesh is no stranger to the open air and the eyes of the curious.

"I kept thinking about [the Henry James novella,] "The Beast in the Jungle," Nichols recalls. 'Let's have animal skins.'"[11] The wardrobe choice of leopard-print for her lingerie (and later for a coat she wears) feels inevitable by the time we see it: we've long since identified her, via Benjamin's subjective terror, as the teeth-bared predator. The tension in what transfixes Benjamin at this moment is complicated, at the very least, by his physical desire for a desirable, half-naked woman; the ambition to be an adult, not the child-like plaything of the adults; the reverberating knowledge that what he suspects Mrs. Robinson of doing with him is "the sickest thing"; the imminence of danger at being caught by Mr. Robinson's return; and the ever-present sense of social etiquette: a young man must politely obey his elders. All the while, Nichols frames the shot so that the portrait of Elaine hangs like an unspoken thought between them.

"What are you so afraid of?" Mrs. Robinson says, taunting Benjamin's natural fears of social and spiritual taboo, as well as of the maternal carnivore, clearly desirous of devouring her young. Actors are always quick to celebrate the joys of playing the villain, a truly wicked character who chews scenery and steals scenes with an innate disinterest in social convention and team play. Therein lies the pitfall of excess, of caricature. The best, scariest performances retain an evil character's humanity: purely alien monsters are less interesting psychologically than the messier hybrid of monstrous humans. Mrs. Robinson is a force of un-nature. Yet Anne Bancroft's skillful performance demonstrates that her misanthropy is fully human and begins at home. Of Bancroft's legendary performance, Hoffman said admiringly, "I think Anne and Mike Nichols made a very critical decision, [...] which was not to judge the character. It's Nichols's style — he walks that edge of really going as far as he can without falling over the cliff, into disbelief. It's not caricature. That's the highest compliment for satire."[12]

Or, if it *is* caricature, it's in the same key as the rest of the film, which sees the world through the eyes of a naïf who caricatures the world. Eventually, during their cataclysmic "conversation," Benjamin learns that Mrs. Robinson's own possibilities to discover her genuine identity and values were aborted by her family's decision to have her marry Mr. Robinson as the result of an unplanned pregnancy. At the most basic level, Benjamin *gets* her — the frustration, the sense of having been passively conveyed to her present predicament. "We suddenly understand her — her bitterness, her deep pool of sadness. It's the key to her character, Buck Henry believes: 'That's when I realized that I knew Mrs. Robinson. That she had *been* Benjamin. She is a very intelligent and cynical woman. She knows what's happening to her.'"[13] While it hardly softens the vision of misanthropic terror she projects as a response, it reveals the very human roots of her disintegration. (It is also, as we will see in examining the film's conclusion, her final condemnation: she's willing to aid and abet the continuation of the cycle.)

Some of the most strident anti–*Graduate* rhetoric focuses on the perceived misogynist representation of Mrs. Robinson's character (particularly in the long conversation between Benjamin and Mrs. Robinson); critics also direct accusations of misogyny at the way Elaine behaves, especially with Benjamin. These ambiguous projections of femininity require careful study, precisely because of what they tell us about Benjamin — not the women. Farber and Changas seem to have understood the ironic point of view in *The Graduate* when they refer to Bancroft's portrayal as "a young man's deliciously provocative sexual fantasy come to life."[14] The film's narrative distortions of Mrs. Robinson are a result of the preoccupations of its protagonist; the nightmare quality of the affair and the cinematic prettiness of the courtship of Mrs. Robinson's daughter Elaine could not feel more different, because they are

6. The Locked Womb

wide swings of a young man's affective pendulum in violent response to emotional forces around and within him.

It's odd and ultimately troubling, then, that Farber and Changas protest Benjamin's eventual downgrading of the relationship with Mrs. Robinson to nothing more meaningful (or pleasurable) than "shaking hands": "what seems an astonishing blindness to Mrs. Robinson's very real sexiness is to be taken as a moral victory,"[15] they write with libertine disapproval. David Denby complains, "The movie's view of her is priggish; all she wants, after all, is sex with a nice-looking boy."[16] These objections to Benjamin's sanctimony also imply an argument in favor of the affair, as if Benjamin's and Mrs. Robinson's mutual satisfaction is all that is at stake in the hotel room. Farber and Changas conclude that *The Graduate* is a "real failure" because, despite being "to a large extent about sexuality," the film is prudishly "fastidious" in its rendering of sex.[17] Tom Reck is more blunt. *The Graduate*'s attitude toward sex [...] is, in short, an anti-sexual attitude." Reck takes the seemingly counter-intuitive position that "for anyone interested in recognizing it, Mrs. Robinson is easily the most admirable character in *The Graduate*." What Reck admires is Mrs. Robinson's frank willingness to see and express her desire: "what she needs is a simple distraction from her own disillusionment with upper-classism, from Los Angeles suburbianism [sic], from marital disunion [...] pure and simply, a sexual orgasm."[18]

Reck believes, rightly, that there's a double-standard in a Hollywood ideology that celebrates the sexual appetites of the young and unattached (as in the example he gives, Elia Kazan's phenomenally dated 1962 sexual psychodrama *Splendor in the Grass*) yet "condemns [Mrs. Robinson] for her audacity" in wanting sex with a physically fit younger partner. But this is neither sexism nor ageism on the part of the filmmakers. Why in fact are both Mrs. Robinson *and* Benjamin condemned by the larger point of view of *The Graduate*— the one whereby we see not only the world through Benjamin's eyes, but also Benjamin exposed in all his callow hypocrisy? Not because they have sexual appetites, but because they have, apparently, nothing else — certainly no sense, for instance, of the distorted, one-dimensional selfishness of their carnality, which is the antithesis of "making love." Nor is there a sense of the transgressed power dynamics of the nuclear bond: much of the Freudian imagery in the film's first act serves to underscore a betrayed unspoken trust, the child taught the unhappy ways of the world by a manipulative surrogate of his mother.

The larger effect of *The Graduate*'s depiction of domestic rot seems consonant with the persistence of the fouled nest in American family life, a theme of Nichols's first feature film as well. In *Who's Afraid of Virginia Woolf?*,

Nichols's adaptation of Edward Albee's corrosive satire on George and Martha as the First Parents of a fractious American empire, George may be a "swamp," but Martha is the howling, emasculating banshee. Like Elizabeth Taylor's Martha, Anne Bancroft's Mrs. Robinson carries the banner of womanhood to the nearest mudhole and makes us feel the mingled pleasure and pain of self-abasement. In Martha and Mrs. Robinson, we understand that a longer chain of causality can be traced beyond woman-troubles or misogyny to an illness in the culture at large, one that devours men and women alike. It is true that Mrs. Robinson is the most demonized source of cultural sickness in *The Graduate*, but comparing her back story to her husband's, for instance, or to the potential future for Benjamin if he toes the party line, makes clear that, ultimately, the rot in the culture is not at its core "female." *The Graduate* doesn't hate or condescend to women; it presents the point of view of a character held fast in terror and thrall of women.

Mrs. Robinson, nearly nude, announces her intention to "go to bed." Briefly, the action moves outside of Elaine's bedroom, only to return there when Benjamin, the disobedient boy who has lost what little nerve he had, is reprimanded by a stentorian Mrs. Robinson for his failure to obey a menial command. As a consequence, she literally sends him to the child's room in the house. The scene on the stairs is comic but, in its Freudian dimensions, the most horrific moment of punitively twisted maternalism until the actual consummation night. Dustin Hoffman channels his inner six-year-old on the staircase, his arms shambling as he ascends and descends. Off-screen (the psychological distance between them growing even as it wrenches them closer to an unhealthy but inextricable attachment), Mrs. Robinson barks orders. The neutral-site solution of Elaine's room is her master-stroke (and by extension Webb's, which Henry and Nichols were wise enough not to tinker with): the child would display profound hesitation before finally entering the master bedroom or bathroom where the risk of the parent's exposure would be so great, and the familiarity of the child's room thus becomes the most likely site of incipient sexual abuse of power. Benjamin stumps like a scared grade-school child into the room where, in the glass reflection of Elaine's portrait, we glimpse the overwhelming reality of Mrs. Robinson's fully naked body as she steals into the room, shuts the door, and turns the lock. The trap is sprung.

A series of quick cuts — the reflected image in the portrait, Benjamin's reverse shot ("oh, God"), flash cuts of various erogenous zones on Mrs. Robinson's body, more reverse shots of Benjamin's nearly but not-quite averted gaze ("oh, my Christ") suggest the profane violence of the moment. The parallel to the legendary shower scene in *Psycho* (Alfred Hitchcock, 1960) is necessarily inexact yet nonetheless striking. Both scenes are dominated by overbearing mother-figures, weak sons, the male gaze, the objectified female body rendered as a series of "parts," and the slashing of matter by montage. Mrs. Robinson presses her naked flesh against the already locked door, a second fail-safe to anyone emerging unscathed. Benjamin can leave only over her nude body. Her smoothly delivered patter has the ring of practice (confirmed by her worldly nonchalance, even faint boredom, at the next meeting, to begin the affair at the Taft Hotel: perhaps, it may occur to us, she's been through all this before). We barely hear her rehearsed pitch. Like Benjamin's, our attention is commandeered by the explosion of visual imagery: flash cutting between shots of Benjamin's anguished yet titillated face, squeamishly looking and not-looking, a gaper at a car-wreck, and brief shots of Mrs. Robinson's breasts and womb interspersed between longer shots of her face, the only part of her still heavily made-up (and thus covered — the mask always in place). He's a good boy encountering the seductiveness of the bad. His profanity here is as religious as it is blasphemous: he knows that they are both being undone by each extra moment of fatal lingering.

We have the sense in reflecting upon the shower scene in *Psycho* of the terrible ambiguities of the shower-murder: Norman's mixed desire and revulsion, Marion's moment of cleansing from her "madness" in stealing the $40,000 sent down the drain with her spilled blood. The ambiguities of Benjamin's visual deflowering are, ironically, summed up by Mr. Robinson mere moments later when, in the midst of giving Benjamin "a piece of advice," he observes, "Ben? You'll never be young again." Nodding, Benjamin laments plaintively, "I know." If Mrs. Robinson's forced penetration into Benjamin's childhood womb-space was begun in his own bedroom, the rape's next stage is enacted in yet another childhood room. The final consummation of the rape will be enacted in yet a third bedroom, this one neutrally located at the Taft Hotel, where Benjamin becomes, if only as a result of still more psychological violence, an active participant in his own deflowering.

7

"Ben? You'll Never Be Young Again."
(16:30 — 21:00)

Mr. Robinson returns home (an off-screen, diegetic exaggeration of squealing tires and a car door's slam that, again, foregrounds Benjamin's subjective hyper-awareness), temporarily breaking the spell that Mrs. Robinson's Morgana has cast. She will have to continue her work another night, though the ironies of Mr. Robinson's "piece of advice" to Benjamin downstairs are not lost on us: in the bankruptcy of Mr. Robinson's vision of the adult world, where 21 is "a helluva good age to be," Benjamin ought to be sowing a few wild oats with all takers. Inadvertently, Mr. Robinson has resumed the pitch begun upstairs by his own wife. In Benjamin's hurried escape from the locked room, we see in close-up that, for the first of many times, he touches Mrs. Robinson's flesh — though this first time it is merely to press her aside at the hip and fumble the locked door open. His track-star training comes to good use in the next shot: a foregrounded tumbler of bourbon poured for him by Mrs. Robinson earlier and left to sweat on ice at the bar serves as finish-line reward for the soft-focus figure racing down the stairs and back into the sun porch. He's falling right into the social swing of things: Benjamin on the Braddock-Robinson fast-track to success, a rat-race best washed down with a stiff drink.

"Is that Ben's car out front?" says Mr. Robinson. Played by Murray Hamilton, he is a golf-bag carrying caricature of sun-burned good health hiding inner rot; eight years later, Hamilton was the ideal casting choice for the self-interested, myopic mayor of Amity in Steven Spielberg's *Jaws* (1975): a man who would literally feed his children to the predator at the risk of lost commerce. The entire ensuing "conversation" between Mr. Robinson and Benjamin is actually, in keeping with the epigrammatic line, people talking

7. "Ben? You'll Never Be Young Again." 95

without listening, a monologue of quiet but profoundly unreflective desperation by Mr. Robinson. Mr. Robinson's mournful assertion that Ben will never be young again implies his own sense of annihilation by time: Mr. Robinson is another of this film's hollow men, and he sees more of the same for the generation he and his partner have produced. There is no warning to escape the rat-race in Mr. Robinson's words; there is only the despairing encouragement for Benjamin to enjoy the last consequence-free years of his life, the ones that will nonetheless precipitate consequences. (Knowing the full history of the Robinsons, as we soon will, we can appreciate the depth of denial such a philosophy requires.) *The Graduate* is at its darkest in drawing conclusions about social reality whenever the generations meet for conversation.

The lighting is similarly *dark*. Ron Howard points out the low-key lighting choices in *The Graduate* as one of the methods the filmmakers employ to manipulate tone: "In some ways it's a traditional kind of sex comedy, but it's not shot like a screwball comedy. It's shot like a drama. Look at all these dark rooms and tense moments."[1] Where comedy would typically have been shot on a set flooded with key-light, Nichols and Surtees opt in scenes like the two conversations between Benjamin and Mr. Robinson for a low-key, chiaroscuro lighting design, in which shadows mix with grotesquely distorted highlights to create expressionistic tension. Nichols credits Surtees with the contrast between the brighter mood of the drink with Mrs. Robinson before they go up together to see Elaine's portrait and this encroaching darkness after the locked-room solicitation. "When we come downstairs, back to the bar," Nichols told Harris, "the lighting is entirely different from the first time we were there — it's a dark and scary place because Mr. Robinson is scary and drunk, and she's *really* scary when she comes in [after getting re-dressed]." Nichols the neophyte remembers asking Surtees if this was okay, to change the lighting when "nothing has changed." But of course everything has changed — Benjamin will never be young again, and Surtees the veteran assured him that a new scene admits its own formal logic.[2] The logic of everything we see and hear in *The Graduate* must be understood through Benjamin: A room turns dark in *The Graduate* when Benjamin perceives its lurking danger, not because someone has flicked a switch.

The shadows sit most heavily in this scene on Benjamin's face, splitting it in two. Mr. Robinson offers Ben a drink, then, unbidden, pours them both a scotch, Mr. Robinson's drink of choice, failing to note either the bourbon already in Ben's glass or Ben's stated preference (a default also set for him, by Mrs. Robinson, within the hour past). He sits Ben down and tears open a cigar with his teeth, spitting the rag-end into a corner of the room. The uncivilized violence of the act elicits one of those involuntary whimpers from Ben. In the background of the shot, in soft-focus, wait the stairs. Like Benjamin, we retain the after-image of that brightly lit flesh we've just glimpsed. As Mr. Robinson begins the slow, condescending wind-up for whatever pitch he means to toss at Ben ("How long have you and I known each other? How long have your Dad and I been partners?"), we can't help wondering what Mrs. Robinson will do. Despite the brevity of screen time (the film is less than 20 minutes old), we have a sense of Mrs. Robinson's audacious power. She seems completely wild, untamed — yet we know in hindsight that her entire life has been a restless pacing within a cage.

That Mr. Robinson, however unknowingly, is counseling Ben to enter into the affair begins to seem nothing more than par for this particular course. A door slams off-screen, upstairs. A moment later a soft-focus figure appears, descending the stairs in the same dress she'd so recently shimmied out of, and Mr. Robinson hurries to conclude his pitch: "Take things as they come ... Have a good time with the girls and so on." Without any greeting for her husband, Mrs. Robinson orders Benjamin to sit back down and heads for the bar. The dysfunction between husband and wife is apparent immediately. But then, isn't Mr. Robinson's attention to the golf course rather than to the party thrown by his partner evidence that the dysfunction is not limited to this household? It's been dark for hours; the presumption is that Mr. Robinson has finished his round of golf and then spent more time at the nineteenth hole, avoiding the party and lubricating for another evening at home. With no more interest in greeting her than she in greeting him, Mr. Robinson asks if she thinks his philosophy sounds like "good advice." Since this is precisely the philosophy that led to Elaine Robinson's conception in the back seat of a Ford, one might reasonably assume neither would find such advice particularly "sound." However, she tersely concurs.

Something sinister is in the air (and the lighting, and maybe the whiskey): without looking at or even liking each other, the Robinsons have nonetheless demonstrated a shared bond. Each resents the bondage. Yet each seeks to protect it at all costs (all the talk at the Berkeley boarding house about a divorce is pure ruse: there they sit in the places of honor in the church as Elaine marries Carl Smith at film's end). Theirs is the worst sort of habituality, a greater mockery of marriage than any divorce, each the other's prisoner in the "ol' castle," as Mr. Robinson calls it. They're Southern California's variation on George and Martha, the fun couple from Nichols's first film. One would think that, if only Benjamin can escape the castle-hold this night, the story he will live to tell will keep him free of loveless marriage for the rest of his days. But this errant knight will have to make a series of potentially devastating mistakes before the final castle-storming, and even then, the success of the quest will be left terminally ambiguous. "Doesn't he look to you like the kind of guy who has to fight 'em off?" says Mr. Robinson, addressing his question from off-screen to Mrs. Robinson, in close-up, around whose head swirls a spider's trap of complex shadow. "Yes, he does," she says, amused that, once again, her voice can carry such effortless, devastating double-meaning: in three words, she makes Benjamin sweat while leaving her husband a cuckolded fool. Mr. Robinson appallingly ends their interview with one final pitch: to sow some of those wild oats with his own daughter, Elaine. The incestuous layers are beginning to pile up, since he's just admitted he thinks of Ben as if he were his "own son."

Nichols has *The Graduate* humming along in a particularly high-performance gear, piling on the good choices as the action proceeds with edited inevitability to the birthday party. We cut to the exterior of the black-and-white house again, Benjamin stumping down the sidewalk towards his car, released for the moment from the asylum. The Robinsons make a showy act of connubiality in the doorway, Mr. Robinson's possessive paw around his wife's shoulder. Mr. McGuire was on to something: Plastics are everywhere. Benjamin totters on the brink of buying in. "I'll see you soon, I hope," Mrs. Robinson calls. Nichols and O'Steen edit in one last Benjamin mouse-squeak as a rimshot, and then they insert Mr. Braddock's overlapped voice to build causation to the next scene. As Benjamin hurdles with track-star agility into his convertible, we hear Mr. Braddock crank up his ringmaster's delivery: "Ladies and gentlemen, your attention please — for this afternoon's feature attraction!" In similar fashion, the next scene (of the birthday party) will transition to the scene beyond it (at the Taft Hotel the night of Benjamin's capitulation). These voice overlaps reinforce "the protagonist's sense of alienation and estrangement,"[3] writes Paul Monaco, yet the three scenes in this sequence of the film — graduation party and aftermath, birthday party, and consummation of the seduction — have a cumulative effect, sealed by the voice overlaps, implying that Mrs. Robinson has accomplices in her seduction of this innocent; it is in fact an unwitting, corrupt conspiracy that includes not only her husband but also Benjamin's own parents. Nichols talks about the causal implications of the voice overlaps as "an organic thing: This thing that happens now leads to the next thing. They are the same. They are interlocked."[4] Ultimately, the world Benjamin witnesses is all one vast locked room. His apparent hair's-breadth escape from the Robinsons' "castle" is an illusion.

Having already made the sound cut, Nichols and O'Steen now cut visually to Mr. Braddock in the backyard of his house. Here are the Braddocks in their element, preening. The voice overlaps have made clear that, for Benjamin, there can be no escape, no stage door he might slip through to avoid the performances the adults have planned for him. He will be moved around as they see fit, like any other piece of luggage. Ben's dark epiphany during this scene in his own backyard (at the bottom of the deep end of the swimming pool) is that to be an adult is to connive, indifferent to anyone but oneself. It's the single road he travels from this moment in the film — as he turns 21— until his next epiphany, in a West Hollywood strip club with Elaine.

8

The Birthday Party
(21:00 — 24:00)

In Mr. Braddock, we note the social performance anxiety rife among the nouveau riche in Beverly Hills. (He's clearly made a pile of money, yet we see in a later scene that he still does the tedious work of skimming his own pool. Production designer Richard Sylbert calls the narrative a "pressure cooker of two families."[1]) Mr. Braddock has populated another party ostensibly thrown for his son with his own friends and their children, none of whom is remotely Benjamin's age: several subjective camera points of view from his own eyes and later his son's reveal that adults and very young children exclusively compose the population of invited guests. The Robinsons are once again conspicuously absent; perhaps they weren't invited after Mr. Robinson's graduation party snub. The overlapped dialogue of the carnival barker continues, then stops. Benjamin is nowhere in sight. The low camera-angle up on Daniels turns his head into that enormous solar presence we first saw in Benjamin's room, dominating the frame.

Even without Benjamin on-screen, we are still in Benjamin's psychological point of view. Mr. Braddock, an enormous magnetic force in his son's consciousness, also projects as pathetic in this scene, scrabbling on his thin white ankles back to the cabana door to peer inside. "Are you ready in there, feature attraction?" he calls. Anxious about neglecting his audience, he rebounds, saying, "Listen, now I'm going to ask for a big round of applause to bring this boy out here, all right? Now wait a minute. Oh, let me amend that: to bring this young man out here ... because today he is twenty-one years old!" Cheers ensue: his audience has correctly identified their own performance cue. When Benjamin does not emerge, however, the heckling begins: "Let's get on with the show!" jeers the voice of one of Mr. Braddock's contemporaries. Nichols the former comic renders the scene for maximum comic discomfort. The heckling from the crowd intensifies (Mr. Braddock's "But first I have a few words to say" prompts the anonymous retort, "You always do!" The best Mr. Braddock can improvise is, "Ho ho ho ho — look who's talking"), which confirms his sense (as well as ours) that the act is dying.

He huskily reverts to coaxing his son out *on stage*. The implication is of a parent exasperated by his young child's bashfulness. "You better get out here, Ben. I can't hold 'em much longer!" Beyond the self-conscious, good-natured irony in the remark — these are "our good friends," we remember him saying the night of the graduation party, and surely good friends would be indulgent of his efforts to please them — there is the desperate vulnerability of flop sweat. We sense that, for these adults, the "attraction" (in the connotative sense of entertainment, of course, but also as denotative gravity or magnetism) of one's offspring is that they redound to their parents' reflected glory. The prime Beverly Hills real estate, the big house, and the pool are all specimens of one sort of cultural talisman, quite easily matched, however, by the mere flashing of a competitor's equally legal tender: Sylbert told Carringer that the film was "about keeping up with the Joneses," and this meant adopting a design in which, despite the factual differences between the Braddock and Robinson homes, where any detail that is black in one is white in the other and any surface that is rounded in one is squared off in the other, the houses are in essence "identical."[2] The point of differentiation in such competitive brinksmanship, then, must transcend what can be bought. In *The Graduate*, the behavior of the Braddocks can be interpreted as their announcement of a bloodline of hereditary excellence. Potentially, the most valuable possession (because not purely an item for purchase) of the men and women in this milieu is a son or daughter of distinction. Benjamin's quantifiable success as an award-winning scholar and star athlete corroborates the Hollywood production of his life Mr. Braddock has been fashioning for more than two decades — indeed, since Mr. Braddock's own collegiate days on the fast track. That he "can't hold 'em much longer" thus comes too close for Mr. Braddock's comfort to a *vanitas* admission.

"Dad," says Ben, off-screen. "Can we just talk about this for a second? I'd like to discuss this." Predictably, his father does not hear. The hoary cliché that children should be seen and not heard takes on prescient significance in establishing the psychology of Mr. Braddock, who turns back to the crowd, single-mindedly intent on maintaining both the mask and the masque. His sunglasses at this point suggest that he is not only deaf but also blind to how his life has unfolded. Soon his son will have donned his own pair of shades, aping the adults' costuming choice as well as their manners. "This boy — I'm sorry," he says, the second time he's had to correct himself about Benjamin's

8. The Birthday Party 101

developmental status in less than a minute — "this young *man* is soon to continue his education as a Frank Halpingham Award Scholar, but before he does, before he does...." Anxiety mounting, Mr. Braddock trots back to the door and hisses, "You're disappointing them, Ben. You're disappointing them!"

On the contrary — we know that in these brittle social competitions, such improvisation is an unexpected entertainment, to see a rival locked in a struggle of wills with his chief calling card. Something useful does emerge in Benjamin this day: hardly what can be called a sense of genuine adult responsibility, but at least a willingness to play hardball. His father's act is dying, and Benjamin is the one who's killing it. Though his initial attempts at adult autonomy are desperately wrong, Ben has begun the slow and painful process of moving himself out from under his father's thumb. "Dad, can you listen?" he asks, but his father is too busy shouting to notice: "He is going to give us a practical demonstration of what I feel safe in saying is a pretty exciting birthday present." He makes one last joke on his own conspicuous consumption and corrupted priorities (thereby betraying his own obsessive awareness of them): "And it better work, or I'm out over two hundred bucks!" Unspoken in the reference to the scuba gear is the apparently secondary possibility that, if it doesn't work, he could also be "out" his only son and heir. "Okay then," he says, scrabbling a last time to the door, which he pushes finally, brutally open: "let's hear it now for ... *Benjamin BRADDOCK!*" — the emphasis, typically, stresses the surname and its reflected glory.

The entire focus of the scene shifts with the next shot. Though we have been viewing all of the preceding through the lost-in-the-funhouse psychology of Benjamin, we only now get our first birthday glimpse of him (and, by extension, of his father's "pretty special birthday present"): in stark contrast to the gleaming white fixtures of the house's interior, Benjamin is sheathed entirely in black. He has become the plastic scuba diver from his childhood aquarium, his parents' insistence on his child-like relationship to them forcing him to remain arrested in the womb. We have seen, however, that Mrs. Robinson has brought psychological complications to the womb of his arrested adolescence. Nichols presents the rest of this scene and the overlapped dialogue to the succeeding scene at the Taft Hotel as an argument for the complicity of the Braddocks in the trespassed womb. The larger focus-shift of this moment of *The Graduate* is from the ego of Mr. Braddock to that of his son. It's Benjamin's big debut. The performance anxiety is all Benjamin's once he takes the stage, and in Benjamin's role as "adult," Mrs. Robinson will be his greatest heckler.

Still inside the house, but aware of the waiting crowd, Benjamin takes a first tentative step towards the camera, then another, big flippers flapping.

The door is open, his privacy stripped from him. For the first and only time, he is referred to as "Benjy," his infantilized identity unmistakable. His father continues to reel off circus patter about the show he's orchestrated, his last production starring his son: "Well, folks, this remarkable young man is going to perform for you some spectacular and amazing feats of daring in water that is over six feet deep!" Though Daniels' delivery is a masterful comic lampoon, we're only half-listening: unlike the previous two minutes, in which Hoffman is off-screen while Mr. Braddock dominates, the next two minutes, in which Hoffman is again off-screen, have a different resonance. Hoffman and the audience merge with the camera; we don Benjamin's mask, breathe with him. These are the sounds of silence — "what was happening in Benjamin's head," Nichols's stated goal for point of view beginning with the sound design.[3] Subjective camera angles provide Benjamin's point of view: on his father and mother, coaxing him forward like proud parents exhorting their infant to toddle in an 8-millimeter home movie; on the ridiculous assemblage of onlookers, amused by the spectacle of Braddock and Son; on his own flippered feet negotiating cement steps and testing the water at poolside. The film's identification with Benjamin is now complete. When he enters the womb/pool, so do we — though some twenty minutes later in the film, darkness, our "old friend," will spare us a vision of his entry into Mrs. Robinson.

The scuba performance is a wonderfully complicated visual metaphor of Benjamin's ambivalence: he toddles out of his childhood home into the backyard, but regresses as if in a child's tantrum by sulking at the bottom of the pool. The lapped voice-over phone exchange between Benjamin and Mrs. Robinson that concludes the scene indicates that this return to the womb is no longer purely maternal but sexually charged. In Charles Webb's novel, the scuba performance is not the direct and final catalyst of the affair implied by the film; in fact, in the novel the scuba performance serves as the expedient to a more dramatic attempt to escape, via the road trip. Webb's intentionally emotionless narrative renders the Braddock men as hollow:

> "What's all this about?" Mr. Braddock said.
> "I'm leaving after breakfast on a trip," Benjamin said, sprinkling sugar on his grapefruit. "I have no idea where I'm going. Maybe just around the country or the continent. Maybe if I can get papers I'll work around the world. So that's that."
> "Well what's the point of it."
> "The point is I'm getting the hell out of here."
> "Mr. Braddock frowned at him. "This doesn't sound too well thought out," he said.[4]

The significance of the trip is that Benjamin Braddock is smart enough to see he has no future here with these people in this place, where his future is a foregone conclusion of advanced schooling, professional apprenticeship, and similarly conspicuous consumption. (Later in the conversation in Webb's novel, Benjamin asserts vehemently that he has not been educated.) The significance of the *failure* of the trip is that Benjamin has the native intelligence to see all this but no imagination to see a viable alternative. He is a sterile product of his environment. And while he knows he ought to be elsewhere, he's going to have his sugared grapefruit first.

As a narrative, the film improves on the book, not so much by eliding the trip (which was in any case a necessary expedient of telling a cinematic story in under two hours) as by making clearer the symbolic causation of the graduation and birthday parties and the consummation of the affair. Webb's narrator tells us, "Two days after he got home from the trip Benjamin decided to begin his affair with Mrs. Robinson."[5] There is no catalyst. Even the effect of the two days is ultimately to diminish the despairing impact of the failed trip, as it blurs into Benjamin's perceived litany of failures, including the pointlessness of his past education or continuing on with the Halpingham Award. In Henry and Nichols's conflation of weeks into days that, in their overlapped editing, seem all part of the same waking nightmare, other conflations emerge: of mothers/lovers, of aquarium and pool with the pre-natal womb, of domineering, condescending, hypocritical adults, of performance and the anxiety that permeates it.

Webb chooses cool disaffection to characterize his narrative's point of view, but the effect Webb desires to convey is undercut by the choice of a predicate like "Benjamin decided." The sheer lost-ness of Benjamin Braddock in *The Graduate* in both its novel and film versions is better served by Hoffman's childlike confusion and passivity, in which the "decisions" he appears to make are actually endgames enforced by the pressures of circumstance. No single image in the novel matches the symbolic power of Benjamin as rendered by the subjective camera, emerging from the pool water framed by the diver's goggles, in what Robert Beuka calls "an odd reimagining of the birthing process."[6] This is, indeed, Benjamin's birthday, and yet the unnatural quality of this whole experience is accentuated as both Mr. and Mrs. Braddock's hands reach down and push Benjamin—the camera, us—back under. The show must go on. On his birthday, amidst what Glenn Man calls "the coded images of death,"[7] Benjamin drowns.

9

An "Affair" at the Taft Hotel
(24:00 − 36:00)

Mr. Braddock's "two hundred bucks" have been well but fatally spent: the scuba gear works, and the Braddocks have lost their son. Glenn Man writes that, "As the underwater camera pulls away from a medium to a long shot, Ben recedes into a little figure in the watery tomb, isolated and insignificant."[1] We presume that he will remain in the deep end until his summoned audience has departed. We may also presume that, despite not having seen what was advertised, they will leave having witnessed a perhaps even more entertaining spectacle: a son "drowning" in his father's grandiosity, and a father "drowning" in his own flop sweat.

What exactly drowns with Benjamin when he ends the party by not resurfacing? We can understand Benjamin to have released himself from the subjugation of the social eye: he has behaved badly in public at two parties in his honor. However, he will remain preoccupied with what people "think" while weakly resisting Mrs. Robinson's overtures, and Hoffman's comic scene with screenwriter Buck Henry as the desk clerk at the Taft Hotel lampoons his continuing awareness of maintaining the appropriate social appearances. Whatever else may have been drowned in the deep end, what surely has found its watery grave is a sense of filial servitude. All pretense of the former relationship to his father has been washed away at the end of the birthday party scene. (Much later in the film, when Benjamin has lost both generations of Robinson women, he gazes wistfully out his bedroom window to the pool below, where his father wields a pool skimmer. Though indistinct in the distance below, Mr. Braddock's exasperation as he sees his son is unmistakable: we know he's thinking that this should be Benjy's job.)

Benjamin, now 21, has made a choice, grown a backbone, become active. Yet the cinematic language that Nichols, Henry, Surtees, and O'Steen employ is spectacularly ambiguous. In Henry's final draft of the screenplay, expanding on a visual effect Nichols had carried with him into the production,[2] the camera is suspended within a helicopter, and the shot that ends the birthday party zooms out as the helicopter zooms up, to a composition that includes hundreds of Beverly Hills swimming pools, a checkerboard of aqua and palm leaves and red-tile roofs. While there is something appealing about adopting a Hitchcockian strategy (as in the helicopter shot after the gas explosion in 1963's *The Birds*) of a shot that zooms out to a God's eye-view of Benjamin's predicament as a mere existential dot in a chlorine sea of materialism, it's the sort of move that Nichols tends to sidestep in the final cut. The point-of-view emphasis remains on Benjamin, submerged. Robert Carringer, writing about the film as formative in Hollywood's evolving depiction of Los Angeles, nonetheless observes that "there may be only one completely unequivocal Los Angeles image in the entire film: the backyard swimming pool"; Sylbert told Carringer in an interview that the pool "was deliberately intended to stand metonymically for Los Angeles as a whole."[3] The potential progress implied in Benjamin refusing to be the automaton of his father is undercut by the visual equation of pool and diver with aquarium — the image we've long since identified with womb-stuck retreat and stasis. The narrative moves forward; Benjamin stays put. And sure enough: he renounces his parents' autocracy only to submit to Mrs. Robinson's. Meet the new boss, same as the old boss.

Wisely, the production resisted the temptation to depart from Benjamin's far more limited sense of the world and his predicament to make a grand, omniscient pronouncement upon Los Angeles. The camera in the final cut moves in a slow zoom out from a full shot of Benjamin submerged in his diving suit to a long shot, still under water, in which Benjamin's image is all but lost. Meanwhile, a telephone conversation begins between Mrs. Robinson and Benjamin, overlapped on the blue vacancy of the pool. The continuum of montage causation, facilitated by the sound overlaps, has moved us from the scene of Mrs. Robinson's naked proposition to this moment of Benjamin's acquiescence. Here O'Steen finally cuts to the visual image of Dustin Hoffman in close-up, cramped in a telephone booth at the Taft Hotel,[4] sweating — and, for the first time, smoking. His dissolution in womb water has begun.

Several forms of uninitiated humiliation under the experienced gaze of the adult world ensue over the next hour of the story's time. Benjamin fumbles his room request to Henry as the desk clerk and winds up in a receiving line of strangers for the Singleman Party in an adjacent ballroom. He subsequently lies about his name to this same clerk, one of the many lies that will haunt him and eventually the first of the lies to be flung back in Elaine's face (by, among others, a dwarf bellboy). He can't seem to get a waiter in the

Taft Hotel's bar to notice him. He bumps into and nearly unmoors a cocktail table. Most important, he endures the persistent condescending smile of Mrs. Robinson both in the bar and later in the hotel room. Benjamin suffers for his sin before he ever has a chance to commit it. Such punishments pale before those that still await, however: he has expressed a desire to be "different" than the adults around him, but as he sinks deeper into the swamp of their world and values, his betrayed instinct will be the sharpest goad in his tanned flesh.

Henry's inspired cameo appearance as the desk clerk who peers without hesitation through the mask of Benjamin's unconvincing and increasingly agitated savoir faire is a triumph of Nichols's continued use of literal point of view, first introduced in the previous scene when we don Benjamin's scuba mask. A very funny subjective-camera, shot/reverse-shot begins their exchange: Henry's desk clerk busies himself, glancingly aware of Benjamin/the camera, tracking Benjamin's timid drift across the lobby. Based on interviews with production designer Richard Sylbert, Carringer reports that "a section of the actual lobby was cordoned off and the set of a lobby was built in the space instead."[5] Henry clearly relishes delivering one of the funniest ironic lines in the film: "Are you here for an affair, sir?"—doubly so because the line is his own, not borrowed from Webb's novel. Despite the screenplay's fidelity to the detail and script-ready dialogue of the original text, some of the best lines originate in Henry's adaptation. Hoffman also makes the most of this exchange, staring open-mouthed at the camera as if the clerk is a clairvoyant. Hoffman enjoys telling the story that he and Nichols settled on a callow youth's awkwardness at buying his first package of prophylactics at a drug store as an approximation of the uneasiness of Benjamin struggling for possession of the room key. For the second time in a scene centered on the radioactive sexuality of Mrs. Robinson, Benjamin has difficulty with keys. Their function as fumbled phallic signifier prepares us for Mrs. Robinson's hypothesis later the same evening that Benjamin's nerves stem from "inadequate" performance—his father's deepest fear, as demonstrated poolside.

Mrs. Robinson soon joins him, asks if she may sit down and if she may have a drink (so much to teach young people these days), then commands a drink from a waiter when Benjamin appears incapable. Henry adds another layer of teeth-gritting comic humiliation after Benjamin finally secures the key: in the novel, Webb has Benjamin return to Mrs. Robinson in the bar (with a detour to the desk clerk to assure him he has managed the transport of his "luggage," the toothbrush), but Henry adds a brief exchange in which Benjamin, at a fever-pitch of anxiety about being discovered, clandestinely calls Mrs. Robinson again from the cramped phone booth. He explains the reasons for his stealth and prepares to end the call. Mrs. Robinson asks, "Benjamin, isn't there something you want to tell me?" She has cruelly left the question in the rhetorical abstract, thus allowing Benjamin either to interpret the question as a request for data (*What room number?*) or to interpret it as he does — a maternal nagging after rote politeness, beginning with his neglect to open her car door when he has driven her home from the graduation party. "Well," he says, "I want you to know how much I appreciate this." Having invited him to embarrass himself, she now underlines his gaffe by cutting him short: "The room number, Benjamin. I think you ought to tell me that."

The camera lingers on her after the exchange, not him — but far from a shift in point of view, this is nothing less than a rendering of the anxious verisimilitude of Benjamin's imagination, picturing her as he agonizes over his latest gaffe. At ease in her leopard-print coat, she smiles. It is a smile of pleasure, rare enough in this film, and thus worth noting, especially from her. Richard Corliss laments that the film does not bother to humanize Mrs. Robinson with "a wry smile here and there," to allow her to emerge "from the shadows of her caricature as the neurotic Black Widow."[6] Bancroft's complex smile in this scene can't quite fit Corliss' description, since we know it has been produced by provoking another's amusing misery, but then again, Benjamin's perspective on her is not one that imagines her happiness but rather her delight in cruel divertissement. "Check, please," she says, in command. No one knows who is in control better than Benjamin does, and the film's point of view reminds us of this (and of his growing resentment). Though during the phone call two panels of glass and an expanse of lobby separate Benjamin and Mrs. Robinson, her delight in making him squirm is palpably a rendering of his point of view. Her monstrousness is a projection of Benjamin's inferiority complex.

Anne Bancroft's unconventional, masculine beauty is perfectly suited to the role of Mrs. Robinson. Her deep voice, dark, angular features, and trim, non-voluptuous body bring the right androgynous chemistry to the cinematic reality of Mrs. Robinson. Of all the casting triumphs in *The Graduate*, Hoffman's may be the most enduringly celebrated for its audacious unconventionality, but Bancroft's is the most essential because she not only must carry within her a palpable source of all Benjamin's insecurities but also her own. She is, in Benjamin's paranoid fantasia, both victim and villain, both male and female, mother and whore, master and slave. Her whole life shaped by a single betrayal not only by her social milieu but also by her own desire and female organs, Mrs. Robinson has never again reproduced, hardening herself into conformity with the patriarchal hypocrisy of male "freedom." (Consider Mr. Robinson's elegy for his lost youth or Mr. Braddock's frantic performance anxiety by the pool for evidence of the emasculated reality beneath the surface of masculine "freedom" in *The Graduate*.)

Mrs. Robinson thinks her husband's manly advice to a young man on the cusp of adulthood is so "good" because it has been assimilated as her own philosophy. In the relationship with Benjamin, she is not only the "mother" usurping and subverting the rights of the womb, but she is also the "male." She will adjourn from the hotel bar to conclude the rape she has perpetrated in methodical stages since the night of Benjamin's graduation party. Interesting, then, that eventually she and Mr. Robinson concoct the public story (mainly for Elaine's benefit) that Benjamin has raped *her*: he takes advantage of her, so the story goes, in a moment of vulnerability and confused weakness (brought on, with social plausibility, by alcohol abuse). That Elaine countenances this story even long enough to demand Benjamin's explanation indicates either an utter unfamiliarity with her mother's invulnerability or a daughter's default understanding of social deference to the words of her parents. (There have also always been critics lining up to call Elaine vacant.[7]) Elaine is Benjamin's equal in proceeding with life upon received rather than lived experience: by the end of the film we still haven't learned very much about the aptitudes or interests of either of these young people, but we know they will always at least share in common childhoods full of similarly patronizing experiences of the way the adult world operates.

Wielding the hard-won key and the illusion that he has asserted his own will, Benjamin enters the cell to which he has sentenced himself for the summer and immediately begins experimenting with lighting: he is the neophyte performer, heir to his father's performance anxiety, exploring the stage before opening night, alone with his nerves and self-doubt. He prefers darkness, all things being equal, which foreshadows the reprise of "The Sounds of Silence." Rounding off a comic touch with the desk clerk, he enters the bathroom and uses his single item of luggage, the toothbrush. We even get another of those trademark, terrified whimpers — the last, as it happens. After this, for what it's worth, he will be a man. It seems all the more painful, then, that as the inevitable knock comes on the door, he is the actor setting himself behind the rising curtain, hitting his mark, fixing his face into a masked lampoon of breezy self-assurance. The experience is so wrong that it denatures him. Benjamin is wrong for the part in which he has cast himself, though the show will run, to decidedly mixed reviews, throughout the rest of a long, unhappy summer.

Nichols, Bancroft, and Hoffman imbue what follows with beautifully interpreted readings of the lines provided by novelist Webb and screenwriter Henry but also with spectacular improvisation. Neither Webb nor Henry envisioned Benjamin's awkward clasping of Mrs. Robinson's breast, which provides an organic prompt for one of the key exchanges between Benjamin and Mrs. Robinson during the deflowering. However, all are in concert in having Benjamin's self-conscious tics exposed in their first kiss. Mrs. Robinson pauses to finish a cigarette. Webb writes, "Benjamin waited a few moments, then brought one of his hands up to her shoulder. He bent his face down, cleared his throat, and kissed her. Then he lifted his face back up and nodded again." Henry's script clearly carries forward the throat-clearing as a comic device to underscore Benjamin's sense of performance, as if about to make a speech; the inhaled and held cigarette smoke is Henry's comic embellishment, a broad parody of youthful ardor, here poisoned by ineptitude and nicotine.

In exasperation, Benjamin finally asks, "What should I do?" Her response is prime Mrs. Robinson. *The Graduate*'s queasy confusion of roles is so complete that the maternal gesture is, at this moment, also the erotic gesture: a hushed diffusion of his anxieties, a comforting touch, a mutual stimulation. In other words, it can't get any worse than this. And then it does. Instead of taking him gently in hand, she offers what this hopelessly sad world of social anxiety and predation often counsels: "Why don't you watch?" The line has echoed down through the cinematic decades in scenarios as distinct as Hal Ashby's *Being There* (1979), David Lynch's *Blue Velvet* (1986), and Steven Soderbergh's *sex, lies and videotape* (1989); and it finds its roots in the ambiguous mixture of power and impotence in the pre-shower scene of Norman Bates peeping on Marion Crane in *Psycho*, with its lingering redolence of Norman's bitter reference to "the cruel eyes studying you." *Why don't you watch?* is as telling a line as Mr. McGuire's "Plastics" for incising the malignancy beneath the skin of this culture. All is performance: people don't interact; they act. (Yet for all the often frenzied or furious motion, there is little or no movement: they are stuck. Again one is reminded of Norman Bates, instructing Marion in his parlor just before he peeps on, then knifes her: "I think that we're all in our private traps — clamped in them. And none of us can ever get out. We scratch and claw, but only at the air — only at each other. And for all of it, we never budge an inch.")

To Benjamin, so desperately insecure, Mrs. Robinson's suggestion that he watch seems a mercy. He snaps stiffly back into his lampoon of breezy factuality, crossing his arms and preparing to be entertained. He is so pathetically unconvincing as an audience that he makes Mrs. Robinson, that most plastic and thus accomplished of social actors, uneasy; she busies him with errands, and he also makes a self-conscious botch of these. Webb and Henry enjoy a comic double entendre on male potency with the reference to "wood" hangers; in a symbolic gesture that stretches credulity, Benjamin appears not to understand how to detach a wooden hanger from its security clasp, though surely a family as well off as the Braddocks has taken hotel-bound vacations. Nichols and Surtees cant the cinematic frame at a dutch angle as Mrs. Robinson sheds her social skin, and the leopard prints of the predator re-emerge. Benjamin totters on the last slippery slope of his old sense of the world, where adults are adults, repositories of secret knowledge of right and wrong, and children who test the limits of what is permissible are instructed in inheritable wisdom. No wonder he is the child instinctively re-attracted to a maternal breast. But this breast offers no solace or nourishment.

There are many brutal moments in *The Graduate*'s case file of Mrs. Robinson's summer-long seduction of Benjamin Braddock, from the initial, lethally playful way she opens up her private life (and legs) to this impressionable, obedient boy, to the moment she clasps a thick tuft of his hair and admonishes him never to date his daughter, and on to the final moment of the summer, when "the autumn winds blow chilly and cold" in Paul Simon's "April Come She Will," as Mrs. Robinson willingly forces the affair's exposure upon her unsuspecting daughter. In Benjamin's unsettled mind, Mrs. Robinson projects as a monster of misanthropy. Among all these outrages, however, she is arguably at her most lethal as she takes Benjamin's virginity.

Benjamin has three times made the move he understands himself as the male of the species to be expected to initiate in the social transaction of sexual intimacy: in the clandestine call from the hotel's phone booth that ends with his failure to provide the room number, in the awkward kiss that literally goes up in smoke, and in this touch that ends in her oblivious attention to an insignificant stain. Ironically, given the fact that they are "here for an affair," Mrs. Robinson commands but then rebuffs all his advances. Her unspoken instruction in these colossally mixed signals is clear: this is her show. Hoffman remembers that, during the rehearsals he undertook with Bancroft under Nichols's sharp directorial eye, Nichols initially envisioned the poignant ineptitude of Benjamin's glomming of Mrs. Robinson's leopard-printed breast as a horrible caricature of the child at his mother's breast. Anne Bancroft, however, found and inhabited Mrs. Robinson's terminal indifference. Her shed blouse in hand, she scrubs at a stain during Benjamin's awkward overture, surprising Nichols and Hoffman into laughter with her return bit of improvisation. Even amidst the laughter, Hoffman the actor worked to stay in the scene: he turned away, walked to the far end of the room, and, giving in to the infection of hilarity, banged his head softly against the wall. Nichols immediately added the improvised responses by both actors, along with the initial improvisation that started it all, to the shooting script. The revelatory truth of each physical action in this small, poisoned moment assures us that, whatever else takes place, pleasure will be neither primary objective nor outcome for the two participants.

In the brief argument that ensues, Benjamin reveals his full acculturation to the anxiety of social appearances. *What others would think* is his only basis for the wrongness of this moment, not his own heart, his own innate sense of the horrible nearness of Oedipal transgression. "Oh no, Mrs. Robinson, I think you're the most attractive of all my parents' friends": a fruitfully comic line that underscores the unnaturalness of their contemplated intimacy. With his rekindled sense of the traditional courtship dynamic expressed in his suggestion that they see a movie, he offers what he thinks is a socially viable way to be together. It is, of course, ridiculous. What would others think, after all, if these two shared any form of social companionship? And of course, what would he and Mrs. Robinson have to say to each other? (She will make this very point when he advocates for their "conversation.") Benjamin's counter-proposal to an affair carries within it all the truths they must ignore if they are to go through with the assignation.

Mrs. Robinson, tired of batting her prey between her rough paws, now settles in to the kill. She introduces that most fearful of all words for the socially anxious, and it fills the room like a gas: *Inadequate.* Robert Beuka sets *The Graduate* in a tradition of narratives articulating suburban anxiety, associated with "the imprisonment of the female, the unmanning of the male, and in a more general sense the spiritual bankruptcy of its adult inhabitants." This louvered cell at the Taft Hotel is a physical manifestation of this malaise.[8] "Would this be easier for you in the dark?" she asks him. It reminds us of Paul Simon's line that opened the credit sequence of the film, about to be reprised: *Hello darkness my old friend....* Despite her diction, the last priority on Mrs. Robinson's agenda is Benjamin's ease. Yet she also invokes the spiritual state to which she's accustomed herself. Darkness will be the default during their most tortuous on-screen moment together, the extraordinary ten-minute "conversation" Benjamin commands them to share and then, having proverbially gotten the thing he wished for, commands them never to attempt again.

At the final moment of their consummation scene, a wavering Benjamin, taunted once too many times with his father's failure of adequacy, finally opts for the dark side. His voice tightens into a terse, imperative instrument, much like his misanthropic mentor's. "Don't move," he commands her. The command is thematically edgier than Webb's original moment as rendered in the novel:

> "Stay on that bed," Benjamin said. He removed his coat quickly and dropped it on the floor. Then he began unbuttoning his shirt. He walked to the bed to sit down beside her, then reached behind her head to remove several bobby pins. Mrs. Robinson shook her head and her hair fell down around her shoulders. Benjamin

finished taking off his shirt and dropped it on the floor. Then he put his arms around her and eased her down onto her back on the bed. He kissed her and kicked off his shoes at the same time. Mrs. Robinson put her hands up at the sides of his head and then moved her fingernails up through his hair and finally wrapped both her arms around him and pressed him down against her until he could feel her breasts flattening underneath his chest and the muscles trembling in her arms. She pulled her mouth away from his and pushed it against his neck, then pushed one of her hands down between them to the buckle of his belt.

"Please," she said.

Benjamin raised his head up several inches to look at her face. Her eyes were closed and her mouth was partly open.

"Please," she said again.[9]

In contrast to Webb's version of Benjamin's command ("Stay on that bed"), Henry's version of Benjamin's command ("Don't move!") accentuates the larger problem of stasis that characterizes all these lives; the command may be compared to the bookended imperative he makes to the wedding party at the end of the film, swinging the cross. The juxtaposition of his terse "Don't move!" as the affair starts, to his impassioned, repeated "Move!" as Benjamin and Elaine exit their inherited social circle might be thought to imply a spiritual progress, but the film's larger point of view must be understood to ironically undercut such an interpretation: Benjamin *thinks* he has moved, but as the final moments of this film amply demonstrate, he has remained consistently on the treadmill.

For those more familiar with the cinematic than literary text, Webb's version of this consummation scene also surprises with the nakedness of Mrs. Robinson's need — the imploring solicitousness of her repeated plea. It's the sort of poignant moment that the film must leave out, because it's precisely the sort of vision of Mrs. Robinson that an anxious, bullied Benjamin in the film could not be expected at that moment to have. (Indeed, the "conversation" scene provides us intimations of Benjamin glimpsing Mrs. Robinson's vast melancholia beneath the no-nonsense exterior, but Benjamin proves a less-than-adept antenna for receiving the vibrations of her vulnerability.) Nichols's version of *The Graduate* explores Benjamin's point of view by noting how a young man's reasonable critiques of the jaded adult world can be transformed by his solipsistic imagination into a variety of tragicomic caricatures: everybody's picking on poor Benjamin. Thus our last image of the film's first act is of Mrs. Robinson in close-up, canted from low-angle, but she is not the needy creature of Webb's novel, begging for a young man's sexual generosity. "Don't move," Benjamin commands in the film, and she certainly is immobile — but with that dark smile of the entertained once again creasing her face. She is amused, diverted. The light goes. A door slams. Something in *The Graduate* and in Benjamin Braddock has ended. Hello darkness.

10

"Drifting"
(38:00—46:00)

"Don't move," Benjamin commands. It will continue for some time to be his philosophy during the film's second act.[1] As *The Graduate* begins, we're made specifically aware of his passive conveyance into and through his life: on the plane, on the LAX moving walkway. He is compelled to enter his graduation party; compelled to drive Mrs. Robinson home, see her inside, view Elaine's portrait, fetch Mrs. Robinson's purse, etc.; compelled to perform his scuba march at the birthday party; and, despite the illusion of what appears to be a willful, contrarian initiative in calling Mrs. Robinson after the birthday party to accept her solicitation, compelled to a spite-filled consummation of their affair. There has been movement in Benjamin's life, but not genuinely of his own making—and not to anywhere "different."

As the screen fades in from black with "The Sounds of Silence" reprised, an "associational montage [...] reinforces the inner sense of Benjamin's feelings of alienation and ambivalence" and "draws out Oedipal dimensions that Hollywood melodramas [...] would only have obliquely implied."[2] As in the title sequence, the frame invites us to meditate on the stationary form of Benjamin Braddock. We note a key difference between the images at the opening and in this musical montage roughly one-third of the way through the narrative: in the opening, Benjamin was motionless but compelled forward. In this newly introduced montage sequence, Benjamin is motionless and, as he himself will characterize it at montage's end, "drifting." Three adults—his parents and Mrs. Robinson—comprise what appears to be the entire population of his life. Three settings abut claustrophobically during the montage: the pool where his parents have so recently humiliated him (and which the film has painstakingly identified with the womb-space of his childhood bedroom), the house where he has grown up, and the Taft Hotel room where, in the ostensible assumption of his culture, he has "become a man." The echoes of the title sequence reach beyond soundtrack and his motionlessness, however: his face is still resolutely glum, even grim. And in the reprise of Paul Simon's song about silence, Benjamin and the three people surrounding him exchange no words. His dissolution has passed beyond the spiritual to infect the physical realm: the track star smokes, drinks beer on his inflatable raft, watches television at home or in the hotel room. He's gone to seed. The montage sequence intensifies our vicarious identification with Benjamin's point of view, in which to be at home or in the hotel is all one. To be laying on an inflatable raft or on a post-coital Mrs. Robinson is all one.[3] It is an indistinguishable morass. Nichols calls it Benjamin's "emotional suicide."[4]

Nichols and Sylbert worked assiduously to accomplish this effect in the set design. The black and white decors already much in evidence at the Braddock and Robinson homes likewise become the prevailing motif of the Taft Hotel. This demanded the oddity of an all-black headboard at the hotel, which in Benjamin's close-ups would be indistinguishable from the black pillows Sylbert's team dyed as a visual match. Nichols and O'Steen thus could juxtapose a shot of Benjamin propped against a black throw pillow in the Braddock home with a black headboard at the hotel, demonstrating the psychological confusion of Benjamin's point of view. Rick Lyman writes admiringly of the use of the white shirt that Benjamin pulls on and painstakingly buttons as he moves from the pool into his parents' house: "Though there has been no apparent cut, he is no longer in his parents' house, but in a room at a nearby hotel"; in fact, we have very clearly noted the cut between shots as Benjamin enters an interior space wearing the buttoned white shirt. Lyman's claim that the cut is invisible derives from Nichols and O'Steen's manipulation of our assumptions about continuity, usually used in film grammar to facilitate the viewer's orientation, but here used to deceive and disorient us, just the same way that Benjamin's days slip deceptively by.[5] Richard Sylbert, production designer of *The Graduate*, acknowledges that the shot was a committee-brainstorm with Nichols and cinematographer Surtees, directly borrowing from montage strategy in François Truffaut's *Jules and Jim* (1963). "[T]hose are the people we admired, the New Wave," says Sylbert. "We came to Hollywood to change things in Hollywood."[6]

In a poignant moment during the montage, Mrs. Robinson's tenderness as she sits beside Benjamin on the bed teeters ambiguously near maternal before slipping fully over again into the erotic. He is stretched on the bed, and she unbuttons his shirt as if he's her little boy waiting to be readied for sleep. She is in control. They are silent. Pleasure is something we must read contextually into the reality of their actions, since they betray no unambiguous evidence of pleasure. O'Steen's montage puts us in the disconcerting place, via a series of carefully orchestrated cuts, to watch Benjamin get up from what we thought was this hotel bed to close the door through which we thought we just saw Mrs. Robinson emerge to unbutton his shirt — only to have the door shut off a breakfast nook where his parents stare at him in helpless disapproval. The effect is hermetic: he is never genuinely alone, yet never in communion. His days and actions are fluid, relative, joyless. As he later characterizes this chapter in his life to Mr. Robinson, he "might just as well have been shaking hands."

We're reminded of the Freudian dilemma inherent in his drifting by more associations of the pool with the maternal — although alienation rather than Oedipal residue now seems the central characteristic of this association. Benjamin peers through drawn blinds at the relentlessly cheerful L.A. sun and prepares himself for reentering the pool. Cut to a shot of the statuesque Wilson, nearly a head taller than either of the men in the family, working in the kitchen as her son passes wordlessly by. She turns to watch him wistfully as he strides without hesitation to the diving board and knifes into the depths. The composition is reminiscent of paintings by artists like Eric Fischl or David Hockney, who charge scenes of quotidian pool recreation and sunny domesticity with primal sex iconography. A cut to Benjamin skimming along the pool floor in rhythmic breaststrokes ought to be preparation for what comes next, given all the disorienting juxtapositions of situation during the montage sequence and the inevitable returns to Mrs. Robinson. David R. Shumway points to the use of Simon and Garfunkel in this montage sequence as a clear example of the mediation of experience through Benjamin's consciousness, providing a sense of fatalistic nostalgia about actions he knows must have an end even as he (and we) engage in them.[7] We recognize via the lyrics that this passage of the film is nearing an end: after "The Sounds of Silence," Paul Simon's "April Come She Will" has ticked away the summer months, lamenting (as Benjamin strokes along the pool's floor) that what may once have seemed like love has been dissolved by entropy. The last line reminds us of Mr. Robinson's lament, "You'll never be young again."

And still the jump cut that follows is as startlingly humorous and devastating whether we have anticipated it or not. The camera follows Benjamin, showing the impressive finishing kick that would have made possible his trackstar success as he vaults from the water onto a waiting raft. The raft is the final visual object of psychological association in the montage sequence: as the coda of guitar notes subsides, the raft onto which Benjamin thrusts himself becomes Mrs. Robinson — the climax of the sequence, indeed. The composition (black headboard, Benjamin's back and shoulders obscuring all but Mrs.

Robinson's impassive face) is standard mid-1960s cinematic intimacy, in the days just before the old production code censoring various forms of human venality was supplanted by the ratings system that permitted franker pictorial reality. The evidence is abundant, if carefully cropped, to support our recognition of just-completed sexual intercourse. What's especially striking about the shot as it lingers is the ambiguity of Mrs. Robinson's post-coital mien. What in the first instant seemed lassitude or indolence now appears to be a more sinister state: zombification, even death. She's post-pleasure. However, the distance from pleasure appears to be something more aptly measured in years or decades rather than in seconds.

Yet Nichols and O'Steen offer still another wrenching juxtaposition at montage's end. Returning to the voice-overlap technique with which they began and ended the birthday party sequence, Nichols and O'Steen insert the exasperated voice of William Daniels as Mr. Braddock: "Ben, what are you doing?" It is an intensely rhetorical question: the cinematic inference we're invited to draw is that these fluid situations through which Benjamin has drifted all summer long have finally sloshed together into a single crisis: his father *knows*. The disgust in Mr. Braddock's voice is palpable. It gives voice to our own dissatisfaction with the turn of this narrative. (We have all the evidence we need that this will not be a pleasant narrative to negotiate for another hour if Benjamin and Mrs. Robinson insist on remaining together.) Most tellingly, however, Mr. Braddock's disgust gives voice to Benjamin's consciousness, which has never stopped knowing what his heart and his social brain have told him. As he will say to Mrs. Robinson during their "conversation," half to hurt her, half to expel some of the vapors of self-reproach he's been breathing, "This is the sickest, most disgusting thing I've ever done." The cut to Mr. Braddock towering over Benjamin on his omnipresent raft indicates, however, that Mr. Braddock's disgust is limited: he's accusing Benjamin of sloth, not lust. The logic of the montage sequence, punctuated with this last voice overlap, here locks into place: the only source of its point of view can be Benjamin's mind, drifting detached from his body through an Ecclesiastes of days and nights. Nothing is new under the sun; all is vanity; childhood home, pool, and carnal hotel room have blended into one long disenchantment.

The low-angle shot of back-lit Mr. Braddock is a photographer's nightmare, and one can imagine Surtees initially objecting and then, meeting Nichols's implacable artistic authority, digging deeper into his bag of photographic tricks and muttering under his breath about how Ford and Wyler used to do it. Nichols blocks Daniels on the set directly in front of the California sun, so that as his agitation bobs and weaves his form, the sun bleeds past his head,

10. "Drifting"

blinding Benjamin (and us). Fortunately for Benjamin, whom we see in high-angle on the raft in the next shot, he wears the ubiquitous sunglasses of this Beverly Hills set—the paradoxical mask of isolating conformity. Prompted by Mr. Braddock's question, an acid exchange ensues, far franker in its hostility than their first conversation the night of the graduation party:

> BENJAMIN: Well, I would say that I'm just drifting, here in the pool.
> MR. BRADDOCK: Why?
> BENJAMIN: Well, it's very comfortable just to drift here.
> MR. BRADDOCK: Have you thought about graduate school?
> BENJAMIN: No.
> MR. BRADDOCK: Would you mind telling me then what those four years of college were for, what was the point of all that hard work?
> BENJAMIN: You got me.[8]

As in that early, stillborn conversation about Ben's future, Mr. Braddock attempts a full eclipse of his son—but Benjamin has discovered the joy of rebellion. Elaine M. Bapis writes, "Floating and drifting mock the value of work, so vital for the parent generation,"[9] leading to her excellent insight that "Rejection of materialism as a means of generational legitimacy was [...] contingent on literally being able to afford to rebel. [Benjamin's generation's] revolt occurs after the fact, after Beverly Hills affluence and university education have given them the choice to do so."[10] The saturation of colors in the high-angle shot of Benjamin belies the usual psychological weight of the subject when viewed (and thus diminished) from above. It's Mr. Braddock who seems ephemeral, desaturated by sun-angle and his son's sudden failure to play the part in which he's been cast. Yet the illusion of Benjamin's self-possession is very short-lived. (Self-possession remains beyond him throughout this film. He is always shifting from one punctilious attitude to the next; as we will see, even in Berkeley, wooing Elaine towards an elopement, his default setting remains squarely within the code of social conformity.) Mr. Braddock hems and haws his way through a conciliatory speech that turns peevishly salty just at the wrong time, as guests arrive. He is bordering on a reprise of the father-son drama they enacted by this pool earlier in the summer, and he quickly backs down, reticent about providing a public encore of his private shame.

"The Robinsons are here," chimes Mrs. Braddock, echoing her musical inflection from the night of the graduation party when announcing the arrival of the Carlsons from Tarzana. First Mr. Robinson steps into view, far left, then Mrs. Robinson, at the frame's other edge. The parents loom over Benjamin like four giants in the haze, admiring a young child in the bathtub. Mr. Robinson returns to the familiar thought that torments him, a good-natured envy of "taking it easy": "That's what I'd do if I could." Who, precisely, is stopping him? As his patter continues, he again pimps his daughter, while Mrs. Robinson remains silent, watchful. Mr. Robinson's mindless hobbyhorse of inter-family dating is forcing an issue between the families. The brief scene ends with another condescending parental prompt to social nicety: "Say hello to *Mrs.* Robinson, Benjamin." The scene's last shot is of a hazy, desaturated Mrs. Robinson in close-up, the lighting subject to heavy lens diffusion; Monaco points out that the lens diffusion and other formally invasive strategies are intended by Nichols to convey "the mood of the picture as interpreted from the protagonist's point of view."[11] The just-ended montage sequence has enveloped the film in Benjamin's existential fog. This diffused shot dissolves into a medium shot of Benjamin, naked to the waist, in a steamy bathroom. He is shaving, though as in a later scene at the boarding house in Berkeley, he doesn't quite finish the job. Again, Nichols and O'Steen use overlap to create a hermetic inevitability in transitions. When a scene shifts to the next scene, the rhetoric of O'Steen's montage suggests, the emphasis is less on chronological continuity than on psychological cause-effect or comparison. Mr. Braddock's criticism of a raft as suitable summer companion becomes Benjamin's own referendum on what he's been doing all summer long, with such joyless faithfulness.

When that hazy close-up of Mrs. Robinson dissolves into a hazy bathroom that Mrs. Braddock enters, without knocking, just as Mrs. Robinson entered his bedroom the night of the graduation party, the film makes its most overt equation of the Freudian dynamics of the affair. (In fact, this scene between mother and son was originally to be played in Benjamin's bedroom, until Hoffman had the insight that the bathroom would provide even more intensified ambiguity.[12]) These women in Benjamin's life acknowledge no boundaries to access—nor does Benjamin command that they respect a boundary. He continues passively to accept their trespassing advances. Both mother and son in this scene carry themselves with the nonchalance of a habitual action: Mrs. Braddock has apparently never stopped wandering in and out of her son's intimate spaces. What's even more notable is her frank presentation of herself: voluptuous in black peignoir set, suggestively raked off one bare shoulder, she is a glamorous Hollywood cliché of availability. Since she's in a steamy bathroom with her nearly naked son, however, we register and simultaneously do our best to reject the cliché: enough that Benjamin is with Mrs. Robinson all these nights. What Benjamin does with his nights is precisely his mother's agenda during this interlude, and in their brief, halting conversation, Mrs. Braddock comes on like a "modern" but jealous lover: demanding to know if there's someone else, even as she acknowledges his sexual

10. "Drifting"

autonomy. Nervy with her accurate thrusts of conjecture about where he's been keeping himself all summer, Benjamin lies (badly). Then he cuts himself.

The analogy to castration[13] when Benjamin slices his thumb is consonant with Benjamin's surrender of personal and sexual autonomy to maternal authority; it is even possible to read the sliced thumb as an intentional diversion on his part, since it does not come in any act that might be considered part of the routine ritual of shaving. The graphic close-ups of the razor pressed to his throat and then, as Mrs. Braddock asks if he meets someone at night, of the razor slicing open his phallic thumb, resonate with the primal imagery of an early Martin Scorsese short, made in 1967, around the time Nichols was first mulling Charles Webb's novel as his debut in film. In *The Big Shave*, Scorsese offers the simple image of a young man — Benjamin's age, *draft*-age in contemporary context, as he first lathers his face, then scrapes it clean with a straight razor. As the short continues, so do the young man's confident strokes, even when it is appallingly evident, amidst the pints of applied fake blood, that he is mutilating himself. The film ends with the oblique caption, "Viet '67," contextualizing all we've witnessed within the systematic mutilation of young American servicemen and their implacable Southeast Asian foes.

When Scorsese and Nichols linger on images of young men shaving, they emphasize one of the few *toilette* rituals of the male of the species. Cinema has of course capitalized on the typical cosmetic regimen of the female, the camera staring in close-up wonder at the irony of beautiful women presenting self on a daily basis through make-up, the preparatory rite of theatrical artifice. Hollywood film culture does not traditionally appoint men the same level of presentation anxiety, but the shaving ritual, with its subtextual anxiety about appearing civilized rather than a product of the natural wilderness, points to the visual mediation of the masculine self in society. For young men, shaving incorporates the additional anxiety about progress in the ongoing journey to adult masculinity. A beard — even if shaved back to smooth skin, is an external sign of an overwhelming internal preoccupation.

The young man in *The Big Shave* keeps blindly shaving long after the goal of pleasing social presentation has been lost in a welter of red rivulets and gashes. Although for Scorsese the scene carries personal resonances of Catholic guilt and retribution as well as despair,[14] its comparison to Benjamin's first shaving scene in *The Graduate* has more to do with Benjamin's reality in a civilization that commands self-conscious, dogged attention to the cultivation of a public face, risking all the potential distortions and mutilations of the genuine self. His impassive face has hardened to implacability. He has begun to sport the sunglasses that work so well in deflecting the penetrating gaze of the Southern California sun — and of his competition in Southern

Californian social striving—and so he seems as naked without his shades as without his shirt in the bathroom. The gash in his thumb is made more startling by the full saturation of hue in another scene whose palette is otherwise neutralized by almost exclusive reliance on diffused black and white.

Yet for all the garish intrusion of her son's red blood into the colorless space, Mrs. Braddock either does not notice or does not care to acknowledge his wound. (The implication is thus that the cut serves him right.) Even as she claims not to want to "play games," Mrs. Braddock begins to stride away, effectively assuming the role of the spurned lover. Defaulting to filial duty, he stops her, though he has no comfort to offer. "Benjamin, I don't want to pry into your affairs," she says—that dreaded "a" word, and we hear her utter it off-screen; Nichols and Surtees point the camera's scrutiny at Benjamin. Rather than have Wilson talk directly to the camera, making us Benjamin as when we don the scuba mask, we enter Benjamin's point of view via this other, equally effective strategy *The Graduate* employs, objectifying Benjamin's proximate self-image under the camera's gaze, as in the scene with Buck Henry's desk-clerk, or that first shot of the pool-side door thrown open to reveal the hiding son in his wetsuit. These shots may not be visions seen literally through Benjamin's eyes, but they are projections of his self-consciousness as he stands vulnerable or self-accused in the glare of the social eye, of which, like a good graduate, he has developed a painfully acute awareness.

The vision of a half-shaved, hangdog Benjamin under examination by his mother is thus more about Benjamin seeing himself exposed than about his mother exposing him. Mrs. Braddock adds a brief maxim: "I would rather you didn't say anything at all than be dishonest." She shows him her back, and Benjamin is left petulantly calling for her to wait. For this reason, the jump cut to his quieter command, "Will you wait a minute please?" does not seem at first to *be* a jump cut. The less desperate tone in his voice suggests that he has managed to retard his mother's retreat. Yet something is wrong with this picture. Literally so: a mere trickle of ambient light through window blinds only accentuates that he has settled in the dark—a disquieting place for a tête-à-tête with one's mother. Benjamin clicks on a bedside lamp, and key light floods the colorless Taft Hotel room where Benjamin and Mrs. Robinson have come for the continuation of their "affair." His body stretches familiarly across hers. The film's associational montage wrenches tighter that clear comparison between mother as lover, lover as mother in this sequence moving from the post-shower bathroom with his mother to bed with Mrs. Robinson. His failure to talk to his mother directly influences his guilty attempts to legitimize his time with Mrs. Robinson *through* conversation. He remains the dutiful boy, even in the lowest depths of his social trespass.

11

"Conversation"-Stopper
(46:00 — 55:00)

One of the key thematic assertions of *The Graduate* is that open, honest conversation is in short supply yet necessary for the health of human community. Most of the film's satiric depictions are of human community in disarray, alienated by deception, substance abuse, adultery. In this scene, the longest in *The Graduate* at nearly ten minutes, Nichols the accomplished theater director recognizes the enormous ironic power of a genuinely honest conversation, the kind that can only reveal the truth. He gives two fine actors a set, script, and each other and lets them work. Benjamin naively enters into this conversation, advocating for it, because he believes at some abstract philosophical level that mutual exchange between human beings is redemptive. His naïveté is not in believing this but in hoping that such a conversation with Mrs. Robinson might be used to legitimize the fundamentally illegitimate, when all it can reasonably be expected to do is reveal the truth. The conversation that ensues, one of the most extraordinary theatrical set-pieces in the history of the Hollywood Renaissance, *is* redemptive: it shines the stark key light of truth over and over again on these characters' sorry circumstances, no matter how many times they attempt to retreat to the literal and metaphoric cover of darkness. Any conversation they have can only remind them of how little they have to talk about. Yet both for their own reasons eventually choose to ignore this redemptive truth and plod on in their unhappy affair.

Despite the flamboyance of the film rhetoric in almost every scene prior to the conversation, Nichols chooses to accentuate the static properties of the relationship between Mrs. Robinson and Benjamin in this scene. A single camera set-up, shot at medium distance from Mrs. Robinson's side of the bed, prevails for the majority of the scene. A lamp on the other side of the room, outlined by the faint light leaking past the closed window blinds, becomes the most dynamic object in the room when the lights are out; at various times, intent on clarity, each participant will switch on another lamp, atop the bedside table on Mrs. Robinson's side, in order to underscore an objective. Whole minutes audaciously go by with the room in darkness, the "old friend" of Paul Simon's song. For this reason, it is specious to claim that the scene is formally uninflected and presented naturalistically. The trope of the lamp as source of illumination verges on overuse in the scene, and at least once becomes a logical misstep, at cross-purposes with the established organic pattern of metaphorical use by the characters within the scene.

Benjamin and Mrs. Robinson typically turn the light on as an act of rhetorical aggression. When Benjamin, his mother's veiled accusations from the bathroom still on his mind, stops Mrs. Robinson's hungry advance and switches on the light, he is inviting them both to look at this stunted thing they have created, all flesh, no spirit. Having spurned his initial gambit, she switches the light off again with equal aggression, and if the scene had ended there, after less than two minutes, with Mrs. Robinson's clinically direct assertion that they have nothing to say to each other, it would have been an effective dramatic means to confirm his alarm about their wrongness. The dramatic punctuation of the light being extinguished might even have ironically illuminated his future course. Yet Benjamin remains essentially passive. His posture as the light goes out the first time is the comic trope of the ostrich hiding its head in sand: he kneels on the bed with his head buried in his pillow and his hands. The scene might have ended here, but the point is to provide a dramatic opportunity for Benjamin to stop burying himself from the truth of his life and to see what he is becoming. Besides, as he admits at the end of this conversation, he can think of no other place to go, nothing he'd rather do. With no new objective to strike out toward, Benjamin is left to watch this relationship continue to devolve (he can watch it very well, even from the intermittent dark: anticipating an observation Mr. Robinson will later make about himself, Benjamin can see so well because he has been accustomed to the dark for "quite a while"). At the most practical level, the scene must continue past this first possible end-point in order to introduce Elaine. But to watch the consistent failure of Benjamin and Mrs. Robinson to take to heart and act upon what they learn from their conversation is the scene's great tragedy and its dramatic triumph. For now, asked to humor Benjamin by providing an alternative topic (she once again mocks him and his parents by suggesting they have this proposed conversation about his "college experiences"), Mrs. Robinson floats the seemingly neutral topic of "art" out into the darkness. Given what we eventually learn about her past, we can decode her suggestion as a veiled acknowledgment of her anger over an unresolved issue, a signifier of her long-nursed resentment.

Later in the conversation, the light snapped on again has rhetorical resonance, when Mrs. Robinson wants to be as clear as possible about her daughter and the ground rules she means to impose: she deftly switches on the light while lunging for his scalp. Her manner here is of a mother pushed to the borderline between scolding and abuse. She turns on the light because she wants to shame him into seeing and acquiescing on her point. Why, however, does she turn on the lamp at the end of their conversation about art, when she is revealed at her most vulnerable? Surely this is a state Mrs. Robinson would always be intently committed to keeping concealed, *in the dark*. There's a failure here of the scene's internal logic, ultimately a rare instance of a failure of directorial nerve. Having audaciously presented a scene of psychological illumination in near-total physical darkness, Nichols waffles on whether Mrs. Robinson's long-lost humanity can be glimpsed without a literal spotlight on Anne Bancroft's wistful expression. Wouldn't her tiny "Kind of," sent quavering out into the darkness, have been enough?

Perhaps the insistence on our seeing Mrs. Robinson just then can be attributed to the importance Nichols places on her vulnerable admission. Nichols calls it a "beautiful, crucial moment," "the key" to understanding her character.[1] Not surprisingly, given the film's faithful monitoring of Benjamin's point of view, this is the moment when Benjamin (from whose point of view all unfolds) comes closest to illumination about Mrs. Robinson's humanity, after she has revealed that art was her major in college and he has all but called her out on her stated lack of knowledge about the subject. But seeing each other's humanity is not in their best interests if their object remains to exploit and be exploited by the other. With the light on, Benjamin studies her, weighing options of what he will say next. He chooses to be socially gracious in providing her a way out of the conversation ("I guess you just kind of lost interest in it over the years")— but in the context of the project of connection he's called for them to undertake, this apparent sympathy is actually just one more failure. He has learned something genuine about her, only because she has, extraordinarily, allowed him this glimpse of herself. And he politely backs off, neither pressing his sudden power advantage nor exploring his sudden entrée into her psychology. All the while Bancroft's face is turned away from him and toward the camera; in the lamp's light, we can see that, far from a two-dimensional villainess, Mrs. Robinson in fact harbors a complexity the film never quite allows us to enter, because it is a film committed to rendering Benjamin's callow perspective, and he never quite allows himself to understand her.

Critics of *The Graduate* like Reck, Farber and Changas decry the film's turning away from Mrs. Robinson's full humanity after this in the narrative as, at best, the filmmakers' timidity or, at worst, their misogyny. It's important to recognize that Mrs. Robinson will return to this physical and verbal vulnerability once more in the scene — when Benjamin resorts to verbal abuse — and again, Benjamin will destroy what small chance there is for some deeper understanding between them. The conversation scene may tangentially be intended to draw parallels between Mrs. Robinson's ruination, now ancient history, and Benjamin's own, in process, but the main point of the scene is ultimately to encapsulate the profound hypocrisy of Benjamin Braddock — someone who both believes high-mindedly that conversation is what humanizes us but who also shuts down conversation, who avows self-righteously that the only appropriate thing to do is end the affair but who also allows the affair to continue, who gives his word that he will not take out Elaine Robinson but then almost immediately afterward does so. The reason we don't learn more about Mrs. Robinson in the conversation scene is because Benjamin refuses to learn more about Mrs. Robinson, and her identity as an ogress throughout the rest of the film comes as a direct result of Benjamin's psychological need to demonize her as a means to justify his own continued iniquities. He needs the very real human drama of his life to be transformed into the melodrama of a fairy-tale: Can he really be a sinner if he's an innocent victim abused by the spell of a monster?

What the scene's vacillation between light and dark, vulnerability and aggression does not reveal is a series of practical choices made by Nichols and O'Steen to render the substance of the "conversation" scene as originally envisioned by Webb and purposefully reduced by Henry. Harris writes that the production slowed to a day-after-day standstill for the filming of this scene. The problem was that Nichols the celebrated Broadway director had fallen in love with its "two-character, one-set, dialogue-based style [that] seemed to belong on the stage, not on screen." As written and duly recorded on film, "it threatened to stop the flow of the rest of the movie."[2] Nichols had two good reasons, then, for attempting to find a way to cut the scene by at least a third: first, he needed to respect the audience's expectations for how a filmed narrative's rhythms will be different from those of the stage; as important, he needed to tell a story that would conform to the traditional length of a feature, typically kept to less than two hours to promote the maximum number of daily screenings. (The film eventually ran at the tidy length of 106 minutes.) Apart from whatever rhetorical effect is conveyed by the illumination or plunging into darkness of the hotel room, Nichols found his way to cut an eventual total of six minutes from the scene: each time a character turns a light on or off represents a careful excision of dialogue.[3]

With or without light, the words these two people speak illuminate — for us, to them — the reality of their condition. All they have in common, it

11. "Conversation"-Stopper

Benjamin Braddock (Dustin Hoffman) and Mrs. Robinson (Anne Bancroft) attempt a humanizing moment of "conversation" at the Taft Hotel, joyless site of their assignations during the summer after his graduation. The formal, depersonalized name by which we know her and the animal-print wardrobe she wears mark Mrs. Robinson as a caricatured object seen through Benjamin's callow point of view. Only in rare moments, as when their conversation has drifted toward her own thwarted youthful ambitions as an art major in college, does Benjamin's point of view allow us a glimpse of her vulnerability and need. Typically, he must view her as the predator; a moment later, she will grab his scalp and insist he have nothing to do with Elaine.

becomes clear, is their deception, hardly a topic for pleasant pastime, let alone for use as a cornerstone in building a relationship. We assume Mrs. Robinson means that they have nothing in common when she asserts they have nothing to talk about, but it may actually be the case that they have all the wrong things in common, and that discussion would be pointless. Farber and Changas contend that her claim "doesn't expose her shallowness, as Nichols seems to have intended, it exposes *Ben's*."[4] Given what they are transacting in this hotel room most nights of the week, perhaps it is most appropriate to acknowledge that they're both shallow. Robert Coles calls the entire conversation "a brilliant parody of silence — between a man and a woman who do not really make love but go at it night after night, again and again, without the slightest evidence that anything else can possibly happen between them."[5] They skid off one topic after another: how she perpetuates the deception with Mr. Robinson (no trouble at all, since the Robinsons are no longer sexually intimate); art (once her major subject in college, though she has learned not to care about it, along with all the other things she has learned not to care about); and then, finally, Elaine. Though we have yet to meet her (except by the proxy of her portrait), her name has been dropped one too many times by Mr. Robinson for us not to assume she will find her way into the narrative. We learn, with Benjamin, that Mrs. Robinson's pregnancy ended her college career and sealed her marriage to a man whose every conversation returns mournfully to the theme of lost youth and freedom. The Robinsons are poster-children for the violence of social conformity.

Benjamin's eventual deduction about the Robinsons' marriage magnifies his innocence and prurient immaturity: "So ol' Elaine Robinson got started in a Ford" is the voice of lubricious adolescence, and it prompts Mrs. Robinson to express her matter-of-fact desire that they not talk any more about Elaine. From the adulterous quasi–Oedipal bed in which he lies, Benjamin ironically poses the question, "Now why is she a big taboo subject all of a sudden?" All those suggestions by Mr. Robinson, silently endured without any seconding from his wife, have apparently not been lost on Benjamin. In his position as apprentice misanthrope, he senses a small but vulnerable chink in his mentor's armor. While he does not embarrass her about art, he will embarrass her about Elaine: Mrs. Robinson has toyed with him, and he takes a tentative step toward toying with her. His voice tentatively assumes the lilt of cocked-eyebrow pillow talk. "Well," he says, "I guess I'll just have to ask her out on a date and find out what the big deal is." The master-teacher's abhorrence of being thus diminished is instantaneously felt: on comes the light; back snaps his head. "Don't you *ever* take that girl out," she warns, through gritted teeth. The rhetorical objectification of Elaine to "that girl" makes her more taboo, not less. Being caught off-guard by this conversation and the twists of topic results in her redoubled initiative to humiliate. She does everything but make him stand in the corner — and this he imposes upon himself at the very end of the scene, as the frame fades in silence to black.

So commence the attacks on both sides: she admits he's not "good enough" to date her daughter, and he calls her a "broken-down alcoholic." Their genuinely honest conversation has pulled back all the layers of social deceit to reveal the darkness of the void. The next step seems obvious: they must part. That they do *not* part suggests the monumental cynicism of Mrs. Robinson's spirit and the passivity of Benjamin's life. "I'm getting out," he has vowed to her, but she talks him into staying via insultingly transparent rationalizations. The shot of her foregrounded leg, with Benjamin diminished in the background next to a closed door, recalls the earlier image in her sun porch the night of the first seduction. For all the apparent activity of his summer, little has changed for Benjamin. The fact is, Benjamin can imagine no place else to go. (Given the rest of the film, this failure of imagination amounts to the story of his life.) What appears to be his movement toward Mrs. Robinson has always been in reality a movement away from his materialist, manipulative parents. To underscore this seeming lack of alternatives Benjamin can conjure for himself, the film during this section continues to bottle him in a world whose entire breadth encompasses a few square miles of Los Angeles: his Beverly Hills home and the Taft Hotel. The conversation finally, painfully ends with a wide-screen shot of two fighters in their opposite corners and Benjamin's whipped request, "Let's not talk at all." The screen fades to black: a second false ending to the film, a second dead-end in a Taft Hotel room.

12

Elaine
(55:00—1:10:30)

    Benjamin studies the back panel of a cereal box while his parents try to sell him Elaine Robinson. He does not speak, does not even seem to hear. Cut to the pool where, scuba mask on, Benjamin maintains his sullen retreat. Mr. and Mrs. Braddock revolve around his black raft like awkward sea predators. Mr. Braddock typically blusters, a flurry of hapless activity; Mrs. Braddock waits patiently, then springs her trap: she is prepared to invite "*all* the Robinsons over." Can she possibly suspect what she has proposed? Somehow she knows at least that this has the requisite negative force to produce motion. The matriarchy remains the ultimate repository of power over Benjamin, and he no longer has a place to hide: when Benjamin submerses himself in the womb-water, we see the Braddocks' legs kicking in the background. Benjamin recognizes no asylum here, as there was when he abruptly ended his birthday party. On that occasion, Nichols and O'Steen used the voice overlap of Benjamin's call from the Taft Hotel to imply causation: the birthday humiliation impels Benjamin to an equally drastic response. Another inference of this editing strategy becomes apparent when we hear it used again now, as a doorbell rings underwater. Benjamin has reaped the whirlwind by inviting Mrs. Robinson into his hermetic world. There is no place of refuge from her now: these three adults are everywhere Benjamin turns. This is his curse, but it is also a kind of grace. Without further avenues of escape, he must eventually confront and even own responsibility for his life.
    The doorbell is the Robinsons'. A jump-cut to Mrs. Robinson on her sun porch, the predator at rest in her jungle-fringed lair, introduces a stunning zoom and track to her baleful displeasure in close-up, a melodramatic flourish of pure cinema that puts Bancroft in the company of cinematic Furies like Joan Crawford. Farber and Changas complain that, while Nichols has treated

Mrs. Robinson's characterization with "respect" until now, from this point forward Nichols "turns her into a hideous witch, an evil Furie maniacally insistent on keeping Ben and her daughter apart."[1] They argue that her motives are "much more intense and tortured than Ben suspects — mostly, presumably, an envy of youth and a fear of being cast off for her daughter — and deserve his sympathy, not his moralistic outrage." Their insight is dead-on except in imputing the denigration of Mrs. Robinson's character to Nichols rather than to Benjamin. Benjamin needs for her to be the villainess.

Mr. Robinson's delight in procuring his daughter for Ben is as out-of-scale as his wife's silent censure. He defaults to the bar and reprises his deafness to Benjamin's drink request, far more interested in the comic miscommunication depicted on an episode of *The Newlywed Game* than on Ben's choice of liquor or the fact that he's handing liquor to this boy at all in the moments before he drives away into the night with his daughter. The subject under debate on the game show is again about shaving — this time a girl's legs: more evidence of the ubiquitous preoccupation with appearance and presentation in every corner and cranny of the culture. Mr. Robinson excuses himself to hurry Elaine, leaving the two fighters as we last saw them, in their neutral corners at opposite ends of the frame. But the bell has rung, and Benjamin weaves gamely forward into the next round against the veteran. His alibi sums his passive life: "Look, this was not my idea. This was my father's idea."

Finally, the film more than half over, a second young person enters the frame, her father possessively at her side, the leer on his face poorly suppressed. As Elaine, Katharine Ross offers Benjamin an alternate version of femininity, beyond Mrs. Braddock's brassy bigness or Mrs. Robinson's hungry hunter. Ross as Elaine is demure, soft-featured, a boy's fantasy of the girl-next-door. Benjamin stands to receive her while, off-screen, Mr. Robinson begins a barker's build-up worthy of his business partner, Mr. Braddock. To his daughter, he says disingenuously, "Well, I want you to keep your wits about you tonight." As Nichols and O'Steen cut to Mrs. Robinson, still glaring and unmoved, her husband continues, "You never know what tricks Ben picked up back there in the east." Another sound overlap, this time a sports car engine at high RPM, ushers in the dissolve from Mrs. Robinson to the back of Elaine's head, hair whipping in the L.A.-freeway wind at night: mother supplanted by daughter, generation for generation.[2] We seem suddenly to be in another movie, not the one where we have known only a fancy hotel and a couple of houses in Beverly Hills. It's a glimpse of what appears to be freedom, though it is little more than a web of illusions created by the tonal shift underway from the first to the second half of the film. Robert Beuka writes, "The cinematography of the second half of the film underscores the immensity of this change, as Nichols's sumptuous rendering of such monuments as the San Francisco Bay Bridge, the UC-Berkeley campus, and Berkeley's student thoroughfare, Telegraph Avenue — not to mention the focus on wide open highways and the sheer prevalence of driving footage — positions the second half of the film in marked contrast to the first, which, with its unyielding emphasis on the generic backyard and swimming pool, paints the suburb as a most confining milieu."[3] The wild, lane-weaving ride with Elaine feels like nothing less than a jailbreak. However, Benjamin in the symbolic position of the driver's seat betrays no glimpse of self-determination. He drives furiously, on a mission, answering Elaine's innocent attempts at conversation with abortive monosyllabic responses. His promise to Mrs. Robinson to make the date a perfunctory satisfaction of competing adult demands appears to be in little jeopardy.

We think we have seen Benjamin at his low ebb, when he cruelly insults and is insulted by Mrs. Robinson but cannot keep himself from crawling back. On this first-date-from-hell, however, we see that there are still lower depths. He can become, ineptly, his image of Mrs. Robinson. Yet his ineptitude and Elaine's innocence keep him from tipping over this final brink. The next three minutes are an encyclopedia of passive aggression directed against an undeserving victim, Benjamin's fantasy of pretty innocence dragged through Benjamin's version of mud. Elaine in her white coat totters after Benjamin as the fast-striding track star negotiates the busy sidewalks of the Hollywood Strip. It's night, but the shades stay on. He passes the clubs where he could have been spending his summer evenings, seeing the Doors at the Whiskey with people his own age. Where he turns in, at the strip club, is another variation on where he has been all summer long: a club filled with adults at least a generation older than himself, dedicated to the pursuit of exploitative performance. Elaine in her bundled white coat is as conspicuous as the stripper. Both are exposed objects, presented for exploitation. Benjamin talks the maitre 'd into a stage table, and Elaine stands by the table long after Benjamin has sat down. Shot in low-angle, the composition layers one young woman on the other, two versions of the same lustrously long-haired form. "Sit down," Benjamin commands. An obedient child (like Benjamin himself), Elaine sits.

In the cut to Benjamin we get our first subjective camera angle that has the possibility of being from outside his point of view. When we've looked at him in confrontations with the Taft Hotel desk-clerk or his parents, the gaze seems to be about his self-consciousness, rather than what they may see. But the shot of his implacability across the table from Elaine provides a sense of her mystification as well as his own careful performance of the role he has set for himself for the evening. In providing an invitation to feel Elaine's horror, *The Graduate* has transposed its allegiance to include a second soul, also innocent, also preyed upon. The transposition identifies clearly the film's solidarity with innocence and possibility when beset by manipulation. The glimpse of Benjamin is of the adult he is about to become. A cigarette dangles from the track-star's lips. Even in the gloom of the club, where the point is presumably to see the show, his sunglasses remain. (In a study in Hollywood's shifting ideological iconography, Benjamin's aping of what he understands to be seasoned cool presages 1983's *Risky Business* (Paul Brickman), where a callow youth hungry for adult, sexual experience and professional success becomes a player in both arenas. Joel Goodsen's character, played by Tom Cruise, in his Wayfarers and with his dangling cigarette, is the true mirror-image of Benjamin — identical, yet reversed — because it is offered without irony. While Nichols intends his character's iconography to project soul-numbness, Paul Brickman directs Cruise as the entrepreneurial *wunderkind* who outmaneuvers the sharks of commerce and seduces the penthouse call-girl — the college-boy's fantasy, updated by the death of the Sixties.)

And so *The Graduate* makes to sacrifice its next virgin. Elaine's eyes watch Benjamin; off-screen, he muses aloud, "Why don't you watch the show?" The focus on ogling sight in this scene will shift in an instant to humbling insight. A smart Berkeley coed, Elaine nonetheless has no answer to Benjamin's apparent animosity for her. She's as mute in the face of outrage as Benjamin has been. He denies disliking her when she poses this question to him directly. Elaine is at a loss for her role in this obvious production, even as her doppelganger on stage enters upon her climactic "great effect." The stripper notes Elaine's discomfort and makes her an unwitting partner in her act, stooping to whirl her tassels over Elaine's head. Shot-reverse shots of Elaine enduring this humiliation and of Benjamin consuming it culminate in a shot of him removing his shades and a close-up of her tear-streaked face. He lunges at the stripper and the spell is broken — more than one spell, in fact: the one just cast by stripper, drummer, and Benjamin upon Elaine, as well as the misanthropic spell he and Mrs. Robinson have been under together for months. Released from her spell, Elaine runs. Released from his spell, Benjamin pursues. Elaine is in the typical predicament of Benjamin: retreating from cruel manipulation. Benjamin, however, is in a new position for the first time: moving *toward* rather than away from an objective. The final 45 minutes of *The Graduate* depict Benjamin in a new gear: drive, rather than reverse or his long-time default position, neutral. What remains to be seen is whether all this motion is genuinely linear or merely circular.

Such forward movement hardly implies obstacle-free progress, in any case. Benjamin's summer of misbegotten choices dooms him to a series of painful confrontations and additional poor judgment. The first confrontation awaits him on the Strip, where, amid the hurly-burly of a long, ill-lit tracking shot populated by strangers and punctuated by a maddening soundtrack collage of competing musical motifs, Benjamin tries to tell Elaine something. Against her better judgment, no doubt coaxed on by curiosity to unearth some rational explanation for his behavior, she stops to listen. His explanation, however, is the familiar one he's already attempted to little effect on her mother just prior to leaving the house: "This whole idea, the date and everything, it was my parents' idea. They forced me into it." This summation not only describes his past and present but her future, the "shotgun" wedding to Carl Smith.

Understandably less than enchanted by this explanation, she resists his advances. Then the one-time apprentice misanthrope reaches a little deeper and plucks out an epiphany: "I'm not like this. I hate myself like this." Improbably, he presses her into a kiss. More improbably still, she does not utterly recoil. What are we to make of such acquiescence? The film's narrative has long since established Benjamin as a blank slate awaiting someone's marker. Elaine, lately Benjamin's victim, proves just as pliable. She is another obedient, unreflective child on a parental fast track to conformity, handed over by a father who might just as well be closing on a real-estate sale.

For Elaine, the good news is that all Benjamin's ulterior motives are a temporary skin he has tried on (like a scuba suit), a graft of misanthropic anxiety rejected as he contemplates the pain he has provoked in the strip club. Benjamin may have been numbed to his own pain, but he is acutely aware of hers. He is no sadist. For Benjamin, such cost to others costs both them and him too dearly. (It's what Mrs. Robinson uses to coax him back to bed: she acts "hurt.") Benjamin is able to see what Mrs. Robinson either can't or won't, that the act of diminishing another provides only the illusion of one's own empowerment. "I hate myself when I'm like this": this is self-hatred that could heal. However, it takes demonizing Mrs. Robinson for Benjamin to accomplish this insight.

In their genuine, honest exchange in the hotel room, Benjamin and Mrs. Robinson have come to a mutual acknowledgment of their shared void. Though each of them is powerless to act on this insight, this does not negate conversation's totemic power to *provide* insight. The two-shot of Benjamin and Elaine in his car provides a vision of a conversation that constructs rather than deconstructs a relationship. Benjamin describes for Elaine his experience of being an apprentice misanthrope, "this kind of compulsion I have to be rude all the time." He asks, "Do you know what I mean?" Henry's screenplay offers Elaine a critical response: "Yes I do," she says around a bite of burger. In their easy, instant intimacy, *The Graduate* implies that each may have found another who understands. She knows about compulsive rudeness; it's all around her. His groping attempts to explain this phenomenon have her nodding her approval, even as they lead him to a series of refining corrections of his own insight. Ultimately, he concludes, the problem is one of systemic passivity and victimization. He can't blame a person or even a group. It seemed to him at first to be a nefarious web of "rules" made up by "all the wrong people," when in fact, he says, "No one makes them up; they seem to have made themselves up." Aaron Cooley identifies this previously inchoate recognition as a crucial moment for Benjamin, because he has articulated "the vital essence of reification."[4] It marks what appears to be a turning point in Benjamin's life, though Cooley muses, "trying to step out of the reified world is fraught with personal and private contradictions."[5]

A bland confrontation with the young men in the next car results in an intensified solidarity for Benjamin and Elaine. The social performance of post-adolescence at the drive-in is one more kind of conformity for Benjamin and Elaine to avoid. (The incident may provide some small measure of insight into a characteristic of Benjamin's personality that so incensed Jacob Brackman in his *New Yorker* essay: why Benjamin seems so disillusioned by his four years of college, which apparently had no lasting intellectual or social effect on him other than alienation. "In life, of course," writes Brackman, "Benjamin would have met hundreds of his peers — heads, revolutionaries, and some who would not fall so easily into categories — who shared his sense of America's disorder, and he would already have begun to work with them on new conceptions of community, and of sanity. At the very least, he would have had a friend who felt as he did."[6]) Benjamin and Elaine display no interest in the prevailing social scene at the drive-in, which all looks less than genuinely counter-cultural anyway — but which, despite Brackman's protestations, does *not* mean it does not reflect what many drive-ins must have looked like in 1967, or remained in spirit where culturally timid or conformist young people continued to gather through subsequent decades.

It's an interesting moment in the film, one Kael derides as yet another failure of nerve on the part of Henry and Nichols[7]: the confined car is a place where the problems of communication and connection the film has so consistently raised are met with a kind of solace, a respite from the social pressures under which Benjamin has typically been caused to perform. Indeed, we do not witness the particulars of Hoffman and Ross' performance, for two very distinct but equally important reasons. One, which the film's critics repeatedly intone,[8] is that Benjamin and Elaine are empty-headed and have nothing to say to each other (which is not precisely true, since they chat animatedly about something, unlike Benjamin and Mrs. Robinson; what the critics mean is that Benjamin and Elaine have nothing to say to *us*, no oracular wisdom that will point a pilgrim's way along a non-conformist's path). The other reason we are not privileged with their conversation is that, in this little red cocoon, they have stumbled upon intimacy — not the mockery of intimacy that Mrs. Robinson and Benjamin have pursued to their mutual displeasure, but genuine intimacy, which Nichols celebrates not just from a strategic but also from a respectful distance, aware for Benjamin and for the film that the pressure of speaking for an emergent revolution is more than any one young man speaking to any one young woman can probably bear. It may be the canny choice of a director who knows that no words can possibly suffice, but it rings with the sympathetic primacy of individualist experience. We must all speak (or fail to speak) for ourselves. If it's a choice guided by the pressures of the marketplace, it nonetheless also delivers the right artistic effect.

Nichols and O'Steen cut from one of the noisiest moments in *The Graduate* (jangled by "The Big Bright Green Pleasure Machine," the Simon and Garfunkel song in the film most likely to stump a trivia contestant) to the pronounced yet companionable silence of the parked car outside the Robinsons' house. The shot is similar to the one in which Benjamin has driven Elaine's mother home from his graduation party at the beginning of the summer. The silence, however, is utterly different. In the earlier shot, Mrs. Robinson seethes with controlling rage, willing Benjamin out of the car and around to her door, up the front steps, into the house, etc. Benjamin and Elaine sit in the spell of a new kind of enchantment, and neither wishes to speak and break the spell. As they extend the evening in search of a nightcap, Nichols the comedian has some fun with a curb and again at the Taft Hotel, reflecting back at Benjamin his erstwhile nighttime-monster, Mr. Gladstone. Escaped again to the car, their shiny red cocoon, Benjamin tells Elaine of his regard: "You're the first thing for so long that I've liked, the first person I could stand to be with." Elaine asks the question that, if answered truthfully, has the power to complete Benjamin's cure: "Are you having an affair with someone?"

Benjamin has heard this word before, but always at the wrong time, in the wrong connotative context, asked by the wrong person. Finally, the right person asks the right question. Her follow-on questions, sober but not salacious, probing without prying, form a catechism for his release from the conspiracy of silence. He describes the affair as "just this thing that happened along with everything else" — a dangerous distancing of himself from its potential consequences. He comes clean with Elaine about everything but the one

12. Elaine

thing that will matter most. (This is the question — his partner's identity — that a decent person can never ask, and so Elaine leaves him in the comfortably familiar burden of his silence.) The construction of the cinematic frame, compartmentalizing them through the car's door and windshield, emphasizes his psychological despair of revealing the full truth of their predicament. Her questions build, and in the loophole left open amongst all the truthful answers, Benjamin sees an illusory glimmer of hope. Elaine asks: "And it's all over now?" His solemn assent must *feel* like truth. For him, it *is* over; for his nightmare version of Mrs. Robinson, however, there is no such thing as over. She will never get over the ruination of her own life, or the need to make someone else pay.

The next two scenes, both in the same location, are literally night and day: a night's tender fantasy of consequence-free attachment, a veritable balcony scene, and the next day's tempest. The narrative, nearly two-thirds complete, has been dominated by water imagery as a form of refuge or retreat. One last time the narrative returns to water, the morning after the date-from-hell-turned-dream-date. Rain hurtles down on the Alfa Romeo, a late-summer monsoon. Benjamin whistles a tune we recognize as "Mrs. Robinson," in a cheerfully defiant stroke against the Greek chorus of Simon and Garfunkel's soundtrack. Glimpsed through the passenger window, a graceful pair of legs runs across the lawn to the car. Mrs. Robinson enters, giving orders. Ron Howard, in his appreciative interview about *The Graduate* with Rick Lyman, refers to the strategy of filming the entire scene with these two anguished people caught together in this tiny space as "such a smart way to shoot this scene. [...] First, it's a very effective way to make it more claustrophobic, which is the way Benjamin feels. Again, it keeps the movie on his point of view. But it's also by far the cheapest way to shoot this."[9] Benjamin attempts a factual assertion of will, but he's never been any match for her. He obeys. "In order to keep Elaine away from you," she says, "I'm prepared to tell her everything." Truth is thus reduced to blunt instrument. "Try me," she dares, her final solicitation of Benjamin. She wears the glint of steely victory in her eyes and at the corner of her mouth. She believes their match is over.

She has underestimated him as much as he has demonized her. The track star runs. Howard's admiration for the treatment of the brief, tense scene in the car is half about aesthetics and half about economics: "All you need is one rainbird," he observes (referring to the gargantuan sprinkler system that, arranged over a set, can produce a storm at the push of a button) — but he then points to the moment in the manufactured rainstorm when, in the midst of an otherwise typically sunny Southern Californian sky, the rainbird cannot cover the full expanse of Robinson lawn. Halfway through Hoffman's soaking run, he enters a dry area beyond the range of the rainmaker, much to Howard's delight.[10] Yet this fault in execution hardly defuses the suspense of the moment. Benjamin throws open the now-familiar arched door, setting a pandemonium of spattering rain (a new rainbird set-up for this shot) and his urgent cries for Elaine echoing through the Robinson "castle." Up the stairs he comes, those same black-and-white stairs up which he was once coaxed like a recalcitrant five-year-old; he barrels past Elaine's virginal defenses raving instructions for how to avoid the inundation bearing down upon them. He should have come fully clean, and he senses that this opportunity, fatally hesitated over, is now gone. Downstairs the door slams, and Mrs. Robinson approaches. As he closes the door to her room, an undressed Elaine squeals in a combination of titillation and scandal.

Surtees frames Elaine's dawning recognition against the slit of her open bedroom door, into which Mrs. Robinson's drowned face appears, in soft focus; illicit sex has infected both Benjamin's childhood bedroom and now her own. Sobering, Elaine says, "Benjamin, will you just tell me what this is all about?" Her amused smile invites him to regain that easy intimacy they'd enjoyed the previous night, a trust that could seemingly surmount any obstacle, even an affair. A reverse shot of Benjamin shows his eyes shift from her to her mother, and in the return to Elaine, Surtees' focus shifts to follow her psychological point of view as she looks where he is looking, at the hard-focus image of his mother. When she turns back, Surtees' slow rack-focus return to Elaine allows us to feel the sickening weight of her awareness. Like the previous night, Benjamin pleads with her not to cry — but crying is no longer her response. Enraged, she rightfully banishes him to the other side of a slammed door. They had shared a conversation, and he has betrayed her trust. He has lied. Most immediately and enormously, he has slept with her mother. Their powerfully affecting conversation of the previous night might just as well have been shaking hands.

Outside the room of the one person he "can stand to be with," he encounters a ghost. It's the dead woman he's been using as a raft during his summer of "drifting." "Goodbye, Benjamin," says Mrs. Robinson, another drowned victim, in drenched and funereal black against the long blank hallway of the Robinsons' second floor. Silence reigns. No image goes further in this film to convey the reality of self-destruction embedded within the vindictive impulse to destroy others. For a third and final time, the film returns to black.

13

"Scarborough Fair": The Berkeley Stalker (1:10:30—1:26:00)

The final third of *The Graduate* has an appropriately different rhetorical feeling than the first 70 minutes. For all but the final minutes of the first two-thirds of the film, Benjamin Braddock is without self-direction, buffeted by the winds of the adult world or simply adrift. The film's settings are hermetic and unvarying. In the film's final 35 minutes, Benjamin *appears* to break out of this confinement, taking to the road in pursuit of an objective: winning Elaine. Although he remains within the grip of a larger spiritual conformity, he seems at least to be acting on his own, as when he announces to his parents that he's come to a "decision" regarding Elaine. While we can see this as a positive step in his self-assertion, we may also see the truth in Mr. Braddock's observation that the idea is "half-baked." Benjamin's self-invention is still a work in progress. The film envelops this last section of his story almost entirely in Simon and Garfunkel's music. Before, his life was as likely to be conducted in genuine silence, the choric commentary of "The Sounds of Silence," the incidental music of Mrs. Robinson's radio, or the cocktail MUZAK at the Taft Hotel. But in the final third of the film, "Scarborough Fair" and "Mrs. Robinson" accompany montages stitching together short vignettes that appear to add up to a new unity of purpose.

This is the good news. The bad news is that Benjamin has become a stalker. Parts of Benjamin's life disturbingly match the stereotypic stalker-profile. He lives in his childhood room and rarely socializes. He has lost interest in education and employment. His routine centers around a pretty young woman's schedule; the young woman is under observation but never aware of his presence. All Benjamin can see, however, is that he is outside of Elaine's circle of affection. Despite being born to privilege (symbolized continuously by his Alfa Romeo), Benjamin has never been more acutely aware of a profound impoverishment.

One final time, as the screen fades up from black, we see Benjamin communing with his childhood retreat, the aquarium. Not only is it our final view of the fish tank, but in the same montage, we also get our last glimpse of the family pool, that ambiguous source of humiliation and retreat, tended by Mr. Braddock. Former solitary refuges offer not even the prior illusion of solace now, because his highly impressionable sensibility has enlarged this one mostly pleasant evening with Elaine into a clarifying night of contact with another soul. In four years at college, he apparently hadn't found anyone who had struck him in this way — hadn't even known to look for such a person, immersed as he must have been in the abstractions of his textbooks. The lack of social and cultural referents in the film is yet another rendering of Benjamin's psychological point of view: he doesn't see the social revolution we know historically is happening all around him, which means the film can't see it either. His inheritance is, at its core, solipsism.

In his car, he prowls Elaine's street. Nichols and Surtees shoot through mirrors and from behind bushes. As the first "stalker"-montage sequence ends, the camera zooms from a medium overhead shot of Benjamin pushed back from his writing desk to the page on which he's been writing. (The image alludes to epistolary sections of Webb's novel, in which Benjamin unburdens himself to both Robinson women, to little effect: Mrs. Robinson is uninterested in his explanations, and he short-circuits the letters to Elaine before delivering them. Much like Webb, Henry felt compelled to attempt a variation of Benjamin's inner-life. Henry's screenplay at this juncture incorporates imagined letters home after having swept Elaine off her feet and away, fantasy vignettes of married life with Elaine, even a dictation of the verbiage on wedding invitations sent out by the Robinsons — but these fantasy sequences, mainly presented as voice-overs, did not make the film's final-cut, precisely because they would have been fantasies within the fantasy of Benjamin's self-serving projections of *all* we see. The fantasy sequences are rendered unnecessary when we realize that the film offers us nothing but his distortions and Nichols's irony.) The salutation at the top of the stationery on Benjamin's desk tells us he's been attempting a letter to Elaine, but the repetitions in increasingly unfocused, dreamy scrawl of her name down the page suggest that he is at a loss for what to say and content to retreat into wishful reverie. The image serves as a kind of distillation of much of *The Graduate*'s point of view: Benjamin's series of imaginatively solipsistic variations on the real life going on around him. The consequences of Benjamin's capitulation to the world handed down to him by the Braddocks and Robinsons have rendered him mute, insensible to make himself understood. He increasingly disengages from the reality of his past to enter what Nichols calls "a kind of fantasy prettiness,"[1] allowing him to pursue consequence-free action.

Nichols illustrates this problem to comic effect in the next scene. As the song closes, the zoomed close-up on the page dissolves to a short, dysfunctional conversation with his parents, which we enter as Benjamin announces, "I'm going to marry Elaine Robinson." He is dressed and holding a suitcase, while his father is still in his morning bathrobe. Has Benjamin been downstairs, trying to move with speed and stealth to avoid his parents' prying interventions? But why, then, is he smiling and speaking with such satisfaction? It seems possible that he has sought out his father to tell him this news, if that is the appropriate term. The moment is ambiguous, then, not only because he is reporting news that is "half-baked" but also because he is reporting it to people for whom he feels a certain horror, given their proclivity for dressing him up against his wishes to entertain their friends. It's a performance, meant to delight but also to confound. Although he has an intellectual awareness of his own crowd-pleasing indoctrination, the habit dies hard. It is feasible to read this scene as a voluntary attempt to regain his parents' approval on the only terms to which they can both agree. It is also the first time he refers to his own plans for marriage. Given the Robinsons' marriage, which he has studied at such close proximity all summer, he might have been expected to be warier of the institution. Yet joining the fraternity of the wedded becomes the sole object of his relationship to Elaine. If they are to be together, it will be as husband and wife.

Whatever his motives for telling his parents, their initial response is nothing short of rhapsodic. Mrs. Braddock in particular is in full throat: the roar of her relief at her son's social conformity borders on madness. Hoffman continues to play low-key when Benjamin is among his elders. They move him around as if he's stuffed, and the small smile with which he has delivered the announcement remains carved into his face. Benjamin endures their growing skepticism and delivers one of the lines that typically produces a big laugh in any audience: "Oh no, it's completely baked." What the audience often misses in the sassy puncturing of the cliché is his next statement: "It's a decision I've made." He has begun to work on his own life rather than wait for others to tinker with it. Nichols the comedian pops the toast to get Benjamin off-stage, but the toaster's punctuation serves also to remind us of a second point of view in the film, one that is aware of the flights of fancy favored by the film's main point of view, courtesy of Benjamin. Maybe Benjamin is half-baked, after all.

From this vignette, we re-enter the musical montage, our first reprise of "Scarborough Fair." Benjamin drives the Alfa Romeo through some of the most pleasing photography of the photogenic Bay Area ever to grace cinema screens, including the extraordinary zoom-out looking northeast, as he crosses the Bay Bridge to Berkeley. Yes, that is a significant practical error to have Benjamin racing along the top level of the bridge headed to Berkeley (everyone knows the view of San Francisco is the one enjoyed by traffic on the top level of the Bay Bridge) — but where is the glamour in having him traverse the bridge's lower level? The symbolism of Benjamin "crossing over" from his previous life of passive submission to what appears to him (and thus to us) to be a new era of initiative and motivation needs — and gets — its visual match in this spectacular shot. Those who have been on the University of Southern California's campus in South-Central Los Angeles know that the sequence that comes next in the montage, as he stakes out Elaine's campus, is at USC, not UC-Berkeley.[2] Such were the vagaries of film-making on Joseph E. Levine's budget. Any doubts about Benjamin's reason for being in Berkeley are neutralized by the rooftop vantage on Benjamin himself: the stalker stalked by the film. As with the popping toast, the shot reminds us that the film has a point of view on Benjamin; the shift from the monster-show grotesques of the Robinsons and Braddocks to the fairy-tale daydream of Elaine is a referendum on Benjamin himself, on his relentless repackaging of rather than grappling with reality.

He settles himself into a room in Berkeley and into her routine. Presumably, his plan is to meet her casually by orchestrated "coincidence" rather than by a formal prompting, as their "chance meeting" on the city-bus will reveal. He will need a base of operations for this reconnaissance, and in the second vignette during the "Scarborough Fair" sequence, he encounters the highly suspicious boarding-house superintendent, Mr. McCleery, played with Silent-Majority outrage by Norman Fell. (Fell would cash in on his short but memorable performance in *The Graduate* by playing an intolerant super for five years on the TV sitcom "Three's Company"; Richard Dreyfuss, one of Mr. McCleery's apple-polishing "boys," also makes a brief appearance at the boarding house, and, in *Jaws*, would express his own disdain for the profit-motive establishment as represented by Murray Hamilton's craven mayor of Amity.) Mr. McCleery's supposition about Benjamin is that only a man with malevolent political intent would show up in a University town without a class schedule. In the patronizing spirit of all members of his generation in this film, Mr. McCleery says he likes "to know what my boys are up to." Although not genuinely an "agitator" hoping to incite Berkeley's Free Speech Movement to revolution, Benjamin is nonetheless unprepared to make a full accounting of his purpose in Berkeley. His natural anxiousness and unconvincing explanation leave him under a vast McCleery cloud he is never able to dispel.

A key question never overtly addressed in the film surrounds Benjamin's means during his sojourn in Berkeley. What is his source of capital for his expenses? Nothing so pedestrian as work — he has reconnaissance to maintain. In Webb's book, Benjamin sells the car and writes Elaine reasoned and passionate letters he fails to post. Henry wisely dispenses with all this plot paraphernalia and lets Benjamin hold onto his car. The car, that most ostentatious symbol of his parents' material hopes for his future, is also his means to DIY travel between southern and central California. In Webb's book, Benjamin is forever dashing to airports; in Nichols and Henry's vision, he's a red dart on California's freeways, and the abandonment of the car has a far more poetic resonance than a cash transaction. Left to speculate on how he pays Mr. McCleery a deposit on the room, we must assume that Benjamin digs a bit deeper into his hypocritical bag of tricks: one must conclude that the Berkeley idyll is underwritten by his father's patronage.

"Scarborough Fair" receives its second reprise. In this montage sequence, genuinely filmed on the city streets of Berkeley (including a cameo of the venerable Moe's Books, still on Telegraph Avenue, still worth the trip), we begin with a long shot of Elaine that racks to a close-up silhouette of Benjamin, still stalking. She lopes onto a city bus and Benjamin breaks into a sprint, beautifully framed through the bus window to offer Elaine's point of view. We see her shock as she collapses into her seat, surrounded by anonymous humanity (or nearly so, since the woman next to her has been cast by Nichols the film scholar as an homage to Federico Fellini, that master of the aestheticized, satirically lampooned point of view: the mountainous woman with the set jaw sitting next to Elaine is Edra Gale, La Saraghina from Fellini's *8 ½* and thus a familiar face to fans of Italian art-movies). The bus has a short, busy route, and Benjamin the former track star easily overtakes it at its next stop; Elaine sets her face for the confrontation she knows is coming. *The Graduate* has formally established Elaine as a second subjectivity through which we may view this world. For Elaine, the only true innocent left in the narrative, that one-night episode with Benjamin was a cautionary experience, a path of deception whose entanglements she believes she's managed, mostly, to avoid. The narrative can thus demonstrate much that is unspoken about her own sense of pampered imprisonment in her parents' world when it eventually presents her as willing to be wooed again by this man who hurt her. Benjamin is the lesser of two evils, ultimately a better bet than a pompous pipe-smoker like Carl Smith (played by Brian Avery as a particularly boorish specimen of that phylum Henry and Nichols referred to as the human surfboards from

Webb's book), whom we discover, in her brief and chilly dialogue with Benjamin aboard the bus, Elaine is riding to meet.

At the zoo, the established meeting place, Carl isn't immediately apparent, but Elaine refuses to reminisce with Benjamin about their shared time in Beverly Hills. She strides purposefully around the monkey house, scowling, until Nichols finally offers us (because Benjamin recognizes Carl as soon as he sees him) a long shot of a tall blond man. He's as Aryan as Benjamin is Jewish, everything Benjamin isn't. In *Play It Again, Sam* (Herbert Ross, 1972) Woody Allen would have fun with this sort of paranoid projection of the anti–Jew, imagining his ex-wife, beautiful, blond Susan Anspach, rolling merrily in the sun-dappled California hills with a tall, blond, virile biker. Carl Smith projects so much of what Benjamin can never be — by genetic inheritance, but also by newly embraced inclination. "He certainly is a good walker," observes Benjamin, commenting on the caricature his point of view conjures. With a train whistling in the background, Carl churns inexorably toward them, waving the pipe, a parody of mature success: the Robinsons' and Braddocks' drawing-board design of the suitable young man. More to the point, he's what Benjamin knows his parents would wish him to be. Clasping a possessive arm around Elaine's shoulders, Carl bundles her away, and she acquiesces like yet another piece of luggage.

Surtees returns to rack-focus to juxtapose a pensive Benjamin with an equally thoughtful ape, and "Scarborough Fair" enters its third reprise. By this point its plaintive performance must begin to grate at the awareness of the filmgoer. Despite the change of scenery and all the emphasis upon movement since Elaine has been introduced, the recycling of this pretty piece of folk balladry indicates an underlying stasis, a new rut to replace the old. Nichols and O'Steen have produced a pattern of formal repetition in the film's third act that reflects the failure of Benjamin to effect positive movement in his life. Carl Smith projects the illusion of such forward progress: he's a "good walker." Although it has appeared that Benjamin has begun a series of sprints toward a goal, Elaine continues to recede. The vignette-and-reprise rhetoric suggests he may have entered upon one of those mythic curses that torment less through the moment's pain than by resignation to its endless return. In Benjamin's point of view, a zoo is a hall of mirrors. The cages are relative, and even the monkeys laugh at him. "Do not tease," reads a sign on one of the cages. For Benjamin's distorting *weltschmerz*, the image that was planted in his brain still remains — an endless recessionary tease, tantalizing him with one night's glimpse of normality before setting him on yet another treadmill.

Elaine's appearance in the night at the boarding house, then, is essential — the only means by which to shift the narrative's burden to a second set of shoulders. Benjamin has borne this weight alone for 80 minutes. Now the film presents him with a second protagonist, who in pushing past his closed door (a gesture reminiscent of earlier invasions by Mrs. Robinson and both Braddocks) demonstrates her attempt to assume an active role not only in his life but in her own. As she bursts in, he's shaving what might as well be the shadow of Berkeley and the Robinsons from his mask. When Elaine demands his version of the story Mrs. Robinson has handed her, a grim fairy tale about booze and rape that Elaine must at some level know rings false, Benjamin eagerly sets about telling her the truth, an equally unpalatable pill for a girl to swallow about her mother and her erstwhile lover. Elaine's scream of refutation brings Mr. McCleery (accompanied, in an energetic bit part, by the youthful Dreyfuss: "Shall I get the cops? I'll get the cops"). Mr. McCleery serves Ben his eviction, projecting a mutual antipathy the film has increasingly foregrounded as Benjamin's organic understanding of the generation gap. When Benjamin and Mr. Robinson have their second "father-son" talk in this same room, the antipathy will be fully and finally articulated.

Benjamin's on-going sense of victimization works to his advantage with Elaine, however: his persecution by Mr. McCleery reminds her that Benjamin is somehow different from a trained monkey like Carl Smith. On the bus out to meet Carl "by the monkey house," Benjamin poses the ambiguously existential question to Elaine, "I was wondering where you were headed." Now she returns this practical inquiry to Benjamin. Despite his avowed position that, "Right now, I don't feel like talking much," she presses him: "What are you going to do now?" He shuts down her questions so summarily that the moment begins to echo the "Let's not talk at all" conclusion to his epic "conversation" with Mrs. Robinson. The soundtrack returns us to yet a fourth reprise of "Scarborough Fair," but, in changing instrumentation to a single recorder accompanied by guitar, signals that this repetitive torment to which Benjamin has been condemned may at last be nearing its end. The long shot from the window, of Elaine's receding form, dissolves into a dark interior, Benjamin asleep. Off-screen, we hear his door open, and an intruder enters. Has Mr. McCleery rallied the local chapter of the John Birch Society? Benjamin leaps up, his response not the more typical "Who's there?" but the more existentially apt, "What's happening?"

The Graduate's meditation on two modes of existence — the culture's fast track v. the counter-culture's exploratory, improvisational drift — is at the center of the film's final 20 minutes. Through Benjamin's gimlet eye, *The Graduate* has satirized the culture that bullies bright, sensitive young men like Benjamin Braddock until they shape up into performing chimps like Carl Smith, after which they devolve into anxious entertainers like Mr. Braddock or sour malcontents like Mr. Robinson. Through Benjamin's disenchantment, the film savages a landscape that binds bright, sensitive young women like Elaine Robinson until they are trophy wives like Mrs. Braddock or predatory misanthropes like Mrs. Robinson. But until now, the film has mostly spared Benjamin and Elaine from its satirical cross hairs, largely because we have been in Benjamin's self-pitying point of view. While there is no dignity to be found in the ridiculous situations into which their culture forces them, we have reclaimed dignity for Benjamin and Elaine by projecting empathetically their puzzlement and frustration. In the next vignette-and-montage sequence, however, accompanied by various reprises of "Mrs. Robinson," Benjamin and Elaine demonstrate a discouraging lack of imagination and momentum. They revert to childhood and the make-believe comforts of conformity.

14
"Mrs. Robinson": The Loneliness of the Long-Distance Runner (1:26:00 — 1:41:00)

The intruder who has entered Benjamin's dark room at the boarding house is Elaine, the stalked object turned stalker, wanting to be kissed. Benjamin obliges and, through a poorly stifled yawn, begins his new repetitive litany: "Will you marry me?" This scene lays out a cinematic deconstruction of the climactic moment in genre romance. The screen is dipped in a chilly blue light. The lovers' faces are utterly obscured. The heroine is glum, the hero groggy. There is no triumphant payoff, no affirming inflection from the soundtrack, which has been eager at other times to respond. "I don't know what's happening," says Elaine, a belated, backhanded response to Benjamin's waking query into the darkness. "You mean you're confused?" asks Benjamin, cotton-mouthed. "Well look, don't be confused. We're getting *married*."

He pronounces the last word in a culturally received hush of reverence. Marriage is the happily-ever-after conclusion to the fairy tales made in studios just down the road from where they've grown up. It is the inviolable, time-honored strategy men and women make before God and witnesses that, in the often-intoned jargon of the wedding rite, *no man may put asunder*. Marriage will be their refuge, Benjamin seems to be telling her — a disturbingly cynical use of the system's own rules against itself. Benjamin is counting on men of the system like Mr. Braddock and Mr. Robinson to be respectful of a civilly proscribed contract at the risk of denouncing their own structures of meaning. As Elaine leaves, having promised Benjamin she will "think about" his proposal, Nichols and O'Steen make a small cut in the shot of Benjamin in profile, his neutral expression leavened in the second shot by a tentative smile. This transformation's process—a dawning satisfaction—will be reversed by the long final shot of the couple on the bus at the end of the film, when smiles fade. The sense that Benjamin is drifting through a dream is reinforced by the end of this shot, after Benjamin has wandered off-screen and back to bed, still yawning: "Good God," he exclaims. Another chance to wake up, ignored. That final shot of the two of them in the back seat of the bus implies the power of finally awakening from a long and familiar, genre-inflected dream to the disorienting complexity of consciousness.

A cut to another scene shot on USC's campus as a stand-in for Berkeley underscores Benjamin's monomaniacal focus on their marriage. He continues to follow her, the stalker legitimized by honorable intentions. "I just don't think it would work," she says to him, entering a classroom. "Why wouldn't it?" he demands, as the classroom door closes in his face. A cut to a different angle of him standing before the closed door suggests the elapse of the class period and his determination not to accept the closing off of this single espied avenue to his happiness. As she emerges, he renews the barrage with a repetition of the same question, and this unproductive debate roves across campus as she meets the schoolgirl obligations of her schedule.

The motif of childhood predominates, and the film launches an aggressive satire of its two protagonists. In gym class, the girls all dressed in their tiny white uniforms, Elaine's attention wavers between Benjamin's threats to drag her off, the back-and-forth of the basketball game, and the promises she's made to the *other* boy, Carl Smith. In proximity to young people's games, the courtship itself has become a game. She nonchalantly chews gum; he acts out. In the library, he wants to compare his own less-than-suave proposal to Carl's, badgering her for details, and she relents: "He said he thought we'd make a pretty good team"—a corny sports metaphor for these children and the game they're playing. Benjamin's immature aggression not only seeks to publicly embarrass her by shouting in the library but, in referencing the creation myth of how "ol' Elaine Robinson got started in a Ford," potentially delivers a more private humiliation only she will understand. The line is funny. But there is real darkness here, a pall cast over their unimaginable future together. There's only one way he can know to make such a reference: intimate access to one of the participants. Can they possibly tolerate this sort of knowledge? Has he told Elaine about the conversation he tried to have with her mother? Has he told Elaine about the circumstances of her conception? Benjamin may have rejected Mrs. Robinson's tutelage, but he still carries some of her venom, and a trace of Elaine's father's bed. A competitive child, Benjamin remembers how she abetted Carl Smith's humiliation of him by the monkey house, and he proves himself capable of lashing out in a very public tantrum that humiliates her, while adding very private barbs that can only deepen her shame.

A cut to an exterior shot of Benjamin and Elaine in a kind of two-person procession past massive, foregrounded brick pillars[1] restores needed solemnity. A campus clock chimes the hour. Neither her game-playing of Benjamin against Carl nor his petulant tantrums has warned them off of what they contemplate. This is, in fact, preparing us for the beauty of that famous final shot of Benjamin and Elaine on the bus. In their childish urgency to have what they want, especially when they're told they may not have it, they rush forward, happy to be pursuing a goal rather than being themselves pursued. Elaine stops between two of the brick pillars and turns to dismiss Benjamin for the evening. Her arms are full of books; the dutiful, obedient girl, she can shift from discussing a life-changing commitment like marriage to researching a term paper at the stroke of a clock. To his question of whether they will be married tomorrow, she can say, unequivocally, no. (Perhaps she has an exam to study for, or a club meeting.) To his follow-up question about the day after that (Benjamin clearly has no other interests or preoccupations cluttering his own mind and schedule), she says, with child-like, sing-song dreaminess, "Maybe we will, maybe we won't." She moves behind a pillar, off-screen, and a voice begins to whistle the jaunty melody of "Mrs. Robinson": we have entered into our final vignette-and-montage sequence. Again, as in the nighttime shot cut to replace Benjamin's somber profile with a smile, we watch his face lit by her return for a parting kiss. But the last time we heard this tune whistled, as Benjamin drove up to Elaine's for their "drive" in the rain, was just before the tempest that brought the deluge. What looms over these two children is their willful naivete that they may, without reifying consequence, forge ahead with their own future.

The montage offers a glimpse of a possible future in the next scene. Shot through a jewelry store's glass-paneled door plastered with logos of plastic credit, Benjamin transacts what must be his purchase of the traditional diamond engagement ring. Benjamin's image is briefly supplanted by that of a family flying a modified freak-flag as they exit the store: the man's hair has grown long, the woman with him, toting an infant, wears a fashionably floppy suede hat. Comparatively clean-cut and mainstream, Benjamin leaves the store visibly whistling, in harmony with the soundtrack, and in the next shot, returns to the room he should already have vacated, laden with flowers and additional presents, the very model of the affluent young swain preparing his romantic *coup de grâce*. (Should we sense trepidation in what he and the soundtrack whistle? In cultural hindsight, of course we should: it's "Mrs. Robinson." But the 1967 audiences who first saw the film would not yet have recognized it; its upbeat tempo thus provides an ambiguous conduit to Benjamin's spirit just before he encounters the full force of reified consequence.) Everything Benjamin has done in Berkeley has cost money—the room, his sustenance, and now these traditional tokens of everlasting esteem; we assume his father's potent credit line can continue absorbing these charges, a nagging shadow of continued dependence amidst the bright flurry of hopeful preparation. A series of shots winds Benjamin up the interior stairwell to his door, where the camera leaves him; Nichols and O'Steen cut to a shot on the other side of the door, where we await his arrival. A soft-focus form, puffing at a cigar, waits with us in the dark: yet another intruder. Benjamin enters, reaches up to pull the light-chain, and shouts in horror at the encountered monster.

Mr. Robinson launches a prepared barrage of rhetorical questions, clearly disinterested in answers: "Do you have a special grudge against me? Do you feel a particularly strong resentment? Is there something I've said that's caused this contempt, or is it just the things I stand for that you despise?" He sits by a rain-spattered window, his raincoat on, his face mostly backlit in darkness. From off-screen, an after-thought, Benjamin replies to this solipsistic line of questioning with respectful reassurance: "It was nothing to do with you, sir." The statement is patently ridiculous, and Mr. Robinson, expecting some such false step, calls Benjamin on it, his strategy to assume the moral and ethical high ground. He manufactures a threat out of Benjamin's clenched fist: the packaged manipulation of all experience is second nature to Mr. Robinson and his circle. Like Benjamin, he can apparently make of his reality anything he wants—except for satisfying. He assures Benjamin, "I can see in the dark, you know—I've been here quite a while." Darkness, the "old friend," visits them all. The shots of Benjamin envelop him just as thickly as Mr. Robinson in this shadowy space, and we sense the existential horror in Mr. Robinson's statement: "quite a while" resonates less as a single rainy afternoon than a lifetime. This is the future Benjamin's been so worried about.

Benjamin attempts to break Mr. Robinson's foregone line of argument: "I'm trying to tell you I don't resent you"—another claim Mr. Robinson has been waiting for, to catch Benjamin in a contradiction: "You don't respect me very much either, do you?" In what must now be heard as a parody of social deference, an old habit dying hard, Benjamin confirms this lack of respect *in a respectful manner*. "No, sir," he says, with embarrassed regret. The response is the first for which the lawyer has prepared no brief. "*What?*" he sputters, stalling for time to formulate a response. Expecting Benjamin to lie, he has instead encountered the truth, and as in the unpleasant realities uncovered by truth in Benjamin's epic "conversation" with Mrs. Robinson, this truth can either set them free or else demand more plastic. Benjamin believes himself to be through with plastic (despite his convenient use of his father's plastic credit throughout his Berkeley sojourn), but Mr. Robinson has staked a lifetime on an artificial sheen of success. Benjamin dutifully repeats his answer, and Mr. Robinson returns to the strategy of painting in bold strokes a caricature of the wild youth's latent aggression and hostility for his elders. He demands Benjamin's "decency to wait until I finish." (This despite the fact he has never waited to hear so much as a drink preference from Benjamin.) Ever dutiful, Benjamin waits.

Mr. Robinson launches his central agenda: the announcement of the impending dissolution of his family's nuclear bond. He expects the announcement to paralyze Benjamin with guilt, because of the sacred force of convention, but Benjamin once again confounds his expectation. "Listen to me," says Benjamin. "What happened between Mrs. Robinson and me was nothing." The statement crystallizes Benjamin's contempt for the plastic culture of deceit he's been made heir to, but it also reflects his own failure to see consequence. All human intersection carries within it the possibility of truth— even the unhappy truths to be encountered in conversations with the Robinsons. Human intersection is never "nothing." Human resistance to the *something* always immanent in human contact is what produces the *nothing* of social hypocrisy and alienation. Benjamin's comic audacity in drawing an analogy between sex and "shaking hands" is both true to the spiritual experience of that sad episode of his life while also serving as a condemnation of *his own complicity* in a plastic culture. Mr. Robinson, never at a loss when back in the familiar landscape of hypocrisy's conveniently malleable boundaries, immediately calls him on it, the man with no interest in his wife suddenly affronted for a perceived slight against her—or at least himself as she is reflected on him as his trophy.

Benjamin, weary of the barrister's brinksmanship, shifts the subject abruptly to his own intentions, a prospective son-in-law addressing the father of the bride: "The point is, I don't love your wife, I love your daughter, sir." Into the shot of Benjamin rises the bulk of Mr. Robinson, another paternal eclipse like the one during the opening conversation between Mr. Braddock and his son. Murray Hamilton's form blocks out Dustin Hoffman's, his left shoulder visually muting Benjamin by obscuring the younger man's mouth. The malevolence and latent violence of which Mr. Robinson has been accusing Benjamin are, for the first time during the scene, given genuine form, and Benjamin's eyes widen in child-like terror of corporal punishment. "All right now, listen to this," says Mr. Robinson, demanding the full attention of others despite his own unwillingness to extend the courtesy. "I don't know whether I can prosecute, but I think I can. I think I can get you behind bars if you ever look at my daughter again. Now I've seen Elaine, and I've made damn sure you can't get to her." Benjamin reaches out a hand, in desperate need of breaking through this thickening wall of resistance, and Mr. Robinson, his legal instincts honed to misconstrue the facts to his own advantage, finds in Benjamin's peaceful gesture an assault. Mr. Robinson agilely leaps across the bed and to the door, where an unexpected ally stands by: Mr. McCleery. In a witty rhetorical flourish, Mr. Robinson says, "You'll pardon me if *I* don't shake hands with you," his voice trembling with an emotion that, knowing what we know about him, can only come from self-conscious pressure to continue a plastic pretense of regard for his family. "I think you are filth," he concludes. "I think you are scum. You are a degenerate!" Mr. McCleery watches all this from the on-deck circle, ready to take his cuts.

In his dismissal of Buck Henry's adaptation of the source novel for the screen, Richard Corliss condemns the film for its vilification of the Robinsons, who are denied the humanity Corliss sees in their counterparts in Webb's novel. One of the examples he cites is, ironically, this last line of invective directed by Mr. Robinson at Benjamin. Corliss implies that Henry added the series of slurs as a dishonest polarizing agent meant to inflame the audience's righteous outrage in sympathy with Benjamin,[2] but a look at the novel reveals that Henry, once again "retyping" (in Corliss' characterization[3]) rather than genuinely adapting the novel, has remained true to the original: "I don't want to mince words with you," Mr. Robinson says in Webb's book. "I think you're totally despicable. I think you're scum, I think you're filth. And as far as Elaine's concerned you're to get her out of your filthy mind right now.'"[4] The larger point is that all of this is mediated by a character's unreliably prejudiced version of his own life, in which everyone is to blame but himself: both Mr. Robinson and Mr. McCleery have become generational bugbears standing, literally, in the way of Benjamin's dreamed-up idea of happiness.

Benjamin stirs into action, intent upon connecting with Elaine by telephone. In these pre-cell-phone days, he despairs of a dime; an inflationary panic provokes him to wave two $10 bills at Mr. McCleery in hopes of securing the necessary change. Mr. McCleery's only response is to threaten the police (what charge, exactly, could he imagine he would press?), and Benjamin's flippant retort, "Can I make one phone call first?" closes the book on his Berkeley idyll. Nichols makes a great show of this corkscrewing interior stairwell, as Benjamin whirls down through the gyre, intent upon escape. It's an acknowledgment of labyrinthine circuitousness, a foretaste of the circuitous route he must still maneuver through much of the lower half of California to find Elaine, a rat conscious of negotiating someone else's maze. Two last shots precede the "Mrs. Robinson" montage's full onslaught: a close-up of Benjamin, his face now a portrait of tense emotion, in contrast to the dull features of the film's early close-ups; and, as Elaine's voiceover reads in a measured tone a series of dictated clichés, a surreal shot of a young woman in a hyper-tailored suit inexorably carrying the letter into his consciousness and the screen into darkness.

As if to express Benjamin's insistent attempts to reject his "old friend," Nichols and O'Steen jump-cut from this darkness to the roar of the Alfa Romeo on a nighttime street. The length of the journey from Berkeley to Beverly Hills is nearly 400 miles. Even undertaken at night, with reduced traffic, at illegal speeds, driving time is likely to be well over five hours. *The Graduate* uses cinema's compressive shorthand to underscore Benjamin's apparent transformation to a driven rather than passive personality. A beautiful, moon-misted long shot of the car's progress yields to another medium shot of Benjamin on the highway, eyes intent on his advancing goal. Then he's on foot, intruding past a physical barrier, the back fence of the Robinson property. Paul Simon's specially recorded instrumental fills in these "Mrs. Robinson" montage sequences pronounce Benjamin's inner state. As he finds the sliding glass door of the familiar sun porch open, Simon's staccato guitar strings beat like an anxious heart. In the belly of the silence and darkness of the Robinson "castle," Benjamin barks a shin in the darkness.

Why, we may wonder, has he found it so easy to ford the defenses of their fiefdom? The answer waits upstairs — and we see him mount these stairs for a final time. He dodges to the right into Elaine's well-lit room, and charged with hope, calls her name. Mrs. Robinson greets him wearing a mask of brisk, emotionless efficiency; she strides from the room, and as he follows her around the vast space of the master bedroom, she reveals her plan for his final neutralization. Like Mr. McCleery and her own husband, she believes Benjamin's case is one for the police, but she will not leave the charge to chance. In a long zoom to close-up that formally bookends her rage the night he comes to pick up Elaine for their perfunctory date-from-hell, she reports his criminal action. Alcohol is so ubiquitous a lubricant of the social wheel that, in the smug satisfaction of "everything quite under control," she even performs the burlesqued social ritual of offering him a drink. At her vanity table, make-up lights frame the mirror as at the cosmetic table of an actress' dressing room: the depiction of the grand, petty artifice of Mrs. Robinson's life is unrelenting. Bancroft even plucks lint from another leopard-print frock in a reminder of her affective distance from Benjamin as she scrubbed at a stain in the seduction scene. Belying what we know from their epic "conversation," Mrs. Robinson must always appear to be anesthetized to all pain, both her own and that she inflicts.

The full revelatory import of her flippancy emerges only gradually, as we pair it with her husband's earlier threat: "Now I've seen Elaine, and I've made damn sure you can't get to her." In their contemporary feudalism, the Robinsons stand smugly certain of their efforts to sequester their daughter in an unknown castle keep or tower. They have steeled themselves to keep their only child away from this physical symbol of their own unhappy lives, prepared to sacrifice Elaine to the same hungry god of social conformity. Elaine has been cloistered in the gown of religious and civil observance, the institution of marriage that has been the Robinsons' ball-and-chain all these years. Cyclicality dominates all action in *The Graduate*. During his apprenticeship to Mrs. Robinson as a misanthrope, Benjamin is first victimized, then victimizes Elaine. Mr. Robinson returns repeatedly to his refrain of lost youth. Benjamin returns repeatedly to his womb-retreat in the confused welter of childhood aquarium, pool, and Mrs. Robinson. In the last third of the film, this cyclical recurrence is, if anything, redoubled by the vignette-and-montage call-response of the "Scarborough Fair" and "Mrs. Robinson" sequences. Now, if we open up our road map of California, we see this repetition expanded to enormous scale.

Back in the dark, Benjamin roars through the night, up the same roads through the state down which he's just traveled. The soundtrack plays for the first time a portion of the vocal version of "Mrs. Robinson" that became a #1 gold record. In the purity of his quest, Benjamin emerges from the darkness into dawn and then daylight. He re-crosses the Bay Bridge, to Berkeley. The staccato tick of Paul Simon's guitar once again accompanies his intrusion, past a watchful German Shepherd, into an enclave of the enemy: Carl Smith's dark, fortress-like, ivy-clad fraternity house. Inside, the prevailing talk is of the commodified futures of individuals, with ribald references to shotgun weddings and an ambiguous request for Carl, "the Make-Out King," to "save a piece" for his friends — "of the wedding cake, of course." This callous jocularity causes an interesting, involuntary facial response in Benjamin. He blinks in an effort to restrain his outrage — a gesture reminiscent of the one we've seen Mr. McCleery direct at him, serving Benjamin his eviction in the boarding house. One might assume that the facile claim of *The Graduate* is for the moral superiority of the younger generation, but the film is ultimately more sophisticated — and less authoritative — than this. The failure of moral vision knows no particular age or gender in the film, and even its protagonists emerge, at the end of their quest, uncertain about a code of conduct going forward. Benjamin's goal, after all, is to secure Elaine for himself through the social trump card of elopement, and Elaine has passed a pleasant Berkeley idyll as two young men vie to possess her hand. Benjamin's McCleery-like expression of hostility may provide us a glimpse of the alienation he developed for his peers while at his prestigious eastern university. Benjamin retreats from Carl's fraternity, equipped only with the knowledge that another six-hour drive back down the state awaits him, and that no tolerance remains in him for a world unable or unwilling to see human connection as anything other than a transaction.

The Graduate launches us into our last musical montage: Benjamin's final ride in the Alfa Romeo. He dives off at a Santa Barbara exit ramp and into a Chevron gas station, where the short vignette with the attendant proceeds over the guitar's slap-slap accompaniment, approximating Benjamin's accelerated pulse and the ticking of time. He mangles a phone book and pounds a wall; he concocts a story for Dr. Smith's answering service about being a cleric-relative of Carl's. (Apparently he's learned some things about his rival Carl and the Smith family during his abbreviated courtship of Elaine, and he's prepared to bluff his way through the rest: his story carries just enough legitimacy and urgent detail to command what cooperation she can offer.) With the answering service's suggested church venue his final remaining object, Benjamin pauses at the office door of the garage to demand direction; the guitar slams into a chord as his hand slaps the nearest countertop. He leaves without heeding the attendant's question about gas, and therefore, it is less than a complete surprise when, a shot later, the soundtrack accompaniment and the car sputter to a stop together. Five minutes remain of the film.

15

More "Sounds of Silence": The Finishing Kick (1:41:00—1:46:00)

As Benjamin leaps from the car with one last cursory look back, he jettisons the final tangible fragment of his past. The former track star enters the finishing kick of this race he's run against his culture. In the ambient silence, we hear only the occasional traffic and the slap of his tennis shoes. The guitar that presided over the death of the car is poised to return, however. It waits in the same breathless anticipation as the audience and, although sprinting block after block, as Benjamin himself. This scene ostensibly about running actually depicts anxious waiting, both for the protagonist and the audience. Tom Tykwer's 1998 film, *Run Lola Run*, posits a young person's sprint across a section of Berlin as a physical test of her desire for union with Manni, her beloved, in defiance of a world of parental indifference, unfaithfulness, and dysfunction. The film celebrates decisive motion, even fetishizes it, lovingly tracking along beside, in front of, and behind Franka Potente for block after block, in and out of slow-motion. *The Graduate*'s strategy of using vignettes stitched by musical montage is also Tykwer's strategy, although unlike *The Graduate*, *Run Lola Run* is only in isolated moments about the protagonist flailing helplessly in paralyzed stasis or resigned retreat, the default dilemmas of *The Graduate*'s first two thirds. When Lola runs, the film's faith in her is absolute, and whenever she fails to arrive in time to extricate herself or Manni from their predicament, the film's narrative grants her another chance. Lola's desire is enough, the film concludes, and the physical expression of that desire, her lung-bursting sprint, is the film's celebration of self-determination. While in a certain sense all her running is also about anxious waiting, the byproduct of the waiting is to discover the effort is all.

15. More "Sounds of Silence"

The joyous equation of youthful exertion to self-determination in *Run Lola Run* is utterly absent in this solo sprint by Benjamin. In a sequence of two shots we watch him run. The first, which takes him from the car to a pavement well up the road, lasts 20 seconds. The emphasis is not on progress or self-determination but on futility. He looks less agile, less technically sound as a disciplined runner than when we saw him buzz across the Berkeley campus while stalking Elaine or when we saw him leaping curbs and dodging pedestrians to catch the bus. In the relative presentations of these two desperate young people impelled by the extremity of their anxiety, Lola in her boots could beat Benjamin in his tennis shoes.

The next shot only magnifies this anxiety: in a long shot, which David Bordwell calls the "archetypal long-lens shot of the 1960s,"[1] Benjamin runs for another 20 seconds straight at a camera equipped with telephoto lens; the diminishing perspective of the frame reduces his effort to the most ephemeral appearance of progress.[2] Only at the end of this shot, as he glances up, turns aside, and the camera pans to absorb his new direction, do we understand the product of his effort. The guitar sounds a triumphant chord as the frame encompasses a modern church building, the First Presbyterian Church of Santa Barbara, its décor the familiar black-and-white world of the Braddocks and Robinsons. Though the antithesis of medieval revivalist monumentality we might have expected from a municipality's "First" church of a mainstream denomination, the design is beautifully chosen for the climactic formal and thematic problems of *The Graduate*. In reality, the building is neither Presbyterian nor in Santa Barbara; Sylbert found it in an architectural book, and after a protracted four-month negotiation, Nichols and company made the special trip to the United Methodist Church of La Verne,[3] a small municipality on the eastern end of the Los Angeles sprawl, because the church's accents fit the general black-and-white pattern of the film's adult environments and because the 1950s modernist design testifies emphatically to a faith in progress. The building possesses a blocky solidity, exaggerated by that climactic guitar chord as we first see it enter the frame. It's a fortress, and, as more chords follow in portentous progression, the church-fortress repels Benjamin's first attempt to enter.

The drama of the moment, the extreme long shot of his figure diminished against this modernist fantasia on the old California Mission-Church ground plan, and the guitar notes combine briefly to allude to an unexpected film genre: Benjamin briefly enters a Spaghetti Western. While there are heroes and villains in this narrative, there can be no question of a moral authority; all these characters have been compromised by their actions. We crave resolution, but we should not be expecting that this resolution is a final word on human responsibility. Yet another layer of genre storytelling may also ironically underlie this climax, however. Mr. Robinson's off-hand remark to Benjamin the night of the graduation party continues to resonate: "Keeping guard over the ol' castle?" Mr. Robinson has subsequently come to recognize Benjamin as the intruder who has breeched the castle walls. In a narrative replete with casual but profoundly disruptive intrusion (every main character has at least one scene in which he or she intrudes on another), the climax depicts a last intrusion, a modern, errant knight on his obsessive quest to possess the forbidden maiden, a damsel in distress. Benjamin manages to find a way into the fortress, through an upper door that leads out onto an odd architectural flourish, a walkway over the sanctuary, in the enormous plate-glass windows at the back of the nave. A zoom to Elaine with Carl at the altar captures the moment as the *real* minister (not the intruder who has claimed to be the Rev. Smith, who will in due course perform an unofficial annulment) has closed his book on this solemn rite, and Elaine submits to Carl's kiss.

Charles Webb was adamant in his novel that Benjamin should arrive before the marriage covenant was sealed. He raged at having his vision of Benjamin as the true conservator of the culture's best values usurped by a cinematic wedding scene of Benjamin as anarchist, and he fired off an angry condemnation of the film's ending to *The New Republic*, whose Stanley Kauffmann had singled out the ending for particular praise. In his letter, Webb claimed that, given the revised ending, the cinematic relationship between Benjamin and Elaine will not be any less illicit than the one between Benjamin and Mrs. Robinson — for Webb, they're both simply cut-and-dried cases of adultery. Interesting that the original satirist of the my-way-or-the-highway, black-and-white world of the adults in *The Graduate* would himself fall prey to the compulsion to simplify morality to its social function.

Benjamin's morality is still in gestation as the film ends, as is Webb's[4]; so, it would seem, is the audience's. One of the important reasons this film has touchstone status in the culture is that it invites the audience to work through the problems of point of view in much the same way that a character must come to a recognition about his or her life. Webb's neat narrative trick of eluding moral ambiguity by having Benjamin arrive before the ceremony has been completed is precisely what Nichols and Henry don't want for their narrative: Harris writes that "Henry and Nichols located *The Graduate*'s comic center in [Benjamin's] complete failure to live up to his own standards, and, unlike Webb, they came up with an ending in which it's not clear if Benjamin triumphs by meeting those standards or by discarding them."[5] In fact, it's not clear if Benjamin triumphs *at all*. Via its ironic point of view on everything in the film, including the protagonist whose subjective point of view dominates much of the narrative, *The Graduate* seems to know more about genuine connection as a moral act than Benjamin does; in the modified ending at the church, he's following an instinct, hoping that what has happened with Elaine is not just "different" but richer than what happened with her mother.

Nichols and O'Steen cut from the kiss, which carries with it the sinking, genre-inflected sensation of Benjamin's having come so close but arrived too late, to a close-up of Benjamin, whose blasphemous profanity as he stands above the church floor recalls his verbal reaction to Mrs. Robinson's first solicitation, in the intimate precincts of Elaine's childhood bedroom. He bows his head, closes his eyes, a suggestion of prayerful meditation. Benjamin's profanity serves as a kind of counter-invocation against the perversions perpetrated in this solemn assembly by the Robinsons, reinforced by another long shot of Benjamin's diminished figure. In this extraordinary shot, Mrs. Robinson in the right foreground of the frame witnesses with satisfaction her daughter's capitulation. The church has few witnesses ("the arrangements were so rushed," after all). In this traditionally joyous moment, there is scant evidence of joy.

Looming like the persistence of conscience in the window above the sanctuary where Mrs. Robinson sits in the foreground, Benjamin is transfigured by the diffused glow of California sunlight through gauzy window treatments. He is dressed in white canvas from head to toe, his arms raised in helpless supplication. The soundtrack's dominance by the music of Paul Simon, emotional conduit to Benjamin's point of view, here is subordinated to the traditional Mendelssohn march, as performed with a heavy hand by a myopic church lady. In the next cut to Benjamin in close-up, his head still bowed, his eyes closed, he is a figure of agony. *What God has joined* ... and yet, is that what he has witnessed? Much interpretative chatter in the first flush of the film's success was devoted to this image of Benjamin in the window, the Christ-figure, a living, breathing fragment of stained glass. Hoffman and Nichols have shaken their heads at this for decades. "'The clincher was the reviews all saying this was Benjamin's Christ moment,' says Hoffman [to Harris]. "It was a fix. That's all it was. You gotta love critics."[6] Nichols adds, "Benjamin's arms are not *outstretched*. [... O]ur thought about Benjamin up there in the church was like a moth fluttering at a window."[7]

The "fix" to which Hoffman refers is one of those Hollywood production stories that unwittingly create (secular) icons. The plate-glass window of the church in LaVerne was a valuable piece of property, and the minister of the church, standing by during the production to oversee just this sort of happenstance, objected when, in the first take, Hoffman pounded on the glass with all his might to interject his will upon the proceedings below. The glass quivered and shook, and the minister was prepared to call off the agreement for which the company had persisted so long. Nichols came to Hoffman and asked him to find another way to transmit his urgency, and the director sold the clergyman on granting them a last attempt to salvage the shot. The film cuts from the church organist to a close-up of Benjamin. What Hoffman settled on was the modest rapping on the glass that survived the final cut. As his eyes open from his former attitude of prayer, Hoffman delivers one of the great cinematic shouts of a name, as powerful as the calls for Shane or for Stella. And he begins tapping at the glass. The tapping, born out of expediency, is equally suggestive of helplessness and persistence. We might reasonably expect the film's first reaction shot to be a cut to Mrs. Robinson, but instead we see Elaine, and only then do we get the reaction shot of a battalion of Robinsons and guests, the women formidable in their righteous anger. The next cut, to a celestial long shot of Benjamin, eliminates any evidence of the people and their ceremony below. He continues his wailing and his tapped Morse code of desperation, a moth-saint trapped under glass. His longing has become ethereal, more transfiguring than the light. Yet it is also dim-witted, childish; he's a toddler in the cry-room seeing the person he wants withheld beyond his reach, and whose loud petulance means to make everyone pay for his unhappiness. And like a toddler, when Benjamin eventually gets what he wants in *The Graduate*'s final shots, he looks confused by how little having his desire gratified seems to have helped.

The next shot of Elaine admits subjective sound: in her ear (and in ours, because Elaine is now our co-protagonist), Carl Smith demands, "Who *is* that guy? What's he doing?" Odd that Carl doesn't recognize Benjamin as the other monkey who had been vying for Elaine's attention at the zoo: the contrast between Benjamin, who seems to have absorbed enough information about Carl to have found his way here, and Carl, who can't be bothered to recall a competing suitor for his betrothed's affections, casts Benjamin in the better light — a point of view manipulation that can hardly surprise us by now. A cut to the Robinsons emphasizes their newfound solidarity: Mr. Robinson vows to "take care" of Benjamin, but Mrs. Robinson rests a hand on her husband's hand, pacifying him. What love has failed to join, hate has bonded. "He's too late," she reassures him, overwhelmingly convinced by the weight of her own experience that the social proscriptions of marriage are forever. The next shot, held in close-up for an audacious 20 seconds, reaffirms *The Graduate*'s reconfiguration as a dual-protagonist narrative. At the crucial instant, all balances not on Benjamin but on Elaine. Benjamin has come to "rescue" her, but she must be equally instrumental in "rescuing" him. In Berkeley, Benjamin's wishful effort to reconnect with Elaine had to be joined to Elaine's independent action, her two intrusions upon his rented room. Now, as we hear on the periphery Mr. Robinson's barked command to Carl, his new son-in-law, to "Get Elaine ... stop her," Elaine begins a slow, inexorable recessional from the ceremony. The tight framing still manages to provide evidence at the edges that Carl and her father have joined her in the aisle. Having proven unable to carry out his putative father-in-law's first order, Carl looks in deference to Mr. Robinson for further instruction. Mr. Robinson stares up at the window in a mixture of loathing and a dawning fear of Benjamin's implacable resolve.

None of it would matter, of course, if Elaine's attention could be redirected. The hyperbolic length of the shot is expressionistic. David Bordwell calculates the average shot length of *The Graduate* at a remarkable 17.8 seconds, and the patience of this method is never more pronounced in the film than at its climax, when the audience might reasonably expect a reversion to the traditionally explosive editing solution of fast cuts.[8] Trance-like, Elaine moves slowly in the direction of Benjamin's voice, her eyes directed up toward the window, and the film pauses, waiting for her to make a choice. Benjamin's own behavior is similarly exaggerated; the tapping and calling continue even now that he clearly has her attention. It's as if he's *gotten* to her, but has yet to get *through* to her — or to see through the problem himself. A look back at Benjamin's epiphany in the strip club suggests his awakening then was a similarly gradual process. The barrier between Benjamin and Elaine in the strip scene was physically manifest by his sunglasses, mask of a Beverly Hills social set he has been groomed to join. The film emphasizes Benjamin's recognition in the strip club by having him remove his glasses and, in seeing her, see himself and *what he's doing* (a substantial answer, finally, to that rhetorical question his father had posed to him poolside as he drifts atop a raft and Mrs. Robinson). In the wedding scene, the barrier of the glass can't quite elide his wracked voice or figure. The focus is on Elaine and what she sees and hears — the 20 seconds in which she stares up at Benjamin, the rough saint under glass, and, in a series of quick cuts to other angles of her vision, what she sees ahead for herself as a result of her social capitulation to the will of the Robinsons and the Smiths.

The 20-second close-up ends as she stops her procession down the aisle. Her jaw squaring, she turns to look to her family's side of the aisle. A powerful five-shot sequence follows, in a pronounced rapidity of six seconds that seems even faster after that prolonged 20-second close-up. A cut to a zoomed close-up of Mrs. Robinson from Elaine's subjective point of view shows her, teeth bared, hurling mute obscenities up in Benjamin's direction. Beside her in the next shot, Mrs. Robinson does the same. It's what comes next — a cut back to Elaine, and the shot of Carl that follows it — that breaks the spell, much as Benjamin seeing Elaine's tears causes him to undo the tasseled spell cast over the strip club. Nichols and O'Steen return to Elaine, in a shot framed so that Carl Smith is recognizable beside her. She turns away from her parents to look at him. The cut to a shot of Carl staring into the camera, his mute invective directed at *her*, is a subjective-camera gaze through Elaine's eyes into the blond, blue-eyed, human-surfboard abyss her parents have rushed to arrange for her. The five-shot sequence concludes with a final shot of Elaine's upturned face, her eyes returned from some unknown, unarticulated alternative future. She meets Benjamin's last "Elaine!" (the twentieth of the scene) with a single, shattering, "*Ben!*" Roughly two and a half minutes remain in the film. What her anguished cry has shattered is Benjamin's own illusion that marriage is fundamentally a civic transaction; he is not, as Mrs. Robinson has judged him, "too late," and marriage is finally a commitment of souls, not social-security numbers, blood types, or tax brackets.

For two minutes, *The Graduate*, so long about passivity and drifting, becomes an action movie, rich in witty genre allusions, as knight battles castle guard for lady fair or gunslinger rides against the mob. The showdown with Mr. Robinson at the bottom of the stairs is believably resolved in the younger man's favor, and Mr. Robinson slumps to the ground like the villain in a Western. Benjamin drives into a scrum of the wedding party, Carl Smith receiving the brunt of his force; the wedding aisle fills with a tumbled mass of middle-aged matrons. Mrs. Robinson manages to avoid this welter, however. She braces Elaine by the door and shrieks, "Elaine! It's too late!"

The shot is framed so her leopard-print hat and collar are pronounced in the foreground, but we see Elaine as she defiantly answers, "Not for me!" That Mrs. Robinson slaps her is a revelation of the misanthrope's diminished power over her environment. She slaps at Elaine because she has nothing left, a big cat declawed if not quite denatured. Nichols and O'Steen cut to a wider angle for the second slap, one that admits Benjamin's whereabouts in the melee. Knowing that the chaos he's caused in the aisle will soon be sorted out, he reaches for the only weapon available, a large cross in one of the plate-glass windows by the door. When is a cross just a cross? The prop is originally Webb's, adapted by Henry and filmed with hearty vigor by Nichols and Hoffman. Nichols allows that the image is, in Gelmis' word, "supercharged," but reiterates that "it came about through a series of practical decisions and it crossed none of our minds."[9] Indeed, as we have seen, Nichols was intent upon an ironic deconstruction of his "hero," and retaining this heroic imagery from Webb's book allows Nichols and Henry to express how difficult is genuine transcendence. We have entered Benjamin's Christ-complex. Carl Smith and

15. More "Sounds of Silence"

Mr. Robinson, foregrounded in the next shot as they encroach, must fall back as Benjamin swings the cross like an Arthurian sword.

"Move!" Benjamin yells, his new motto, intoned three times, wading into the crowd, as if performing an exorcism. The command intentionally echoes the change Henry made from Webb's book, when as Benjamin prepares to consummate the affair, his imperative "Don't move!" so amuses Mrs. Robinson. Her face still stinging from her mother's slaps, Elaine hovers behind Benjamin, and when his wild swings have widened the gap, they fall back, through the front doors, whose handles provide a convenient scabbard with which to sheathe the cross and bar the entrance, another touch added by Nichols during production.

They are officially outside. A mass of outraged, middle-aged faces presses against the glass door, trapped in their own ensnaring institution. Benjamin in his torn white outfit escorts Elaine in her regal wedding gown at a run from the church, a parody of the traditional emergence at ceremony's end. They have no well-wishers, no shower of rice. Elaine, in a comic touch, still carries her bouquet; she moves well despite the gown and heels. A shot of them passing through a set of small white pillars introduces a drab suburban street and a passing municipal bus, which Benjamin runs beside, pounding its panels, until it admits them. Benjamin stuffs a bill into the slotted change box (one of the wilted $10 bills he'd offered to Mr. McCleery?); money is no object, at least for the moment. The bus is nearly full. They pass all the way through the aisle, to the conveniently vacant back bench, each of them framed in a rear window. What Nichols and O'Steen have been doing with sound now becomes apparent, as the bus accelerates away from the curb, the church, their past. The bus motor is muted, and when Benjamin whoops in triumph, clapping his hands, we hear it as if from a great distance, or through glass. The effect is like the percussive silence we helplessly hear after a great booming explosion. Turning from the windows, beaming, Benjamin and Elaine regard (and are regarded by) a corridor of assembled humanity. Without joy or personality, the bus riders stare in frank but impassive curiosity at this odd couple — the young man in the torn canvas jacket, the beautiful young woman in full wedding regalia. Midway back through the bus another young man, a generation younger than the rest of the crowd, stares at the camera through the familiar mask of sunglasses.

When Nichols and O'Steen cut from this shot of the bus passengers, the reverse shot of Benjamin and Elaine is all youthful joy. They look into each other's eyes. They grin. And the camera gazes at them hungrily in this two-shot close-up for an astonishing 40 seconds. Sylbert acknowledges that this is another New-Wave idea borrowed from François Truffaut, this time from the last shot of *The 400 Blows*.[10] Actually, the correspondence is even more substantial. Nichols borrowed from Truffaut's extraordinary debut film a sense that pace, even at a film's climax, must remain organic to the reality of the character's situation. In *The 400 Blows*, this meant that Antoine (Jean-Pierre Léaud), after escaping from reform school, runs toward the sea — but instead of employing the traditional cinematic rhetoric of cross-cutting between Antoine and his fading pursuers, we simply watch Antoine run. We never see the pursuers again. Marilyn Fabe writes, "Because we are permitted to see an unedited shot of Antoine running for a relatively long time without showing the least indication of fatigue, we are better able to experience along with him the pure adrenaline-fueled exhilaration of his bid for freedom."[11] That shot tracks for 75 seconds beside Antoine; it revels as much as Antoine himself in his movement. The long takes of Benjamin running toward the church, in contrast, meditate on an essential futility in Benjamin's lately-found motion. For both Truffaut and Nichols, the long takes imply the agonized "slowness" of real time, weighed against the spectator's expectation of how time is typically reduced by the cinematic shorthand of editing.

Truffaut's film is even closer to its end than Nichols's as their respective running scenes appear. For Truffaut, the run to the sea provides the symbolism of a vast, uninhabitable horizon that locks Antoine to the land; Truffaut famously employs a freeze-frame as the film's last image to underscore "Antoine's final and definitive entrapment in a system from which there is no escape."[12] Truffaut had entered the project intending to burden Antoine's character with ill-health and passivity, but Léaud's scruffy energy as the film's proagonist transformed Truffaut's vision of the character.[13] Antoine's redoubtable capability makes this climactic cul de sac more painful. The 75-second run, uninterrupted by cross-cut reminders of a system that means to corral him, had given us his false hope. Nichols uses the run to the church to create a similar sense of hope; the glass wall between Benjamin and Elaine as she kisses Carl Smith would seem to be the end of that hope — but the film isn't finished, and neither are the long takes. In the church, Elaine ascends to her full role as Benjamin's co-protagonist when Nichols grants her a long take, newly married but contemplating a coerced and loveless future.

There is no freeze-frame ending in *The Graduate*, but the long two-shot of Benjamin and Elaine on the bus functions in a similar way to Truffaut's formalist flourish as his film ends. The ironic emphasis in both films pits the illusion of freedom and movement against the reality of enclosure and stillness. In the old VHS days, when *The Graduate* and many other classic films were re-formatted for the square-screen television market, the producers of the video version were left with a dilemma. Since they could not include all the

15. More "Sounds of Silence"

visual information of a wide screen in a square format, what would they keep and what would they have to elide? Usually, the choices simply eliminated what was at the left and right extremes of the frame. Throughout the VHS version of *The Graduate*, their choices result in cramped compositions, lost information, and reduced artistic effect. In the sour silence at the end of the epic conversation between Benjamin and Mrs. Robinson, for instance, the filmmakers' original intention, a widescreen vision of two battered fighters in neutral corners, is panned and scanned in the VHS version to focus on Mrs. Robinson as she first unsnaps and then rolls down her stockings. We don't see Benjamin at all in this last moment of the scene, and this is a problem for the videotape legacy of the film, since the effect of this conversation on Mrs. Robinson, while far from negligible, hardly compares to the blow Benjamin's residual innocence has received. His frozen, alienated posture in the corner of the room as the scene fades to black is the scene's true point, and it's lost in that antiquated technology before letterboxing rendered the wide screen's complete vision.

In the last, crucial minute and a half of the film, during the 40-second, two-shot close-up on Benjamin and Elaine, the producers of the video release confronted a similar problem. Although not banished to opposite ends of the frame in the extremity of their alienation, Benjamin and Elaine are in ambiguous proximity, together but also apart. The VHS image could not be formatted to a square frame without bleeding parts of both figures off-screen. The producers chose a pan-and-scan approach, although this time they noted that both participants were equally important. In essence, they cut between Benjamin and Elaine several times, an added series of cuts that reintroduces a visual sense of alienation themed to the final reprise of "The Sounds of Silence." While not Nichols's original intention for the 40-second, uninterrupted shot, with its promotion of accrued anxiety in the audience, the VHS cutting nonetheless articulated their anxiety. A comparison of the two cinematic methodologies, however, ultimately illuminates the brilliance of Nichols's original choice, the one restored in DVD format.

Unlike in much of the rest of the production, where conferences and huddles produced collaborative results, Nichols acted on instinct in setting up this final shot of the two protagonists. Nichols got Hoffman and Ross onto the bus, let them stagger back to their seats, and captured their initial, breathless euphoria as the bus pulled out and they knew that, in essence, they had escaped the Robinsons. But Nichols did not call cut. He asked Surtees to keep the camera rolling, and what the lens began to record, with the unblinking verisimilitude of documentary footage, were the unease and self-consciousness of two young actors working off-script but in character, improvising without any prior opportunity to devise a strategy. Given direction by Henry's screenplay and by Nichols's vision throughout the production, they were in this capstone shot of the film set adrift, without direction: precisely the predicament of their characters. It is a brilliant directorial improvisation by Nichols that evidences a great faith not only in his actors to sense and seize the moment (as they managed to do) but in the cinematic medium to do formal justice to their reality as Hoffman and Ross, scared and beyond script, groping toward the reality of Benjamin and Elaine. Nichols knew what he'd wrought was a long-shot attempt at discovery, and he knew when he saw it that he'd found the punctuation for the rhetorical irony of his film's point of view: "[W]hen I saw those rushes, I thought: 'That's the end of the picture. They don't know what the hell to do, or to think, or to say to each other.'"[14]

Hoffman is the first to blink, looking away from Ross, who follows his lead and also stares at an indefinite horizon. Their smiles, more distant now, usher in the familiar first guitar notes of Simon's song, which the film has long since imprinted on us as a choric lament for failed contact. The initial smiles gone, each of them produces another brief burst of visible pleasure at what they have done — Ross first, then Hoffman. They smile at this point at their own private, unshared thoughts. Their timing is impeccable: as each smiles, the other wears an impassive mask of exhaustion. (Predictably, the VHS pan-and-scan picks each of these moments of animation for focus; what's lost is the sobering vision of the counterpart.) They are, in fact, the recognizable if restrained masks of comedy and tragedy, appropriate to this ambiguous ending of an ultimately ambiguous narrative, a comic story of ruined lives and uncertain futures.

When Hoffman's smile fades, the 40-second shot is exactly half-done. What follows is another 20 seconds of discomfort for all concerned — actors, characters, and, if they haven't put on their coats and headed for the aisles, the audience (Brackman noted in dismay in his *New Yorker* essay that the crowd at his screening were so satisfied by the triumphant escape from the church that they took the 40-second two-shot as their cue to leave).[15] The audience is particularly challenged in this moment: the film has just commanded our emotional participation in the suspense of Benjamin's wild ride up and down the state of California, the rude awakening of the completed wedding ceremony, the anxiety of the wedding-party scrum, the exuberance of their narrow escape. Audiences have laughed and cheered as Benjamin, the canvas-clad crusader, swings the cross, then uses it to bar the door on the infidels: the fairy-tale resolution. They have laughed at the reaction shot of the deadpan bus passengers. But now the film has required their return to quietude. The last 20 seconds of this masterful shot ask us to consider what

The most ambiguous moment in *The Graduate* is its last: happy ending or not? This extraordinary 40-second shot, a directorial improvisation by Mike Nichols, coaxed Dustin Hoffman and Katharine Ross to stay in character long after they expected the take to be complete. What emerged was the actors' improvisatory uncertainty, dovetailing with the sudden disorientation of their characters: they are certain that the future mandated by their parents is not what they want, but uncertain of what might constitute a viable alternative. Nichols, amazed at the mass audience's unreflective assumption of a happy ending, took to predicting publicly that Benjamin and Elaine become their parents.

really happens after the knight saves the damsel or the Western hero rescues the girl, since *love conquers all, happily ever after* is kid's stuff, another plastic confection our culture offers us as a consolation for an often less-than-ideal reality where marriage is hard work and often ends in heartbreak. The medium is aware of itself during this shot — aware of what it withholds (pure triumph), aware of what it offers as a replacement (ambiguity, doubt). During the last half of the shot, Elaine in a chilling vignette turns and regards Benjamin, a point-blank study of his profile; it produces in her no smile or warmth. We project onto that clinical gaze the history of their families, the recent history of his summer with her mother. She wears her bridal veil, but is she bound for a bridal bed with this man? If so, it will be an extra-marital bed filled with ghosts. She is Mrs. Carl Smith in the eyes of the church and the court. And he is her mother's former lover. How will they negotiate the physical and psychological baggage they will carry into this night and the next day and the next?

Glenn Man writes, "The bus scene is appropriate in its open-endedness. If the movie had concluded with Ben and Elaine in heady flight, it would lessen their achievement, and confer upon it the aura of fantasy, wish fulfillment, utopia."[16] In other words, the film would openly foster the misinterpretation many have formed. Man is openly critical of Nichols in *Radical Visions*, not for the popular critics' complaint that Nichols has settled for the fairy tale, but rather because Nichols has held too tightly to the dark edge of his satirical sensibility. This is, of course, a matter of interpretation, and Man's acute analysis of *The Graduate* is not ultimately distorted by his belief that Benjamin and Elaine have not solely developed a distaste for the life they are trying to leave behind but also a positive vision of the future, "the suggestion of possibilities beyond the ordinary and conventional, the promise of a pleasure beyond the daily rituals of life."[17] What Man articulates, in far more eloquent rhetoric, is a variation on Benjamin's opening wish for his life to be "different."

In interviews, Nichols believed that his young protagonists could see what the problems were; his doubts came in whether they would have the imagination to replace a corrupted lifestyle with one that offers greater promise for a life of genuine spiritual fulfillment. The key determination Man makes is to introduce the audience into the equation of resolving the film's open ending: "The doubts and questions raised at the end locate the couple's future actions in the real world, where they should be, where they hold meaning for the audience."[18] Genre formulas, content to satisfy audience appetites for fantasy, appear in *The Graduate* only to be parodied and rejected. *The Graduate* is a narrative that ultimately invites the audience's active collaboration — thus the exponentially increased potential of an audience's interpretative preference for wish-fulfillment via available, genre-based cinematic fantasy rather than an extrapolation to the audience's own real-life predicament as targets of consumer culture. Nichols and his filmmaking team saw Benjamin and Elaine rejecting empty materialism even as their actions reified their likely re-absorption into the drowning pools of consumerist conformity; the rhetorical flourish at the end of *The Graduate* is to invite empathy for Benjamin and Elaine while at the same time proffering a meditation on the potential futility of aimless rather than philosophically informed movement.

Benjamin stares straight ahead, entirely without expression. We have seen this look before. As the soundtrack reprises the opening music over the closing of the narrative, the second half of this shot reprises the first shot of the film, of Benjamin alone in a crowd, anxious but impassive, conveyed without direction into an unknown future. *The Graduate*'s love of cyclical return as a formal means to expressing the characters' existential dread serves as cautionary punctuation to the narrative. This remarkable shot finally ends with a cut to the exterior of the bus, Benjamin and Elaine readily recognizable through their separate windows. "In narrow streets I walked alone," sing Simon and Garfunkel, underscoring our sense that these two oddly matched people who have boarded the bus together may not in fact be *together*. Although the shot tracks after them, the greater acceleration of the bus soon leaves us far behind, and the vehicle conveying the camera glides, like Benjamin's empty Alfa Romeo, to a complete stop before the fade to darkness.

The cut to this final shot outside the bus may be contrasted to the famous edit Charlie Chaplin employed at the end of *Modern Times* (1936), as Chaplin's Tramp and the Gamin (Paulette Goddard) persist, hands locked, against the various forces of society seemingly united in conspiracy to discourage and disenfranchise them. On a country road, all their possessions amassed in two small cloth bundles, they are diminished to insignificance by the weight of a narrative in which all their various schemes and efforts to embrace the American dream of financial independence have met with indifference. Most of their efforts have, in fact, met with incarceration, and the film has offered little cause for a future that looks any different. Joan Mellon writes that the irony of "Dawn," the title card before this final episode of the picaresque narrative, is "blatant."[19] That the Tramp and the Gamin still have each other, then, is the gift Chaplin the sentimental artist offers to his two protagonists (and to his audience). They walk forward, toward the camera and the audience, their faces unbowed. They are a misfit pair, much like Benjamin and Elaine in their mismatched garb, with Hoffman's much-discussed non-classical features a contrast to Ross' radiance. In the penultimate shot of *Modern Times*, Goddard's face in particular is so fresh and shining with undaunted youth that, as she and the Tramp stride forward, their motion seems to lead towards a group hug with the world amassed in theaters. Then Chaplin cuts to a 180° reverse angle: the final shot of the film is of our sympathetic couple walking away from the camera, from us. We are pointedly denied a last lingering look at the Tramp, who would never appear on screen again, and at the Gamin's beauty, and at the joy of their redoubtable communion.

Mellon finds significant the action of the Tramp and the Gamin even before the cut. She calls the movement toward the camera an accusation: "as if they were about to disappear into the lens, as if they were confronting a spectator who would prefer to ignore their existence."[20] Their motion may thus be interpreted as square-jawed defiance — the very emotion we see drained away from Benjamin and Elaine during their 40-second scrutiny by the camera at the back of the bus. When the camera cuts away from the Tramp and Gamin to show us their backs and to see them dwindle up the road, Mellon notes that the action underscores their defiance, and the defiance of their creator: "It is as if Chaplin were raising a curtain between his characters and the indifferent and morally hostile society that has betrayed them."[21] Chaplin asserts a reverence for his characters' indomitable spirit; the venom of his irony is reserved for the passivity of a world that refuses to reward such spirit. At the end of *The Graduate*, however, Nichols employs Chaplin's strategy for the exact opposite rhetorical purpose. To do this requires him to present one of the longest shots of the film. We are afforded more than enough time to gorge on the faces of the two protagonists; our discomfort grows in proportion with their own. We watch disillusionment move across their features like cloud-shadow over landscape. The cut, when it finally comes, offers no solace, because we have seen the protagonists' isolation. The Tramp and the Gamin are "independent in their dignity" as they walk away[22]; Benjamin and Elaine are anonymous in their isolation, part of the lonely crowd as the bus pulls away from the camera and leaves us behind.

PART III
Valediction

But if we're all going to die the moment we graduate, isn't it what we do beforehand that counts?
—Jenny, in *An Education* (Lone Scherfig, 2009)

16

The Legacy of *The Graduate*

At the height of *The Graduate*'s cultural ubiquity, in May 1968, the social psychologist and cultural critic Robert Coles wrote, "In fact neither Nichols nor anyone else has figured out how youths like Ben and Elaine come about, in view of the ornately shabby, empty world that 'nurtures' them, if that is the word. That is the central, haunting question of *The Graduate*."[1] Coles himself is less than specific about what he means by the phrase (and category) "youths like Ben and Elaine." Would such youths have been the type to pass a worn Bantam paperback of Hermann Hesse's *Siddhartha* back and forth, reading of the call to the life of the spirit? Would they have followed Coles down to Mississippi to keep an eye on civil rights? Or would they have missed the easy convenience of their parents' charge cards? Linda Ruth Williams writes that "The final question the film asks is just how post-suburban Benjamin and Elaine's lives will be."[2] Are we to understand Benjamin Braddock and Elaine Robinson as archetypes of emergent iconoclasm? Or are we to understand Ben and Elaine as privileged heirs to their culture's material plenty and spiritual want, the very characteristics Lyndon Johnson so feared for the Great Society?

Part of the pleasure of the film is to continue mulling these questions. In 2000, more than three decades after the film's initial theatrical release, the Braddocks and the Robinsons resurfaced via a London and New York stage production, whose chief dramatic feature was a notorious nude scene, performed by a parade of famous actresses of a certain age, beginning with Kathleen Turner both in the West End and on Broadway. When a production must resort to burlesque to create buzz, there may be a problem. The produced play unfolded like a highlight reel, collecting Buck Henry's choicest bits from the screenplay while revisiting Charles Webb's novel for new "discoveries" about Benjamin. Benjamin's ill-fated three-week trip to find America returns to the narrative, for instance, though one may question whether the trip makes Benjamin more or less sympathetic. Terry Johnson, who adapted the story for the stage, posits a very different pre-trip mood between Benjamin and his father. Johnson gives back all Benjamin's most painfully condescending speeches from the novel ("I want simple honest people that can't even read or write their own name"[3]), but he adds a bloodline context for Benjamin's disillusionment among the nouveau riche: his blue-collar grandfather "built half of Toledo."[4] Johnson even has Mr. Braddock express his adamant (if tone-deaf) "approval" of the trip, stuffing money in Benjamin's pocket (hardly in the spirit of Benjamin's desire to live simply and independently, though at last he takes the cash) and declaring that Benjamin "walk down the stairs" where the graduation party guests are still assembled and "show that bunch of ... *grotesques* down there just what Benjamin Braddock is made of."[5]

Still, following Webb's lead, Johnson's play does not depict the trip itself; in fact, Johnson edits Benjamin's attention span from three weeks in the novel to nine days in the play. Of most interest is where Johnson takes the story off its familiar, well-traveled track, in positing Robinson mother-daughter chats and in extrapolating briefly beyond the endings we already know. The interruption of the wedding is far more civil; Mrs. Robinson even has time to pronounce her unholy benediction on Benjamin and Elaine. Mr. Robinson has threatened to intervene, but Mrs. Robinson reassures him by saying, "Leave them alone and they'll *bore* one another to death."[6] A brief coda, with Benjamin and Elaine together in a cheap Nevada motel room, seems to confirm this; neither young person seems willing to confront the overwhelming baggage that sexual consummation would require, and so they sit together, sharing a box of Cheerios like small children. Johnson's logical ending to *The Graduate*'s narrative, one that he borrows equally from book and film, is arrested development rather than transcendence. It blanches any possibility of triumph, however ironic and thus compromised, from the story we know.

In his 2007 novel, *Home School*, which retains the titular theme of education, Charles Webb himself has projected his original narrative eleven years further into the future, to the mid–1970s. Benjamin and Elaine have two sons and have moved across the country to be away from her mother and near her father; the Robinsons have indeed gone through with their divorce. (Webb's first book is more sympathetic to Mr. Robinson than to his wife.) Benjamin and Elaine have managed to repel all efforts by Mrs. Robinson to re-enter their lives as a doting grandmother. Yet when the local school district feels itself threatened by Benjamin and Elaine's commitment to home-schooling their children, Benjamin improbably enlists his mother-in-law in a sting operation: Mrs. Robinson seduces the school principal and captures the incident on tape to silence his persecution of the home-school arrangement. Webb's vision of Mrs. Robinson in this novel is absolutely black; her only interest in carrying out the blackmail scheme is to gain leverage over her daughter and son-in-law, the grandchildren to be used as barter by both sides.

It's an unpleasant book, although it clarifies what had remained ambiguous all these years: what sort of people Webb envisioned Benjamin and Elaine would become when they finally grew up. It turns out they are weak, grasping, "self-righteous," and "arrogant" (these last two judgments are, from all evidence, correctly charged against them by Mrs. Robinson herself); Benjamin and Elaine are willing to stoop as low as necessary to achieve their own ends. As abominable as Mrs. Robinson emerges from *Home School*, Benjamin is hardly better, and Elaine remains a cipher dominated by the stronger personalities around her. Through a successful exchange of in-law brinksmanship (a decidedly experimental home-school project for the Braddock boys is the game of poker, "to study how people bluff each other"[7]), Benjamin and Elaine manage to evict Mrs. Robinson from a mother-in-law suite she has sponsored for herself in their basement. "'It's not over,' Elaine said, looking up at him. 'Forget the three thousand miles. She's here to stay now. Lodged in our house and in our lives and in our brains.'"[8] Webb's two Benjamin Braddock novels will never be more than cultural footnotes, but because of the cinematic images Mike Nichols planted "in our brains," Benjamin still remains, forever young and worried about his future, "available to us" (to paraphrase Mrs. Robinson) as we encounter the film during our youth, gauging our anxieties about the future we're being handed, then encounter the film again in middle-age, when we can begin evaluating whether we have continued to "drift."

Although the optimism of education as a life-altering phenomenon is the black-comic illusion of the film's title, *The Graduate* has "served as a kind of film-school course for new generations of filmmakers, including Steven Soderbergh, Harold Ramis, Todd Haynes, Mark Foster, the Coen brothers, and Paul Thomas Anderson."[9] To this distinguished list Lee Hill appropriately adds Sam Mendes, Wes Anderson, Spike Jonze, and Whit Stillman.[10] Indeed, silence and communication breakdown may be rife in the narrative, but *The Graduate* began a dialogue that has wended its way across movie screens for four decades. Hollywood is self-conscious about this film. This has resulted in a direct lineage of thoughtful, involving work, although some of the results have been purely superficial. *American Pie* (Paul Weitz, 1999), for instance, parodies *The Graduate*'s first seduction scene as an isolated skit whose classic allusion many in the intended audience would not have recognized; *Wayne's World 2* (Stephen Surjik, 1993) parodies the climactic race in the car in a similar exercise in discursive comedy. Even the unused opening of Buck Henry's screenplay, in which Benjamin's notes for his valedictory speech blow away in the wind, was redacted in Ben Stiller's 1994 Gen-X fable, *Reality Bites*, when this same fate befalls Winona Ryder's character Lainey, a none-too-subtle nickname derived from Elaine.

In Nancy Meyer's 2009 hit, *It's Complicated*, Buck Henry's brief scene as the desk clerk at the Taft Hotel makes another cameo. Jake (Alec Baldwin) has been cheating on his wife with his ex-wife Jane (Meryl Streep). He's just settled in for a movie-night with Jane and their kids; on screen, Meyers shows us Henry as the Taft Hotel desk clerk of Benjamin Braddock's nightmares. Henry's clerk asks, "Are you here for an affair, sir?" Glancing up from the television, Jake beams at Jane: an affair is *exactly* what *he's* here for. It's a moment that confirms for Jane the wrongness of what they've been up to. Jake's tin ear for the painful double entendre of Henry's line forecasts his ultimate failure as a man of commitment: Jake can always be "here," but it will always be "for an affair."

More expansive reference to *The Graduate* emerges in the awkward and unfunny *Rumor Has It ...* (Rob Reiner, 2005), in which Jennifer Aniston's character, Sarah Huttinger, believes she may have discovered that her family is the model upon which "Charlie Webb," an old prep school pal of Sarah's mother, based his novel. Aside from the insulting insinuation that story ideas always have direct real-life correlatives and are never original (perhaps not such a stretch in some Hollywood circles), the plot makes Sarah climb into bed with a legendary friend of the family named Beau Burroughs (Kevin Costner), who has slept not only with her mother but with her grandmother (Shirley MacLaine, trying very hard to be a creditable prototype for Mrs. Robinson). At the time of their assignation, Sarah has only just begun considering that Beau may *not* be her long-lost father — a scenario that prompted A. O. Scott wryly to warn, in the content guide at the end of his review of the film, that Reiner's film "has some sexual situations that are more shocking to think about than to witness."[11] The third act features a happy-ending reunion of age-appropriate lovers, but without a shred of the irony that Nichols wielded in his own narrative — which means that the tone has shifted precipitously and without rhetorical logic from the first half, when we were to understand the film as sex-farce. In other films, Reiner has demonstrated real talent as a director, but while Nichols's early films were cool, even icy satire, Reiner is at his best assuming a warm, affective relationship to his material. Scott remarks near the beginning of his review on the essential irrelevance of *The Graduate* allusions in Reiner's film, given "how uncannily it resembles movies far more recent and, in general, less interesting than *The Graduate*."[12] *Rumor Has It ...* ought to know its storyline is a Hollywood train-wreck and have fun with it; when it goes for the heartstrings rather than the jugular, it loses touch with its own best premise: to make fun of movies just like the one it has become.

Rumor Has It ... would seem to be precisely the sort of warmed-over goulash that passes for the story ideas Tim Robbins' character Griffin Mill endures one after another in the audacious eight-minute opening shot of *The Player* (Robert Altman, 1992). Among the cameos in this opening scene is an appearance by Buck Henry to pitch his idea for "*The Graduate, Part II*." In this fictionalized proposal (ringing with the stranger-than-fiction truth of several decades of Hollywood gossip about a sequel) Benjamin and Elaine are married, have a daughter, and care for Mrs. Robinson, who lives in a room upstairs after a debilitating stroke that Henry promises Mill will be "funny." Even a tone-deaf industry hack like Mill double takes on such a promise, and Henry quickly abstracts the stroke to "some kind of malady." Altman, like Nichols, works the cool end of the cinematic gauge, happy to lampoon the sort of industry minds that would daydream a cynical sequel (or even a well-made but diluted one, like the long-running *M*A*S*H** TV series Altman hated to have associated with his 1970 original).

The Player comes closest to the dark satiric heart of Nichols's film in its manipulation of the film's ending. Mill has killed one writer, but discovers that it was the wrong one; the writer who has been menacing him all along now has the leverage to extort a movie deal. Mill relaxes into the writer's pitch, driving through palm-lined avenues on the way to his idyllic Hollywood-player's home. The writer essentially describes in pitch form the ideal ending he knows Mill wants to hear, and that we watch, as it's happening. *The Player* flouts Hollywood's appetite for restored domestic order; no one watching the film can feel anything other than outraged dislocation as the final and farfetched story-idea becomes cinematic "reality." Yet Altman does not set up the audience quite the way Nichols does: we never entertain the idea of Griffin Mill as hero. He's a weasel from first to last. That's why the confected "happy ending" of *The Player* leaves such an appropriately bitter taste, and with little tonal risk of confused audience reception. In *The Graduate*, Nichols wants us to feel Benjamin's pain, which thus requires a much greater effort to establish distance when it comes time to see Benjamin's actions in the second half of the film. Benjamin begins to think of himself as the hero of the film at just about the time we are obliged to acknowledge that he doesn't have it in him. He can imagine himself as a hero (as long as he selects traditional narrative templates like chivalric knight or gunslinger), but he lacks the imagination actually to become a hero in the real world. Nichols has challenged us at the end of *The Graduate* to be more perceptive than the protagonist's own eyes.

Such films' subtle (or not so subtle) allusions to *The Graduate* work with the film in a different and ultimately less intimate way, however, than films that are *The Graduate*'s true spiritual heirs. To discuss them all would require a different scope than this concluding chapter, but even a representative sample yields compelling evidence of *The Graduate*'s influence. Two of the directors Lee Hill identifies, Sam Mendes and Wes Anderson, have created films intensely committed to conversation with *The Graduate*. Not mere set-piece parodies, Mendes' *American Beauty* (1999) and Anderson's *Rushmore* (1998) adopt imagery and incidents from Nichols's film; they also carry forward the expressive exuberance of technique that Nichols himself later resisted in his own work. In the immediate youth-movement euphoria of the late–1960s, Hal Ashby made *Harold and Maude* (1971), in which a morose young man of privilege bullied by his mother toward a life of superficial consumption meets and has an affair with an older woman — a *much* older woman — who teaches him valuable life lessons. An appealing but less deliberate revisiting of the thematic problems of *The Graduate* emerges in Lone Scherfig's *An Education* (2009), which transposes genders to watch a young woman taken in (in all senses) by an older man. Finally, in another film released in 2009, Marc Webb's *(500) Days of Summer*, *The Graduate* is interpolated in the film's preface and at one of its emotional climaxes. All five of these films feel the presence of *The Graduate* and reflect upon the cultural legacy of its claims.

Webb's *(500) Days of Summer* is the most formally dialectical of the five films in its accessing of *The Graduate*, since Nichols's film literally makes a cameo appearance. In the narrated prologue to the film, we learn that Tom Hansen, aspiring architect, "grew up believing that he'd never truly be happy until the day he met 'the one.' This belief stemmed from early exposure to sad British pop music and a total misreading of the movie, *The Graduate*." As the narrator reaches the punch line of this sentence, writer-director Webb offers us a vision of the romantic Tom Hansen taking form, a pre-adolescent sitting in his childhood bedroom and gaping at a television, where Benjamin Braddock discovers he hasn't quite made it to the church on time and bellows, "Elaine!" In the final cut of the film, as we have seen, Benjamin actually yells her name twenty times; Webb's micro-excerpt manages to squeeze in two, and our memories do the rest. We know this movie, and Webb knows we know it.

16. The Legacy of The Graduate

Webb isn't through with *The Graduate*, however, and his second allusion punctuates an emotional peak in his own film, when Summer leaves Tom. Through the narrative re-shuffling of the calendar that makes *(500) Days of Summer* a meditation on romantic destiny, we already know the romance of Tom and Summer is, in the words of *The Graduate*'s choric soundtrack, "A love once new [that] has now grown old." We have presumed the narrator's pronouncement upon Tom refers to his misinterpretation of the film's ending as happy-ever-after. Marc Webb drops us in the middle of a negotiation late in Tom and Summer's relationship: Tom suggests they might simply go home (he is happy simply to be in her presence), while Summer apparently beats the drum for seeing a film (she is restless, ill at ease under such relentless regard).

The cut to Nichols's extraordinary two-shot of Benjamin and Elaine on the municipal bus at film's end confirms for us that the movie Tom has resisted attending is one of the formative classics of his childhood. And then, in the next cut, we learn why he has been resisting: Summer, watching the uneasy silence grow between Benjamin and Elaine, weeps. Tom's new interpretation of the film is that, when one of the two members of a romantic pairing is uncertain, nothing can keep them together. Outside the movie theater in the next shot, which in the narrative re-shuffle we've seen before as an ominous portent, Summer goes her own way, and Tom knows his doom: that he's misread *The Graduate* as a fairy tale. As such, Marc Webb's film seems to be an adamant acknowledgment of the larger culture's tendency to misinterpret the film's subtext, to fail to see the storm clouds massing over Benjamin's summer of love.

Marc Webb has the advantage of four decades — roughly 500 months — of cultural reception of *The Graduate* to draw upon in his narrative; the two young people represent polemical responses to Mike Nichols's film — at least when in relationship. Yet the film's ending resuscitates the cultural reception of *The Graduate*, as Summer extols the virtues of having discovered, with someone else, what Tom had felt with her (thereby reverting to Tom's initial "total misreading"). Ultimately an apolitical romantic comedy, *(500) Days of Summer* has little interest in the socio-economic condemnations that consume *The Graduate*'s point of view. In *Harold and Maude*, however, unreconstructed hippie Hal Ashby insists upon providing a protagonist whose point of view on his circumstances out-lampoons even Benjamin Braddock's caricatures, yet Harold Chasen is able to resist the torpor of his culture and, through love with an older woman, tune in and drop out.

Harold (Bud Cort) is to the manor born, awash in dark, baronial extravagance of material comfort and familial pretense. Ashby, working from a script by Colin Higgins, projects an old-money, English sensibility onto a central Californian landscape: rich brown interiors, cluttered with antiques and plastered with mirrors, antithesis of the Californian architectural aesthetic of clean lines and light. It's a willful renunciation of the world in favor of nostalgic artificiality. Harold lives alone in all this splendor with his mother, played with monstrous, deranged narcissism by Vivien Pickles. The two Chasens stage an on-going performance and counter-performance of passive aggressive self-absorption: Harold is death-obsessed, staging elaborately gruesome ritual suicides, while his mother assumes an air of oblivious disregard, rightly ignoring the patent falseness of his "cries for help" while failing to recognize Harold's disenchantment with the life of conspicuous consumption she means for him to inherit. He buys and restores a junked hearse. She replaces the hearse with a silver Jaguar (which, as always, is *her* preference, not his, as when she fills out a questionnaire for him that increasingly reflects only her own sentiments). He refits the Jag as a sports-hearse. Other dramas play out on the theme of his love-life (ritual suicides performed for a series of dating-service girls procured for him by his mother) and his professional life (an elaborate con game perpetrated upon his uncle, a disabled military man with portraits of Richard Nixon and Nathan Hale on his office walls). Point of view is, as in *The Graduate*, distorted in the service of a self-pitying protagonist, whose caricatures make Benjamin's portrayals of adult conformity, resignation, and irrationality look like kitchen-sink realism by comparison.

Indulging his feigned infatuation with easeful death, Harold attends a series of funerals, at which he begins to notice another "regular," Maude (Ruth Gordon). She, like Mrs. Robinson, must make the first advances upon a callow youth. She steals Harold's hearse, invites him home for tea and to see her collections, and begins to insinuate herself into his narcissistic loneliness. Unlike Mrs. Robinson, she isn't locked into her own losses (though she nurses her grudges just as carefully); she's able to hear Benjamin when he talks, and she's able to teach him more than misanthropy. She hands him a banjo, involves him in minor municipal law-breaking (including tree-napping), and listens as he confesses the humiliation of having a mother who, in the midst of a party, used the mistaken report of Harold's death as a once-in-a-lifetime opportunity to grandstand her tragic victimization. Maude instructs Harold in individual identity and abhorrence of conformity, on "fighting" for the "big issues." While Maude is no less pretentious than Harold or his mother, Ashby offers her as a crowd-pleasing projection of the counter-cultural left, an original-vintage bohemian. Ashby's audience quickly self-selected, making *Harold and Maude* a cult favorite.

It was a far smaller audience than the one for *The Graduate*. Part of this may be attributed to the unpalatable contemplation of romance between a young man and a woman four times his age, but part of the audience response is also due to the seismic shifts in culture in the brief interim between the films. What Brackman may prematurely have posited in 1968 in *The New Yorker*, that the counter-culture had become the prevailing culture for what would come to be known as the Baby Boomers, had gained further rhetorical traction in middle-American consciousness, such that Archie Bunker and his son-in-law Mike the Meathead could argue the polemical positions Brackman had once claimed were inarguable (because a new generation had recognized the futility of ever getting through to their elders).[13] While the point of view in *The Graduate* enabled facile misinterpretation of its ironies, thus superficially offering the sort of fairy-tale ending audiences will always crave, there was no walking away from the conclusion of *Harold and Maude* with harbored illusions. Ashby literally made his film's ending as subtle as a car crash.

Harold Chasen's Jag-hearse roars through the ending of *Harold and Maude*. The car is every bit the self-conscious statement of identity that his mother had originally intended (or that the Braddocks had intended with their graduation present to Benjamin)—but with Harold having welded on his own statement. The soundtrack comments on his spiritual condition: Maude has just died, and Cat Stevens sings of "Trouble." Ashby, the veteran editor turned director, convinces us that Harold has reverted to the film's opening, an obsessive, theatrical appropriation of death. Maude would seem to be in line to take the blame for this, given her ambiguous end—filled with sermons on reverence for life and refusal to capitulate to fascism during the Hitler murder program but ultimately punctuated by her theatrical renunciation of life to assert her own will even upon the natural processes of death.

Ashby, having provided a series of close shots of Harold weeping as he maneuvers his car up onto the cliffs above the Pacific, cuts to a long shot of the car toppling grandly into a heap of scrap metal on the shoreline, and we assume that Harold has followed his mentor's last action, not her commission (to "go and love some more"). That he has stranded himself atop the cliff with his banjo in the next shot comes simultaneously as both a shock and an inevitable conclusion of having been transformed by his time with Maude. Like Benjamin, he has abandoned the car, symbol of asserted socio-economic status. Unlike Benjamin, however, Harold appears to have returned to the opening of the narrative not to resume his place on its cyclical track but to break the cycle. Benjamin, passively conveyed at the film's opening into a future beyond his design, takes a seat on the bus and is carried into a future beyond the story of the film. Harold, committed to the spectacular artifice of his own destruction (as in the opening scene's "hanging"), stages an elaborate destruction of his artifice — a witty, theatrical reversal of his witty, theatrical negations. We do not know where he is headed next, but the film's spirit — its point of view — suggests it will be someplace genuinely counter-cultural, not merely contrarian. By this point in 1971, Brackman would have been disillusioned by the various so-called Deaths of the Sixties: the 1968 assassinations of King and Kennedy and the Manson murders, the debacle of Chicago and the election of Richard Nixon, the Altamont riot as real-life corrective to the dream of Woodstock, the acrimonious break-up of the Beatles, the shootings at Kent State and other martial misappropriations of force. He would have been compelled to acknowledge the reality of a Silent Majority that continued implacably to pursue an American Dream that Brackman and other counter-cultural apologists had pronounced dead. The box-office champion of 1971 was *Fiddler on the Roof* (Norman Jewison). *Harold and Maude* wasn't in the top twenty. The mass audience that had attended but, in essence, failed to see or internalize *The Graduate*'s black-comic caution failed even to attend Ashby's film.

Twenty-five years later, in *American Beauty*, Alan Ball created a screenplay that takes a look at a Benjamin Braddock type in mid-life, as if Benjamin had succumbed to the dreamy anomie of his fantasy life in *The Graduate* and slept-walk through an intervening two and a half decades. Early in *American Beauty*, the protagonist, Lester Burnham, narrates a primer on his quotidian existence, a distancing technique that exaggerates his alienation and helplessness. Describing himself as "dead already," he clinically dissects his failings as a husband, father, bread-winner: "Both my wife and daughter think I'm this gigantic loser, and ... they're right." The image on-screen is Lester late for his family's morning carpool; he accidentally empties his briefcase onto the front walk and then takes a submissive backseat to his wife and daughter, where he promptly falls asleep. Reflecting on his family-appointed status as "loser," he muses, "I *have* lost something. I'm not exactly sure what it is, but I know I didn't always feel this ... sedated. But you know what? It's never too late to get it back." He's been asleep, it would seem, since around the time Benjamin and Elaine alighted from that Santa Barbara bus, when they and Lester still had their whole lives in front of them.

In the final cut of *American Beauty*, Sam Mendes dispenses with some of the early scenes of Ball's script (much as Nichols had done with Henry's script), commencing the narrative-proper with Lester's pink slip from *Media Monthly* magazine. Lester's reaction to his firing is not predictable devastation but rather delighted liberation (he brazenly extorts a healthy severance package from Brad, a corporate hatchet-man half his age): Lester is, as he describes himself, "just an ordinary guy with nothing to lose," and he's "looking for the least possible amount of responsibility." Lester's reaction to the realities of the rat race are reminiscent of Benjamin's summer of "drifting," the antithesis of all those questions about what he intends to do with his future. Lester fills his nights with surreal fantasies of his daughter's slutty friend Angela (Mena Suvari) and his days by pumping iron and smoking pot in his garage, where he uses the big pay-out to revert to a teenage gear-head fantasy of owning the car of his adolescent dreams, a red 1970 Firebird (choosing an American muscle car over *The Graduate*'s little red "wop job"). In a sense, he has awakened as the teenager who had once-upon-a-time been sedated into adulthood by the culture of capitalist advancement. It's as if that potent narcotic has just now worn off, and we realize, despite our amusement at Kevin Spacey's depiction of mid-life crisis, the debilitating sadness of so much lost time.

He tells his wife, Carolyn (played in a memorable frenzy by Annette Benning), to leave him alone; suddenly she is far too *old* for him, and the lesson she extracts from his rejection is that "You cannot count on anyone except yourself," a lesson she means to impart, in a travesty of loving maternal advice, to her own daughter. Both Burnham women are, like the Robinsons and Braddocks, consumed by the weary work of projecting social identities they believe are necessary for status. Jane (Thora Birch), a beautiful, full-breasted teenager, nonetheless contemplates plastic augmentation of her breasts and, despite semi-goth leanings, goes through the motions as a cheerleader. Her mother's entire life as a would-be real-estate broker is a plasticized rendering of tape-recorded motivational speeches that devolves most chillingly in her lingerie-clad scrubbing of a prospective house for sale and most heartbreakingly in her wailing lament for Lester's empty clothes once she knows she's lost him. The Burnhams live in an immaculate, up-scale suburb like the Braddocks; Mendes presents the house-façade in full shot much the same way Nichols presented the Robinsons' house, a luxurious American Dream behind which lurks a less-pleasant reality. Uncle Charlie's thesis in Alfred Hitchcock's *Shadow of a Doubt* (1943) is that, if you rip the fronts off comfortable American homes of privilege (like the Braddocks' and the Burnhams'), what you'll expose is "swine." Uncle Charlie's misanthropy reposes most concretely in misogyny; he becomes the Merry Widow Killer, relieving "fat, greedy women" of their fortunes and their futures. Both Mrs. Robinson and Carolyn bear the symbolic weight of their respective films' judgments of greedy, grasping consumerism.

In an Afterword about his screenplay, Alan Ball writes, as if paraphrasing Mr. McGuire in *The Graduate*, "We live in such a manufactured culture, one that thrives on simplifying and packaging experience quickly so it can be sold."[14] Carolyn, desperately desirous of success as a seller (and willing to offer herself to the realty "King" in exchange for the keys to his kingdom), becomes Ball's poster-girl for all that is wrong in the culture, much as Mrs. Robinson is emblematic of cultural failure in *The Graduate*. Both narratives are in this sense misogynist fantasies of their male protagonists' anxieties; both make the "mother" the root of rot. Ball, taking a page from *The Graduate*, lets the masculine point of view eventually encounter a more comprehensive vision of the world: "But as Ricky knows — and Lester learns — things are infinitely deeper and richer than they appear on the surface."[15] That Ricky (Wes Bentley) is the repository of an old soul, able to recognize the beauty underlying all the vainglorious material striving, is cold comfort in a narrative in which the old soul resides within an affluent neighborhood narcotics pusher and user; the moment of greatest human compassion is left to Lester, who, in less than a minute of film-time, ages gracefully through his nearly three lost decades, undressing then redressing a suddenly vulnerable Angela. He moves from madness, his chronic teenage religion of surface appearance and fulfillment, to maturity, a larger insight about the insecurities and obsessions of others and the relative wealth of his own life.

As in *The Graduate*, when Benjamin contemplates the tear on Elaine's soft cheek in the strip club, the male protagonist in *American Beauty* encounters genuine innocence in a beautiful, wholesome female form, and his wayward course corrects itself. Angela's slutty patter has all been a ruse; she's afraid and humiliated and hungry, and Lester fills her not with an older lover's predation but with a paternal sandwich and an inquiry about her well-being. In a matter of minutes, he'll be dead, victim of his neighbor, Col. Fitts (Chris Cooper), a man still under emotional lock and key in the world of packaged surfaces. "Man oh man," muses Lester philosophically, unaware and unalarmed as he dies. He's suddenly prepared to die: he's been enlightened. For Sam Mendes and Alan Ball, the voice-over of a dead man offers a hedge against audience misperception, a lesson learned and articulated by a prototypically selfish, shallow person who shares his late insights with an audience presumably in need of similar awakening, to feel "gratitude for every single moment." By contrast, Mike Nichols gives us a callow 21-year-old, without the mellowing that can come from experience. Benjamin is as blank as Lester Burnham must have been "the first time I saw my cousin Tony's brand new Firebird." Benjamin has as much in common with Angela, desperate to slough off the handicap of innocence, as he does with Lester, whose innocence long since curdled into the cynical certainty that experience is a plastic promise. Benjamin never quite gets to enlightenment; Lester gets to enjoy his just long enough for his life to pass before our eyes in the film's coda.

If Lester represents the middle of the three proverbial Ages of Man, and Benjamin is a wide-eyed First-Ager, the two meet as foils in Wes Anderson's

16. The Legacy of The Graduate

Rushmore as Max Fischer and Mr. Blume (Max's father Bert might be said to serve as the final Age, imbued by a Stoic's peaceful acceptance of his life). As in *The Graduate* and *American Beauty*, the majority culture is consumed with *performance*, whether the flashy materialism of private schools and big houses or the elaborate production of Max Fischer's life. Max (Jason Schwartzman) fancies himself a precocious Man of the Theater, staging ever-more-elaborate staged entertainments, the most ambitious of which is his one-man-show as a Rushmore Man, devoted to wearing the crested blazer the rest of his days. He impresses Mr. Blume (Bill Murray), who sends his thuggish sons to Rushmore Academy, and whose steel business allows him to make such sizable donations that Dr. Guggenheim (Brain Cox), headmaster of the academy, is obliged to give him a bully pulpit at mandatory assembly.

Mr. Blume and Max exchange philosophies early in the film. Max takes careful notes during Mr. Blume's address, which seethes with a philosophy of class warfare: "You guys have it real easy. I never had it like this where I grew up. But I send my kids here because the fact is you go to one of the best schools in the country: Rushmore. Now, for some of you it doesn't matter. You were born rich and you're going to stay rich. But here's my advice to the rest of you: Take dead aim on the rich boys. Get them in the crosshairs and take them down. Just remember, they can buy anything but they can't buy backbone. Don't let them forget it." Afterwards, Max massages Mr. Blume with praise, then adds, "Except I disagree with your ideas about rich kids. Because, after all, we don't choose who our fathers are." (Max's shame about his own father provides one of the most overt stimuli for Max's play-acting.) Another day, Mr. Blume comes to retrieve his sons and spies Max, engrossed in yet another Rushmore-related project. He calls Max over and asks, "What's the secret, Max? You look like you've got it all figured out." Looking, despite his material success, like someone far from having it "all figured out," Mr. Blume may be forgiven for presuming to obtain the "secret" of life from as unlikely a source as a child. Max can't quite conceal the smugness with which he answers, via aphorism, Mr. Blume's query: "I think you just have to find something you love to do, then do it for the rest of your life. For me, it's going to Rushmore."

As Max, Jason Schwartzman is an appealing lampoon of Dustin Hoffman's awkwardly asymmetrical appearance. His large, swarthy features out-ethnicize anything *The Graduate*'s many close-ups throw at us, and their function is to provide the same sort of visual cues to Max's social alienation that Nichols and Henry envisioned in re-making the "human surfboard" as a schlemiel. *Rushmore*'s narrative, like *The Graduate*'s, privileges its protagonist's point of view grotesqueries. The characters in *Rushmore*—Mr. Blume;

Brian Cox as the growling, tough-love headmaster Dr. Guggenheim; Magnus Buchan as a foul-mouthed, bullying Scots exchange student; Seymour Cassel as Max's elderly father, maddeningly content with his quotidian life as a barber — are the products of a teenager's cartoon fever-dream, one we often see Max instantly transform into art, as for instance when middle-school children don mustaches and play hard-case, tough-talking narcs in Max's stage version of *Serpico*. Max's point of view is at its most pronounced (and most overtly Nichols-influenced) in rendering his romantic yearnings. Benjamin had his Mrs. Robinson; Max is more fortunate: he has Miss Cross (Olivia Williams) — and the maternal and romantic signals once again get crossed near a child's aquarium. Unlike Benjamin, Max has no mother (and for reasons of class anxiety, can't countenance his forbearing father). Miss Cross, an elementary school teacher who has lost her husband (and some part of herself, since she has largely devoted her subsequent life to perpetuating his memory), clearly enjoys the schoolboy crushes she provokes in both Max and Mr. Blume, but without Max's narrative point of view ever quite impugning her with the sort of villainous qualities Benjamin's narrative imputes to Mrs. Robinson. Rather, Max makes Miss Cross a modern vestal virgin, observing solemn rites in memoriam for her dead husband, Edward.

Rushmore ultimately has a gentler, more hopeful heart than *The Graduate*, even as it continues to invoke Nichols's film and its bleak outlook for much of the culture. *Rushmore*'s birthday party also takes place by that backyard signifier of success, the in-ground swimming pool, and while the twins greedily tear into their presents, Mr. Blume becomes Benjamin Braddock on his birthday, with Bill Murray's ruined face mooning his poolside alienation from his ex-wife and moronic sons. He, too, spoils the party, enveloping himself, via party-splattering cannonball, in the pool's murky womb-water. Miss Cross becomes the apparent solution for the existential woes of Mr. Blume and Max, and in another of the film's overt homages to *The Graduate*, Anderson offers a mid-narrative, dialogue-free montage of juvenile aggression, cut to The Who's "A Quick One (While He's Away)." As in Nichols's film, the soundtrack provides relentless choric commentary, dominated by Cat Stevens (as in *Harold and Maude*, another film about a lost young man in need of an older woman's experience); *Rushmore* ends with The Faces' "Ooh La La," a song of nostalgic regret from a point of view profoundly altered by experience. In his screenplay directions for the scene, Anderson calls this song, which plays as the curtains close and credits roll, "the saddest song of the night."[16]

Why so sad? As it was for Benjamin in *The Graduate*, there remains some question as to what Max knows even at the end of the film: in this narrative, in which curtains pull back to reveal the sub-titled months, the most formally

16. The Legacy of The Graduate

In *Rushmore* (1998), director Wes Anderson creates a loving homage to *The Graduate*'s visual, aural, and dramatic motifs. Jason Schwartzman (front left) plays Max Fischer, an unfocused young man in thrall to a glamorous older woman, Miss Cross (Olivia Williams, far right). Insinuating himself as the third point of an unlikely love triangle is Mr. Blume (Bill Murray), shown dancing with Max's girlfriend Margaret Yang (Sara Tanaka) in the almost-happy-ever-after confection of the film's ending. Like the ending, *Rushmore*'s depiction of Williams is courtesy of Max's point of view, a hyper-romanticized, virginal projection of his own sensibility. Miss Cross comes closest to being deglamorized when, frustrated by Max's obsessive infatuation with her, she crudely verbalizes adult sexuality to disenchant him. *Rushmore*, like *The Graduate*, is a formal meditation on the dangers inherent in wishful distortion of reality.

artificial moment of all in the film is its ending, in which, like a traditional theatrical comedy, everyone is paired off, including the elderly Mr. Fischer to the matronly Mrs. Whitney. Max even has his bittersweet moment with Miss Cross, after adjusting his sights to a more age-appropriate girlfriend. The final play and its after-party have all the texture of spun cotton-candy, and we begin to sense either that the narrative's concluding confections could solidify into the hard-won recognitions of The Faces' lyric (the song reveals the perspective of a significantly older man addressing his grandson, acknowledging the tough lessons life routinely offers the young), or else that the fantasies that dominate much of *Rushmore* could melt, like cotton-candy, into sugary grit.

This residue of ambiguity, despite the overtly chipper tenor of the movie's concluding scene, is the final of *Rushmore*'s many revisitings of *The Graduate*—a formal understanding of and distance from the protagonist's perspectival autonomy. Both Benjamin and Max will for themselves happy endings, but Mike Nichols and Wes Anderson are too realistic to allow them this caprice without introducing a note of ambiguity. Benjamin and Max awaken to the sadness and difficulty of the world. There is substantial reason for hope at the end of *Rushmore*, in Max's undeniable energy and precocity, and especially in the generosity of his closing fantasy, in which he aims to see everyone as happy or even happier than himself. Max may be able to move eventually from self-serving fantasy to art. But as in *The Graduate*'s cyclical structure, which returns Benjamin to a state of uncertain passivity, *Rushmore* undeniably ends back where it began (in a celebration of Max's genius-level—and non-existent—mathematical problem-solving): in fantasy.

In 2009, *An Education* serves to transpose gender, making a female *Graduate* set in pre–Beatles' English gloom. Danish director Lone Scherfig and novelist Nick Hornby adapted Lynn Barber's coming-of-age memoir about Jenny Mellor, whose pedestrian parents dream of their bright daughter's Oxonian upward mobility. Jenny (Carey Mulligan), however, is less certain of formal education as a means of enlightenment: "Studying is hard and boring," she says to the headmistress (Emma Thompson) of her preparatory school, summing up the talking-to she's just been made to swallow. "Teaching is hard and boring. So what you're telling me is to be bored, and then bored, and then finally bored again, but this time for the rest of my life. [...] It's not enough to educate us any more, Miss Walters. You've got to tell us why you're doing it." She seems to be anticipating precisely the sort of empty exercise Benjamin Braddock apparently experienced "back there in the east," where Mr. Robinson imagines they taught Ben "tricks" for ensnaring young women. The scene ultimately plays as a more articulate paraphrasing of Benjamin's retort, "You got me," to his father's exasperated rhetorical question about the value of college.

In one of her least sympathetic moments, Jenny cuts Miss Stubbs, the once-beloved English teacher with whom she'd seemed to share a simpatico: "But if we're all going to die the moment we graduate, isn't it what we do beforehand that counts?" Miss Stubbs replies, "I'm sorry you think I'm dead." Olivia Williams plays Miss Stubbs; she's as deglamorized in *An Education* as she was radiant as the Miss Cross of Max's schoolboy imagination in *Rushmore*, a happy coincidence of casting that demonstrates the vital importance of unpacking point of view in all these post–*Graduate* films. Williams appears deglamorized in *An Education* because she is sublimated to Jenny's post-adolescent sexual fantasies about herself as the Only Girl in England capable of

16. The Legacy of The Graduate

In *An Education* (2009), director Lone Scherfig's casting and subsequent depiction of Olivia Williams (standing) as Miss Stubbs provides an instructive counterpoint to Wes Anderson's presentation of Williams in *Rushmore*. In both films, Williams's character is a projection of the protagonist's point of view. For Jenny (Carey Mulligan, front right), Miss Stubbs is a beloved figure of classroom wit and wisdom in otherwise drab surroundings but also an omen of what awaits bright girls who follow the rules. Jenny's point of view sees only dull browns and grays in her parents' home and Miss Stubbs' excessively deglamorized appearance. *An Education* eventually affords Jenny a fuller recognition (and revision) of her distortions in perspective than either Benjamin in *The Graduate* or Max in *Rushmore* are permitted. Amanda Fairbank-Hynes is seated at front left, with unidentified extras in the back.

sidestepping the cultural trap she perceives the otherwise sagacious Miss Stubbs to have stepped into. In *Rushmore*, by contrast, Williams glows because she is the burnished object of both Max's and Mr. Blume's fantasies of sexual completion. Miss Cross, Williams' character in *Rushmore*, is as much in need of education as any of the other sufferers, and the agents of education come from the margins: little Margaret Yang (Sara Tanaka) and littler Dirk Calloway (Mason Gamble), both of whom are willing to tell Max the truth but also extend an olive branch of forgiveness; there is also, eternally, Max's old, wise father Bert, hopeful (but never insistent, let alone bullying like the Braddocks) that his son will one day decide for himself to be genuine rather than artificial. In *An Education*, Williams' character has the educational goods, and when

Jenny eventually seeks her out at her flat for help that can come from nowhere else in her life, she sees Miss Stubbs (and potentially herself) transformed by context. Providing scenic direction in his screenplay, Hornby writes, "It's a proper Bohemian flat. There are books and papers and pictures covering every available surface. Jenny looks around. Finally, for the first time, we see her in somewhere she can feel at home."[17]

Getting to this place is, like most education, difficult, and fraught with error. Besides insulting and estranging her favorite teacher, she burns bridges with the headmistress. Jenny has chosen instead to pursue an alternative source of education, via an affair with an older man, David (Peter Sarsgaard). David seems to offer what Jenny desires: a sympathetic cultural palate and a willingness to impart the wisdom of worldly experience; he's everything Jenny's hopelessly provincial father, played with hulking insecurity by Albert Molina, is not. The cultural evenings with David (and eventually the overnights as far away as Paris) are, like Benjamin's date with Elaine, as much jailbreaks as social engagements, and their illicit character only intensifies as Jenny's education about David and his business partner, Danny, deepens. Jenny, like Benjamin in *The Graduate*, knows at some level what she ought to be doing, and that secret assignations with an older partner are intuitively a dangerous game. Yet both Jenny and Benjamin are compelled by the conviction that no viable alternative exists for their futures. Each feels a counter-intuitive conviction centered in a young person's first enormous and illusory flush of physical potency and desirability. Jenny ought to be leaving David, returning to diligent study for her exams — in short, she ought to be who she is, a schoolgirl with a shot at Oxford.

The men in Jenny's life all have the potential to project as the kind of monster Mrs. Robinson became in *The Graduate*: her bumbling father, obsequious before David's apparently superior wealth and breeding; Danny (Dominic Cooper), David's partner-in-crime, who never quite rescues her despite knowing David's shoddy treatment of her; David himself, the liar and thief (he steals old ladies' property and Jenny's virginity, but most cruelly, her good sense). That none of these men becomes an extravagantly caricatured monster is a reflection of Jenny's point of view: she is a smarter, less ego-protecting protagonist than Benjamin or Lester or Max. Lone Scherfig and her protagonist are more generous to even the worst people in *An Education* than Mike Nichols and Benjamin were to anyone in *The Graduate*, which marks the generic difference between *An Education*'s drama and *The Graduate*'s satire. Still, Scherfig's film offers insights into the distortions of subjectivity: the lovely Olivia Williams becomes plain in Jenny's point of view because she is the projection of Jenny's worst fears for her own future; her father is a hopeless cultural illiterate; the headmistress is the caricatured voice of Jenny's professional doom ("It doesn't have to be teaching. There's always the Civil Service"); and a young admirer of Jenny's own age is even more maladroit than her father at her birthday dinner.

An Education permits Jenny to see in three dimensions: her own scolding by Danny when she presumes to lecture him from her self-deluded moral high ground; the sadness and despair of the headmistress; the genuine love her father possesses for her; most important, the richer life of the spirit Miss Stubbs conducts beyond the gray walls of the school. As for David, he is both a gentle romantic (dreaming up the affair's consummation in Paris) and a tone-deaf boor (the introduction of the banana). Remarkably, Jenny stands up to him in much more mature and sensible ways than Benjamin ever dreamed of with Mrs. Robinson, and this, too, is reflected in the film's subjective point of view. Our final impressions of David tellingly come with him already off-screen, "out of the picture" as it were: Jenny with her parents in the living room, her jaw set, waiting in vain for David to get out of his car, join them, and accept responsibility for his part in the mess they've made; Jenny standing in front of the house where she now knows David has lived with his wife and family all along, mere unexotic blocks from her own home.

An Education ends happily, and without tonal ambiguity, for all its chastening sadness in the film's final act. We're even rewarded with a glimpse of a girlish Jenny, astride a bike, peddling next to an Oxford boy with James Gibbs' Radcliffe Camera unmistakable nearby: she's made it. Hornby writes that, in Barber's original narrative, David reappears a final time, looking for Jenny at Oxford. Hornby dutifully included the scene, and Scherfig and crew shot it, "but it never really worked," writes Hornby in an introduction to his screenplay. "[I]t didn't give the actors enough to do, apart from restate their positions with as much vehemence or self-delusion as they could muster."[18] As a result, the "Alternative Ending" supplied in an appendix at the end of the screenplay feels particularly unreal, not only because Jenny has moved on in a way that, for instance, Benjamin has not at the end of *The Graduate*, but also because the film had reflected her psychological movement by banishing David from the last fifteen minutes of the film. The reappearance of a diminished David, groveling for another chance while she is clearly in her element in Oxford, is the point of view of a different film, one with a more ironic sense of its protagonist and the supposed progress she's made — a film more like *The Graduate*.

An Education offers the potential for life-lessons not only to its protagonist, but also to the supporting cast. Her parents in particular learn what the Braddocks never bother to acknowledge, that they have been driving, and driving away, their own child by enforcing their tunnel vision on their child's future. Though the ending of *An Education* is bittersweet, it is not ambiguous. Jenny is a better, quicker, more realistic student than Benjamin or even Max; Max sulks in his little house until his friends intervene in his life, but Jenny actively seeks the help she needs (it's what Miss Stubbs has been hoping all along Jenny would ask). We know what Jenny knows at the film's end — no more, no less. While some of her future remains as unrevealed as Benjamin's or Max's, she shows no interest in regression. She certainly displays none of the recurrent, passive surrender of Benjamin, capitulating to the cultural rule of marriage as the inviolable state and riding gloomily in an undetermined direction. She evidences no interest in continuing to spin ego-massaging fantasies like Max does at the end of *Rushmore* (no matter how much less mean-spirited those fabulations have evolved because of his maturing generosity of spirit). There is no revenge scene at the end of *An Education*; the film is as mature as its protagonist. She has moved on. One senses that, as she enters college, Jenny already knows more, and is more practically suited to access and apply what she knows, than Benjamin is capable of as *The Graduate* ends, half a year after his college career is over. Miss Stubbs has taught Jenny that "Action is character." For all the imperative commands to "Move!" at the end of *The Graduate*, no one ever quite got that message through to Benjamin.

Act I of *The Graduate* closes with Benjamin commanding Mrs. Robinson, "Don't move!" By the end of Act III, this same *boy — no wait, let me amend that, this young man* commands the wedding party, "Move!" The echoed variation provides a structural unity that suggests the expected narrative illusion of a character's development. In significant ways, Benjamin has in fact been transformed by his summer after college. Although he didn't learn much at his prestigious eastern university, at least he knows that he didn't. Upon his return home from college, the graduate's callow, obvious alienation makes him a prime recruit for Mrs. Robinson's apprenticeship program and, whatever his caricatured antipathies for her by narrative's end, she has made possible the person he becomes, a young man who is able to see clearly — to see through — the plastic veneer of material success that substitutes for a life of humanity in all its multi-dimensional richness, including the life of the spirit or soul, the genuine meeting place (not board rooms, court rooms, or show rooms) where human beings make contact.

As *The Graduate*'s narrative begins, in other words, Benjamin is a graduate only on paper, a high-achiever who has perhaps jumped a bit higher than many, but without a sense of why. As we watch his dull-witted, obtuse

16. The Legacy of The Graduate

drift through his summer, we may in fact find ourselves questioning the evidence (all second-hand testimony, from his yearbook, his parents, and the Halpingham Award Committee) of how bright he is. He seems fairly ordinary. The flat, unaffected prose of Charles Webb's source material has set this tone. Benjamin is a parrot of his culture until Mrs. Robinson shows him what parroting this culture for too long actually causes. Where would Benjamin have been without the intervention of Mrs. Robinson? It seems reasonable to presume that Mr. Robinson and Mr. Braddock would have beaten the drum for the feudal merging of the families not just via business partnership, but also in an enhanced romantic conjunction. Would Benjamin, without the focusing antagonism of experiences like the epic "conversation" with Mrs. Robinson, have learned the force of his objection to the Robinsons' and Braddocks' way of life, or would his life have become a much less self-conscious "drifting" (the kind he himself would be unable to notice and identify, the kind that Alan Ball and Sam Mendes envisioned in *American Beauty* as Lester Burnham's decades of sleepwalking) into the vague varieties of solipsism and desperation of which the older generation serve as representative types?

It is true that Benjamin is able to articulate to his father, even before Mrs. Robinson recruits him for her school of hard shocks, that he wants his future to be "different." But the irony of the film's title ascribes to the formal processes of learning a sense of purposive production, of raw matter shaped to a refined end. The narrative of *The Graduate* suggests that Benjamin is only prepared to *move on* to a new phase of his life through intensive tutorial from a woman who has had a similar insight about her life and cultural inheritance and has allowed her own capitulation to destroy her from the inside out. This does not constitute an impetus to move on *to* a worthier goal but only *away from* one that must be avoided. In this as in all things, Benjamin's psychological point of view is self-serving. The majority of his efforts at making a "different" future for himself are matters of skewed perspective. Mrs. Robinson sees through the culture but capitulates to the culture, and Benjamin ends her cautionary fairy tale by turning her into a ghoul. He can't help but feel better about himself in comparison, even as he rides into his own future of unimaginative capitulation.

The Graduate's narrative-long meditation on movement and its opposite — stasis, paralysis, willful rootedness — finds a final irony to wring from Benjamin's story in observing that negative movement is valuable but ultimately unsustainable. One must ultimately point *toward* something. In the "conversation" Benjamin undertakes with Mrs. Robinson in their room at the Taft Hotel, they uncover a series of truth-statements to one another about the spiritual bankruptcy of what they're doing. Yet despite the animation with which Benjamin and Elaine seem to converse at the drive-in on their first date, the majority of their dialogue we get to overhear is either duplicitous (his half-confession to her outside of the Taft Hotel) or childish (their courtship banter in Berkeley). The life of easy privilege and spiritual compromise offered to them by their parents is the road they've ostensibly chosen not to take, but their single obsession has been the cultural role-play of marriage as a strategic means of asserting social identity (rather than genuine spiritual union). This interpretation of marriage is the source of so much human wreckage in the film.

The Graduate articulates no alternative cultural roadmap. In its classic scene of dramatic resolution at the church and then on the bus, the narrative both offers and then withdraws the comforts of traditional resolution, of *happily ever after*. To this point, Benjamin and Elaine have demonstrated a failure to imagine a positive counter-cultural response. Their very relationship is predicated initially upon their fathers' wills to see them together and then, as the summer's sins are revealed, upon their rebellion against the parental proscriptions and prohibitions set in place to keep them apart. What has strengthened their bond is a shared outrage for the culture's "rules," the subject of their first (and only) substantive philosophical conversation, the night of their first date. A common antipathy is a start, but it isn't solid footing for a future — hence the displeasure people like Jacob Brackman, in that long *New Yorker* essay, took with the film, which vetoes contemporary consumer culture but does not nominate an alternative. (Nor, in several decades' worth of hindsight, has the culture at large.)

In the third act of the film, Benjamin and Elaine play at positive movement, yet their preoccupation is marriage, and their motives are less than pure. That air of resigned exhaustion that settles over them on the back bench of the bus in the film's penultimate shot may be their burgeoning sense, stripped of the narcotic illusions of their culture, of how difficult a life created whole-cloth, rather than received passively as a birthright, might actually prove to be — as in the endings to John Updike's classic short story, "A & P," in which the narrator "felt how hard the world was going to be to me hereafter"[19] or Raymond Carver's husband and wife in "Neighbors": "They stayed there. They held each other. They leaned into the door as if against a wind, and braced themselves."[20] While Benjamin and Elaine catch their breath and understand the practicalities of even the first night — a wedding night with the ghosts of summer past — the antipathetic forces of the social order may already have driven an inexorable wedge between them.

Mike Nichols's aesthetic resolution in *The Graduate* was and is to provide no easy resolution. His film does not attempt to depict Benjamin and Elaine's groping toward "a richer life of mind and spirit"; it does not put them in line at the Peace Corps or teaching schoolchildren in Watts. It does not explore, as for instance *Easy Rider* did a little over a year later, some of the more celebrated dead ends in alternative culture, including nomadic wandering to "find America," communal living, and drug experimentation. Rather, *The Graduate* posits the inevitable movement of time, so that even a "drifting" is movement in time's stream, and a life not lived in positive pursuit of one's moral vision is a life of passive conveyance into an increasingly disorienting, alienated future.

In his "Great Society" speech, made to the bright, idealistic Benjamin Braddocks and Elaine Robinsons of the University of Michigan in the spring of 1964, Lyndon Johnson challenged his audience and the nation "to move not only toward the rich society and the powerful society, but upward to the Great Society." The movement towards wealth and power, in other words, is not an end in itself but "the foundation on which we will build a richer life of mind and spirit." *The Graduate*'s narrative premise is not to provide a glimpse of that Great Society but to depict the failure of smart people to see beyond material reward and social convention to another, better purpose. Mike Nichols's negative satire offers, in the Robinsons and Braddocks, a vision of an America "condemned," as LBJ feared, "to a soulless wealth."[21] The movement of *The Graduate*, via its two protagonists, would seem to be *away* from this soul-trap, but their final prospect is hardly fond anticipation, and this is where the narrative ends, as the camera slows to a stop, allowing Benjamin and Elaine to recede into that imaginative limbo where the artist's work becomes the audience's task.

Chapter Notes

Preface

1. Jacob Brackman, "The Graduate," *The New Yorker*, 27 July 1968, 65.
2. Robert L. Carringer, "Designing Los Angeles: An Interview with Richard Sylbert," *Wide Angle*, 1998, 113.
3. Nora Ephron, *Wallflower at the Orgy*, 194.
4. Robert Beuka, "'Just One Word ... PLASTICS': Suburban Malaise, Masculinity, and Oedipal Drive in *The Graduate*," *Journal of Popular Film and Television*, 2000, 14.
5. Lyndon Johnson, "The Great Society," in *The Times Were a Changin': The Sixties Reader*, ed. Irwin Unger and Debi Unger, 40.
6. Leonard Quart and Albert Auster, *American Film and Society Since 1945*, 84.
7. Lee Hill, "Mike Nichols," *Senses of Cinema*, June 2003.
8. David Thomson, *The New Biographical Dictionary of Film*, 633.
9. David Thomson, *"Have You Seen...?,"* 340.
10. Linda Ruth Williams, "*The Graduate*," in *Contemporary American Cinema*, ed. Linda Ruth Williams and Michael Hammond, 102–103.
11. Glenn Man, *Radical Visions: American Film Renaissance, 1967–1976*, 48.
12. Hill, "Mike Nichols."

Chapter 1

1. Peter Biskind, *Easy Riders, Raging Bulls*, 18.
2. Richard Corliss, *Talking Pictures*, 362.
3. Peter Biskind, 34, 125.
4. Nick Clooney, *The Movies That Changed Us*, 67.
5. Sam Kashner, "Here's to You, Mr. Nichols," *Vanity Fair's Tales of Hollywood*, ed. Graydon Carter, 189.
6. Mark Harris, *Pictures at a Revolution*, 108.
7. Corliss, 362.
8. Harris, 72.
9. Harris, 361.
10. Robert L. Carringer, "Designing Los Angeles: An Interview with Richard Sylbert," *Wide Angle*, 1998, 98.
11. Barry Monush, *Everybody's Talkin'*, 222.
12. Robert Carringer, "Hollywood's Los Angeles: Two Paradigms," in *Looking for Los Angeles: Architecture, Film, Photography, and the Urban Landscape*, ed. Charles G. Salas and Michael S. Roth, 250.
13. Linda Ruth Williams, "*The Graduate*," in *Contemporary American Cinema*, ed. Linda Ruth Williams and Michael Hammond, 101.
14. Williams, 101.
15. Aaron Cooley, "Reviving Reification: Education, Indoctrination, and Anxiety in *The Graduate*," *Educational Studies*, 2009, 359.
16. Jacob Brackman, "The Graduate," *The New Yorker*, 27 July 1968, 62.
17. Edward Sorel, "*The Graduate*," *Esquire*, May 1980, as qtd. in Monaco, 184.
18. Carringer, "Hollywood's Los Angeles," 250.
19. Cooley, 359.
20. Cooley, 372.
21. Williams, 102.
22. Carringer, "Hollywood's Los Angeles," 250.
23. Elaine M. Bapis, *Camera and Action: American Film as Agent of Social Change, 1965–1975*, 57.

24. Carringer, "Hollywood's Los Angeles," 251.
25. Lyndon Johnson, "The Great Society," in *The Times Were a Changin': The Sixties Reader*, ed. Irwin Unger and Debi Unger, 40.
26. Johnson, 42.
27. Lee Hill, *Easy Rider*, 33.
28. Monush, 222.
29. Joseph Gelmis, *The Film Director as Superstar*, 370.
30. Kashner, 190.
31. Williams, 101.
32. Robert Coles, "*The Graduate*," Trans-Action, May 1968.
33. Carringer, "Designing Los Angeles," 114.
34. Brackman, 34.
35. Williams, 103.

Chapter 2

1. Charles McGrath, "Mike Nichols, Master of Invisibility," *New York Times*, 12 April 2009.
2. Rick Lyman, *Watching Movies*, 26.
3. Bosley Crowther, "Film: Tales Out of School," *New York Times*, 22 December 1967.
4. Bosley Crowther, "Graduating with Honors," *New York Times*, 31 December 1967.
5. Andrew M. Greeley, "Sons and Fathers," *The Reporter*, February 1968.
6. Barry Monush, *Everybody's Talkin'*, 222.
7. Nora Ephron, *Wallflower at the Orgy*, 190.
8. Lee Hill, "Mike Nichols," *Senses of Cinema*, June 2003.
9. John Simon, "*The Graduate*," *Movies Into Film*, February 1968, found at http://web.infoave.net/~dennmac/review5.html.
10. Tom S. Reck, "'The Graduate' Reclassified," *Commonweal*, found at http://web.infoave.net/~dennmac/review4.html.
11. Stephen Farber and Estelle Changas, "The Graduate," *Film Quarterly*, 1968, 41, 37.
12. Pauline Kael, *For Keeps*, 225.
13. David Thomson, *The New Biographical Dictionary of Film*, 4th ed., 633.
14. Paul Monaco, *The Sixties: 1960-1969*, 184.
15. Mark Harris, *Pictures at a Revolution*, 418.
16. Monush, 222.
17. Hill, "Mike Nichols."
18. Joseph Gelmis, *The Film Director as Superstar*, 349.
19. Jacob Brackman, "The Graduate," *The New Yorker*, 27 July 1968, 34.
20. Brackman, 34.
21. Brackman, 38.
22. Brackman, 40.
23. Brackman, 39.
24. Brackman, 39.
25. Farber and Changas, 37.
26. Thomson, *The New Biographical Dictionary of Film*, 633.
27. Brackman, 39.
28. Brackman, 39.
29. Brackman, 39.
30. Brackman, 39.
31. Brackman, 38.
32. Brackman, 34.
33. Brackman, 60.
34. Brackman, 62.
35. Brackman, 65.
36. Brackman, 65.
37. Brackman, 58.
38. Brackman, 65.
39. Brackman, 65.
40. Harris, 396.
41. Sam Kashner, "Here's to You, Mr. Nichols," *Vanity Fair's Tales of Hollywood*, ed. Graydon Carter, 188.
42. Richard Corliss, *Talking Pictures*, 365.
43. Lyman, 26. It must be noted that, when Howard watches the film with Lyman, his attention does not appear to rest on the ambiguities of the protagonist's future; Lyman's recounting emphasizes Howard's enthusiasm with the technical aspects of the storytelling, like the use of rain-making machines in sunny Los Angeles.
44. Brackman, 60.
45. Hollis Alpert, "'The Graduate' Makes Out," in *Saturday Review*, 6 July 1968, found at http://web.infoave.net/~dennmac/review2.html.
46. Gelmis, 370.
47. Monaco, 184.
48. H. Wayne Schuth, *Mike Nichols*, 61.
49. Brackman, 64.
50. Brackman, 64-65.
51. Thomson, "*Have You Seen...?*," 340.
52. Daniel Eagan, *America's Film Legacy*, 632.
53. Schuth, 60.
54. Hill, "Mike Nichols."
55. Gelmis, 375.
56. Gelmis, 376.
57. Robert Kolker, *A Cinema of Loneliness*, 3rd ed., 350.
58. Glenn Man, *Radical Visions: American Film Renaissance, 1967-1976*, 48.
59. Glenn Man, "Ideology and Genre in the *Godfather* Films," in *Francis Ford*

Coppola's The Godfather *Trilogy*, ed. Nick Browne, 117.
60. Harris, 275.
61. Richard Schickel, "Film 67/68," *Life*, 19 January 1968.
62. Corliss, 363.
63. David Denby, "Critic's Notebook: And Here's to You," *The New Yorker*, March 8, 2010, 9.
64. Farber and Changas, 38, 39.
65. Farber and Changas, 39.
66. Mark Cousins, *The Story of Film*, 322.
67. Gelmis, 375.
68. Brackman, 56.
69. Man, *Radical Visions*, 44.
70. Man, *Radical Visions*, 48; Elaine M. Bapis, *Camera and Action: American Film as Agent of Social Change, 1965–1975*, 47.
71. Murray Pomerance, "Movies and the Specter of Rebellion," in *American Cinema of the 1960s*, ed. Barry Keith Grant, 192.
72. Cousins, 322.

Chapter 3

1. Joseph Gelmis, *The Film Director as a Superstar*, 379.
2. Mark Harris, *Pictures at a Revolution*, 27.
3. Harris, 28.
4. Charles Webb, letter to the editor of *The New Republic*, as qtd. in Hollis Alpert, "'The Graduate' Makes Out," *Saturday Review*, 6 July 1968, found at http://web.info ave.net/~dennmac/review2.html.
5. Harris, 397.
6. Harris, 27.
7. Orville Prescott, "Talent Busting Out All Over," *New York Times*, 30 October 1963.
8. Charles Webb, *The Graduate*, 142.
9. David Thomson, "*Have You Seen...?*," 340.
10. J. D. Salinger, *The Catcher in the Rye*, 20.
11. Webb, 26–27.
12. Richard Corliss, *Talking Pictures*, 362.
13. Webb, 39.
14. Webb, 42.
15. Webb, 44.
16. Robert L. Carringer, "Designing Los Angeles: An Interview with Richard Sylbert," *Wide Angle*, 1998, 111.
17. Webb, 38.
18. Gelmis, 370.
19. Webb, 50.
20. Webb, 114.
21. Lawrence Turman, *So You Want to Be a Producer*, 194.
22. Sam Kashner, "Here's to You, Mr. Nichols," *Vanity Fair's Tales of Hollywood*, ed. Graydon Carter, 168.
23. Harris, 47.
24. Turman, 212.
25. Turman, 195.
26. Harris, 50.
27. Harris, 97.
28. Turman, 196.
29. Harris, 362–363.
30. Harris, 119.
31. Dan Georgakas, "From Words to Images: An Interview with Buck Henry," *Cineaste*, Winter 2001, 4.
32. Turman, 196.
33. Harris, 120.
34. Webb, 120.
35. Harris, 121.
36. Gelmis, 370.
37. Georgakas, 4.
38. Harris, 319.
39. Charles McGrath, "Mike Nichols, Master of Invisibility," *The New York Times*, 12 April 2009.
40. Wayne Schuth, *Mike Nichols*, 19.
41. Schuth, 19.
42. Harris, 48.
43. Harris, 49.
44. McGrath.
45. Carringer, "Designing Los Angeles," 105.
46. Harris, 311.
47. Turman, 196.
48. Turman, 195.
49. Turman, 195.
50. Barry Monush, *Everybody's Talkin'*, 221.
51. Turman, 216.
52. Jacob Brackman, "'The Graduate,'" *The New Yorker*, 27 July 1968, 46.
53. Harris, 314.
54. Harris, 315.
55. Betty Rollin, "Mike Nichols: Wizard of Wit," *Look*, found at http://web.infoave. net/~dennmac/review6.html.
56. Harris, 290.
57. Harris, 294.
58. Carringer, "Designing Los Angeles," 106.
59. Harris, 294.
60. Gelmis, 379.
61. Kashner, 174–175.
62. Harris, 274.
63. Harris, 271.
64. Harris, 275.

65. Kashner, 177.
66. J. Hoberman, "Flaunting It: The Rise and Fall of Hollywood's 'Nice' Jewish (Bad) Boys," in *Entertaining America: Jews, Movies, and Broadcasting*, ed. J. Hoberman and Jeffrey Shandler, 198, 225.
67. J. Hoberman, "Dustin Hoffman," *Entertaining America: Jews, Movies, and Broadcasting*, ed. J. Hoberman and Jeffrey Shandler, 198.
68. Harris, 312.
69. Harris, 364.
70. Kashner, 186.
71. Nora Ephron, *Wallflower at the Orgy*, 189.
72. Carringer, "Hollywood's Los Angeles," 252.
73. Harris, 395.
74. Kashner, 190.
75. Gelmis, 349.
76. Harris, 360.
77. Gelmis, 359.

Chapter 4

1. Buck Henry, "'The Graduate': Screenplay" (Dated March 29, 1967). The screenplay may be found at various locations on the internet, including http://sarcasmalley.com/graduate.txt.
2. Mark Harris, *Pictures at a Revolution*, 291.
3. Harris, 313.
4. Linda Ruth Williams, "*The Graduate*," *Contemporary American Cinema*, ed. Linda Ruth Williams and Michael Hammond, 102.
5. Thomas Pynchon, *The Crying of Lot 49*, 13–15.
6. Harris, 313.
7. Edward Sorel, "*The Graduate*," *Esquire*, May 1980, as qtd. in Monaco, 184.
8. H. Wayne Schuth, *Mike Nichols*, 47.
9. Robert Coles, in *Trans-Action* May 1968.
10. Paul Monaco, *The Sixties: 1960–1969*, 183.
11. Monaco, 115.
12. David R. Shumway, "Rock 'n' Roll Sound Tracks and the Production of Nostalgia," *Cinema Journal* Winter 1999, 37.
13. Glenn Man, *Radical Visions: American Film Renaissance, 1967–1976*, 35.
14. Shumway, 37.
15. Aaron Cooley, "Reviving Reification: Education, Indoctrination, and Anxiety in *The Graduate*," *Educational Studies*, 2009, 364.

Chapter 5

1. Jami Bernard, in *The A List: The National Society of Film Critics' 100 Essential Films*, ed. Jay Carr, 139.
2. Kael, *For Keeps*, 224.
3. Jacob Brackman, "'The Graduate,'" *The New Yorker*, 27 July 1968, 56.
4. Stephen Farber and Estelle Changas, "The Graduate," *Film Quarterly* Spring 1968, 37–38.
5. Cooley, 365.

Chapter 6

1. Harris, 314.
2. Murray Pomerance, "Movies and the Specter of Rebellion," in *American Cinema of the 1960s*, ed. Barry Keith Grant, 191.
3. Cooley, 368.
4. Harris, 292.
5. Sam Kashner, "Here's to You, Mr. Nichols," Vanity Fair's *Tales of Hollywood*, ed. Graydon Carter, 181.
6. Robert Enright, "Desiring Ambiguity: The Art of Eric Fischl," in *Eric Fischl: 1970–2007*, Arthur Danto, Robert Enright, and Steve Martin, 64.
7. Enright, 66.
8. Robert Carringer, "Hollywood's Los Angeles: Two Paradigms," in *Looking for Los Angeles: Architecture, Film, Photography, and the Urban Landscape*, ed. Charles G. Salas and Michael S. Roth, 250. Carringer cites Peter Biskind's *Easy Riders, Raging Bulls* as the exponent of a general trend in New Hollywood narratives to depict Oedipal rebellion.
9. Robert Carringer, "Hollywood's Los Angeles," 251.
10. Harris, 313.
11. Kashner, 181.
12. Kashner, 180.
13. Kashner, 180.
14. Farber and Changas, 38.
15. Farber and Changas, 38.
16. David Denby, "Critic's Notebook: And Here's to You," *The New Yorker*, March 8, 2010, 9.
17. Farber and Changas, 40.
18. Tom S. Reck, "'The Graduate' Reclassified," *Commonweal*, found at http://web.infoave.net/~dennmac/review4.html.

Chapter 7

1. Rick Lyman, *Watching Movies*, 28.
2. Harris, 315.

3. Monaco, 108.
4. Joseph Gelmis, *The Film Director as a Superstar*, 370.

Chapter 8

1. Carringer, "Designing Los Angeles: An Interview with Richard Sylbert," *Wide Angle*, 1998, 109.
2. Carringer, "Designing Los Angeles," 107.
3. Harris, 360.
4. Charles Webb, *The Graduate*, 40.
5. Webb, 50.
6. Robert Beuka, "'Just One Word ... PLASTICS': Suburban Malaise, Masculinity, and Oedipal Drive in *The Graduate*," *Journal of Popular Film and Television*, 2000, 19.
7. Glenn Man, *Radical Visions: American Film Renaissance, 1967–1976*, 48.

Chapter 9

1. Man, *Radical Visions*, 35.
2. Dan Georgakas, "From Words to Images: An Interview with Buck Henry," *Cineaste*, Winter 2001, 4.
3. Carringer, "Hollywood's Los Angeles," 251–252.
4. A scarifying footnote involves where location shooting took place in Los Angeles for the scenes at the Taft. The actual location was the Ambassador Hotel on Wilshire Boulevard. In June 1968, *The Graduate* was still a box-office phenomenon when, early the morning of June 5, after winning the California Democratic Party Primary election, Robert F. Kennedy was fatally wounded by gunshot. The hotel went into a two-decade slow decline before closing its door in 1989. For another decade and a half, the prime real estate sat vacant until most of the hotel was finally razed in 2006; the plan is for the Los Angeles United School District to open a $572 million high school on the property (the school opened in late 2010).
5. Carringer, "Designing Los Angeles," 110.
6. Corliss, *Talking Pictures*, 364.
7. For example: Brackman, 54; Farber and Changas, 39.
8. Beuka, 20.
9. Webb, 63.

Chapter 10

1. In *Talking Pictures*, Richard Corliss notes that each of Mike Nichols's first three films evidences his sense of the stage, including "literally, a three-act structure, complete with a fade-out at the end of each 'act'" (362).
2. Monaco, 98.
3. Linda Ruth Williams describes such passages in the film as disruptions of "a linear sense of space and time" (102); she quotes Ryan and Kellner's *Camera Politica: The Politics and Ideology of Contemporary Hollywood Film*, which argues that the montage conveys "the interchangeability of upper-class luxury and cynical adultery."
4. Harris, 361.
5. Lyman, 22.
6. Carringer, "Designing Los Angeles," 112.
7. Shumway, 38.
8. Buck Henry,
9. Elaine M. Bapis, *Camera and Action: American Film as Agent of Social Change, 1965–1975*, 49.
10. Bapis, 58.
11. Monaco, 76.
12. Betty Rollin, "Mike Nichols: Wizard of Wit," *Look*, found at http://web.infoave.net/~dennmac/review6.html.
13. Beuka, 19.
14. Vincent LoBrutto, *Martin Scorsese*, 67–69.

Chapter 11

1. Harris, 317.
2. Harris, 316–317.
3. Harris, 361.
4. Farber and Changas, 39.
5. Robert Coles, *Trans-Action*, May 1968, found at http://web.infoave.net/~dennmac/review13.html.

Chapter 12

1. Farber and Changas, 39.
2. Schuth, 53.
3. Beuka, 20.
4. Cooley, 369.
5. Cooley, 374, n8.
6. Brackman, 61.
7. Cf. Kael, *For Keeps*, 225.
8. Cf. Farber and Changas, 39.
9. Lyman, 29.
10. Lyman, 29–30. Howard's delight is not cruel; it's the fraternal amusement of one director commiserating with another's technical challenges in film production.

Chapter 13

1. Gelmis, 375.
2. The building in front of which Benjamin waits, looking for Elaine, is USC's Edward L. Doheny Memorial Library. This is exclusively a practical rather than aesthetic choice, unlike the reversing of directions on the Bay Bridge. It doesn't require an accountant to understand that it's far less expensive to get a suitably collegiate shot across town than by taking a whole company halfway up the state.

Chapter 14

1. Again, the nearby University of Southern California campus stands in for faraway Berkeley; the pillars belong to the exterior colonnade of the Van Kleinsmid Center of International and Public Affairs.
2. Corliss, 364.
3. Corliss, 362.
4. Webb, 168.

Chapter 15

1. David Bordwell, *The Way Hollywood Tells It*, 126.
2. Bruce F. Kawin, *How Movies Work*, 134.
3. Carringer, "Designing Los Angeles," 110–111.
4. Harris, 397. In an interview with Harris, Webb regrets the "'priggish'" character of his position, postulating that he had created Benjamin's predicament as a close-enough analogy to his own mistreatment by his pregnant girlfriend's in-laws that he was unable to avoid self-righteousness.
5. Harris, 121.
6. Harris, 318.
7. Gelmis, 373.
8. Bordwell, 260–261.
9. Gelmis, 374.
10. Carringer, "Designing Los Angeles," 113.
11. Marilyn Fabe, *Closely Watched Films: An Introduction to the Art of Narrative Film Technique*, 131.
12. Fabe, 131.
13. Naomi Greene, *The French New Wave: A New Look*, 73.
14. Gelmis, 377.
15. Brackman, 60.
16. Man, *Radical Visions*, 49.
17. Man, *Radical Visions*, 48–49.
18. Man, *Radical Visions*, 49–50.
19. Joan Mellon, *Modern Times*, 65.
20. Mellon, 67.
21. Mellon, 67.
22. Mellon, 67.

Chapter 16

1. Robert Coles, *Trans-Action* May 1968, found at http://web.infoave.net/~dennmac/review13.html.
2. Linda Ruth Williams, "*The Graduate*," *Contemporary American Cinema*, ed. Linda Ruth Williams and Michael Hammond, 103.
3. Terry Johnson, *The Graduate*, 24.
4. Johnson, 25.
5. Johnson, 25.
6. Johnson, 101.
7. Charles Webb, *Home School*, 199.
8. Webb, 225.
9. Sam Kashner, "Here's to You, Mr. Nichols," Vanity Fair's *Tales of Hollywood*, ed. Graydon Carter, 190.
10. Lee Hill, "Mike Nichols," *Senses of Cinema*, June 2003, found at www.sensesofcinema.com/contents/directors/03/Nichols.html.
11. A. O. Scott, "A Romantic Entanglement with a Heart of Celluloid," *The New York Times*, December 23, 2005.
12. Scott.
13. Jacob Brackman, "'The Graduate,'" *The New Yorker*, 27 July 1968, 56, 58.
14. Alan Ball, *American Beauty*, 114.
15. Ball, 114.
16. Wes Anderson, *Rushmore*, 121.
17. Nick Hornby, *An Education*, 187.
18. Hornby, 16.
19. John Updike, "A&P," in *Pigeon Feathers*, 196.
20. Raymond Carver, "Neighbors," in *Where I'm Calling From*, 70.
21. Lyndon Johnson, "The Great Society," in *The Times Were a Changin': The Sixties Reader*, ed. Irwin Unger and Debi Unger, 40.

Filmography

These are the films discussed throughout the book.

8½ (1963). Directed by Federico Fellini.
(500) Days of Summer (2009). Directed by Marc Webb.
The 400 Blows (1959). Directed by François Truffaut.
All the President's Men (1976). Directed by Alan J. Pakula.
American Beauty (1999). Directed by Sam Mendes.
American Pie (1999). Directed by Paul Weitz.
An Education (2009). Directed by Lone Scherfig.
L'Avventura (1960). Directed by Michaelangelo Antonioni.
Being There (1979). Directed by Hal Ashby.
The Big Shave (1967). Directed by Martin Scorsese.
The Birds (1963). Directed by Alfred Hitchcock.
Blue Velvet (1986). Directed by David Lynch.
Bonnie and Clyde (1967). Directed by Arthur Penn.
Carnal Knowledge (1971). Directed by Mike Nichols.
Catch-22 (1970). Directed by Mike Nichols.
Charlie Wilson's War (2007). Directed by Mike Nichols.
Citizen Kane (1941). Directed by Orson Welles.
Easy Rider (1969). Directed by Dennis Hopper.
E.T. (1982). Directed by Steven Spielberg.
Fiddler on the Roof (1971). Directed by Norman Jewison.
The Fortune (1975). Directed by Mike Nichols.
Gone with the Wind (1939). Directed by Victor Fleming.
The Godfather (1972). Directed by Francis Ford Coppola.
The Godfather, Part II (1974). Directed by Francis Ford Coppola.
Gosford Park (2001). Directed by Robert Altman.
The Graduate (1967). Directed by Mike Nichols.
Harold and Maude (1971). Directed by Hal Ashby.
In the Heat of the Night (1967). Directed by Norman Jewison.
It's Complicated (2009). Directed by Nancy Meyers.
Jaws (1975). Directed by Steven Spielberg.
Jules and Jim (1962). Directed by François Truffaut.

Lenny (1974). Directed by Bob Fosse.
M*A*S*H* (1970). Directed by Robert Altman.
The Matrix (1999). Directed by Andy and Larry Wachowski.
The Miracle Worker (1962). Directed by Arthur Penn.
Midnight Cowboy (1969). Directed by John Schlesinger.
Modern Times (1936). Directed by Charlie Chaplin.
Nashville (1975). Directed by Robert Altman.
The Player (1992). Directed by Robert Altman.
Play It Again, Sam (1972). Directed by Herbert Ross.
Psycho (1960). Directed by Alfred Hitchcock.
Reality Bites (1994). Directed by Ben Stiller.
Risky Business (1983). Directed by Paul Brickman.
Rumor Has It... (2005). Directed by Rob Reiner.
Run Lola Run (1998). Directed by Tom Tykwer.
Rushmore (1998). Directed by Wes Anderson.
sex, lies and videotape (1989). Directed by Steven Soderbergh.
Shadow of a Doubt (1943). Directed by Alfred Hitchcock.
Short Cuts (1993). Directed by Robert Altman.
The Silence of the Lambs (1991). Directed by Jonathan Demme.
Silkwood (1983). Directed by Mike Nichols.
The Sound of Music (1964). Directed by Robert Wise.
Splendor in the Grass (1962). Directed by Elia Kazan.
Star Wars (1977). Directed by George Lucas.
Sunset Boulevard (1950). Directed by Billy Wilder.
Superman (1978). Directed by Richard Donner.
Taxi Driver (1976). Directed by Martin Scorsese.
The Tiger Makes Out (1967). Directed by Arthur Hiller.
Wall Street (1987). Directed by Oliver Stone.
Wayne's World 2 (1993). Directed by Stephen Surjik.
Who's Afraid of Virginia Woolf? (1966). Directed by Mike Nichols.
The Wild One (1953). Directed by Laslo Benedek.
Working Girl (1988). Directed by Mike Nichols.

Bibliography

Alpert, Hollis. "'The Graduate' Makes Out." *Saturday Review*, 6 July 1968, found at http://web.infoave.net/~dennmac/review2.html.
Anderson, Wes. *Rushmore*. New York: Faber and Faber, 1999.
Ball, Alan. *The Shooting Script: American Beauty*. New York: Newmarket, 1999.
Bapis, Elaine M. *Camera and Action: American Film as Agent of Social Change, 1965–1975*. Jefferson, NC: McFarland, 2008.
Bernard, Jami. "*The Graduate*," in *The A List: The National Society of Film Critics' 100 Essential Films*, ed. Jay Carr, 138–141. New York: Da Capo, 2002.
Beuka, Robert. "'Just One Word ... PLASTICS': Suburban Malaise, Masculinity, and Oedipal Drive in *The Graduate*." *Journal of Popular Film and Television*, 28.1 (2000), 12–21.
Bewes, Timothy. *Reification, or the Anxiety of Late Capitalism*. London: Verso, 2002.
Biskind, Peter. *Easy Riders, Raging Bulls: How the Sex, Drugs, and Rock 'n' Roll Generation Saved Hollywood*. New York: Simon & Schuster, 1998.
Bordwell, David. *The Way Hollywood Tells It*. Berkeley: University of California Press, 2006.
Brackman, Jacob. "The Graduate." *The New Yorker*, 27 July 1968, 32–66.
Carringer, Robert L. "Designing Los Angeles: An Interview with Richard Sylbert." *Wide Angle*, 20.3 (1998), 97–131.
_____. "Hollywood's Los Angeles: Two Paradigms," in *Looking for Los Angeles: Architecture, Film, Photography, and the Urban Landscape*, ed. Charles G. Salas and Michael S. Roth, 247–266. Los Angeles: Getty, 2001.
Carver, Raymond. "Neighbors." In *Where I'm Calling From*. New York: Atlantic Monthly Press, 1988.
Clooney, Nick. *The Movies That Changed Us*. New York: Atria, 2002.
Coles, Robert. "*The Graduate*." *Trans-Action*, May 1968, found at http://web.infoave.net/~dennmac/review13.html.
Cooley, "Reviving Reification: Education, Indoctrination, and Anxiety in *The Graduate*." *Educational Studies* 45:4, 2009, 359.
Corliss, Richard. *Talking Pictures: Screenwriters in the American Cinema*. Woodstock, NY: Overlook, 1985.
Cousins, Mark. *The Story of Film*. New York: Thunder's Mouth, 2004.
Crowther, Bosley. "Film: Tales Out of School." *New York Times*, 22 December 1967.
_____. "Graduating with Honors." *New York Times*, 31 December 1967.
Denby, David. "Critic's Notebook: And Here's to You." *The New Yorker*, March 8, 2010, 9.
Eagan, Daniel. *America's Film Legacy*. New York: Continuum, 2010.
Enright, Robert. "Desiring Ambiguity: The Art of Eric Fischl." In *Eric Fischl: 1970–2007*, Arthur Danto, Robert Enright, and Steve Martin. New York: Monacelli, 2008.
Ephron, Nora. *Wallflower at the Orgy*. New York: Ace Books, 1973.

Bibliography

Fabe, Marilyn. *Closely Watched Films: An Introduction to the Art of Narrative Film Technique.* Berkeley: University of California, 2004.

Farber, Stephen, and Estelle Changas. "The Graduate." *Film Quarterly,* 21.3 (Spring 1968), 37–41.

Gelmis, Joseph. *The Film Director as Superstar.* London: Pelican, 1974.

Georgakas, Dan. "From Words to Images: An Interview with Buck Henry." *Cineaste,* Winter 2001, 4–10.

Giannetti, Louis D. *Understanding Movies,* 1st ed. Englewood Cliffs, NJ: Prentice Hall, 1972.

Greeley, Andrew M. "Sons and Fathers." *The Reporter,* February 1968, found at http://web.infoave.net/~dennmac/review7.html.

Greene, Naomi. *The French New Wave: A New Look.* London: Wallflower, 2007.

Harris, Mark. *Pictures at a Revolution: Five Movies and the Birth of the New Hollywood.* New York: Penguin, 2008.

Henry, Buck. "The Graduate": Screenplay. (Dated March 29, 1967). Available at http://sarcasmalley.com/graduate.txt.

Hill, Lee. *Easy Rider.* London: British Film Institute, 1996.

———. "Mike Nichols," *Senses of Cinema,* June 2003, found at www.sensesofcinema.com/contents/directors/03/Nichols.html.

Hoberman, J. "Dustin Hoffman," in *Entertaining America: Jews, Movies, and Broadcasting,* ed. J. Hoberman and Jeffrey Shandler, 198. Princeton, NJ: Princeton University, 2003.

———. "Flaunting It: The Rise and Fall of Hollywood's 'Nice' Jewish (Bad) Boys," in *Entertaining America: Jews, Movies, and Broadcasting,* ed. J. Hoberman and Jeffrey Shandler, 220–243. Princeton, NJ: Princeton University Press, 2003.

Hornby, Nick. *An Education.* New York: Riverhead, 2009.

Johnson, Lyndon B. "The Great Society," in *The Times Were a Changin': The Sixties Reader,* ed. Irwin Unger and Debi Unger, 39–42. New York: Three Rivers Press, 1998.

Johnson, Terry. *The Graduate.* London: Methuen, 2000.

Kael, Pauline. *For Keeps.* New York: Dutton, 1994.

Kashner, Sam. "Here's to You, Mr. Nichols," in *Vanity Fair's Tales of Hollywood: Rebels, Reds, and Graduates,* ed. Graydon Carter, 167–191. New York: Penguin, 2008.

Kawin, Bruce F. *How Movies Work.* Berkeley: University of California Press, 1992.

Kolker, Robert. *A Cinema of Loneliness.* 3rd ed. New York: Oxford, 2000.

LoBrutto, Vincent. *Martin Scorsese.* Westport, CT: Praeger, 2008.

Lyman, Rick. *Watching Movies.* New York: Times Books, 2002.

Man, Glenn. "Ideology and Genre in the *Godfather* Films," in *Francis Ford Coppola's* The Godfather *Trilogy,* ed. Nick Browne, 109–132. New York: Cambridge, 2000.

———. *Radical Visions: American Film Renaissance, 1967–1976.* Westport, CT: Greenwood, 1994.

McGrath, Charles. "Mike Nichols, Master of Invisibility." *New York Times,* 12 April 2009

Mellon, Joan. *Modern Times.* London: British Film Institute, 2006.

Monaco, Paul. *The Sixties: 1960–1969.* Berkeley: University of California Press, 2001.

Monush, Barry. *Everybody's Talkin': The Top Films of 1965–1969.* New York: Applause, 2009.

Pomerance, Murray. "Movies and the Specter of Rebellion," in *American Cinema of the 1960s,* ed. Barry Keith Grant, 172–192. New Brunswick, NJ: Rutgers University Press, 2008.

Prescott, Orville. "Talent Busting Out All Over." *New York Times,* 30 October 1963.

Pynchon, Thomas. *The Crying of Lot 49.* New York: Lippincott, 1966.

Quart, Leonard, and Albert Auster. *American Film and Society Since 1945.* 3rd ed. Westport, CT: Praeger, 2002.

Reck, Tom S. "'The Graduate' Reclassified." *Commonweal,* found at http://web.infoave.net/~dennmac/review4.html.

Reeves, Tony. *The Worldwide Guide to Movie Locations.* Chicago, IL: A Cappella, 2001.

Rollin, Betty. "Mike Nichols: Wizard of Wit." *Look*, found at http://web.infoave.net/~dennmac/review6.html.
Salinger, J. D. *The Catcher in the Rye*. New York: Little, Brown, 1951.
Sarris, Andrew. *The American Cinema: Directors and Directions, 1929–1968*. New York: Dutton, 1968.
Schickel, Richard. "Film 67/68." *Life*, 19 January 1968, found at http://web.infoave.net/~dennmac/review8.html.
Schuth, H. Wayne. *Mike Nichols*. Boston: Twayne, 1978.
Scott, A. O. "A Romantic Entanglement with a Heart of Celluloid." *The New York Times*, December 23, 2005.
Shumway, David R. "Rock 'n' Roll Sound Tracks and the Production of Nostalgia." *Cinema Journal*, 38.2 (Winter 1999), 36–51.
Simon, John. "*The Graduate*." *Movies Into Film*, February 1968, found at http://web.infoave.net/~dennmac/review5.html.
Sorel, Edward. "*The Graduate*," *Esquire*, May 1980, as qtd. in Paul Monaco, *The Sixties: 1960–1969*. Berkeley, CA: University of California Press, 2001.
Thomson, David. *The New Biographical Dictionary of Film*. New York: Knopf, 2002.
_____. *Have You Seen...?: A Personal Introduction to 1,000 Films*. New York: Knopf, 2008.
Turman, Lawrence. *So You Want to Be a Producer*. New York: Three Rivers Press, 2005.
Updike, John. "A&P." In *Pigeon Feathers*. New York: Knopf, 1962.
Webb, Charles. *The Graduate*. New York: New American Library, 1963.
_____. *Home School*. New York: St. Martin's, 2007.
_____. Letter to the editor of *The New Republic*, as qtd. in Hollis Alpert, "'The Graduate' Makes Out," *Saturday Review*, 6 July 1968, found at http://web.infoave.net/~dennmac/review2.html.
Williams, Linda Ruth. "*The Graduate*," in *Contemporary American Cinema*, ed. Linda Ruth Williams and Michael Hammond, 101–103. New York: McGraw-Hill, 2006.

Index

"A & P" *see* Updike, John
Academy of Motion Picture Arts and Sciences *see* Oscar Awards
Adler, Renata 63
Albee, Edward 92
Alfa Romeo "Spider" (Benjamin's graduation gift) 56–57, 80, 85, 134, 135, 138, 140, 141, 151, 153, 154, 167, 179, 181
All the President's Men (film) 10
Allen, Woody 10, 142
Alpert, Hollis 36
Altamont 180
Altman, Robert 9, 43, 175–176
Ambassador Hotel 199*ch*9*n*4
American Beauty 9, 176, 180–182, 183, 191
American Film Institute 5, 9
American Pie 9, 173
Anderson, Paul Thomas 173
Anderson, Wes 9, 173, 176, 182–186
Aniston, Jennifer 174
Anspach, Susan 142
Antonioni, Michelangelo 73
"April Come She Will" 65, 110, 115
Arkin, Alan 40–41
Ashby, Hal 9, 109, 176, 177–180
Auster, Albert 4
Avco-Embassy Pictures *see* Levine, Joseph E.
Avery, Brian 141
L'Avventura 73

Bad Boy 85–86
Baldwin, Alec 174
Ball, Alan 180–182, 191
Bancroft, Anne 16, 60, 61, 81, 84, 90, 92, 107, 108, 110, 123, 125, 128
Bapis, Elaine M. 5, 21, 48, 117
Barber, Lynn 186
Barthes, Roland 21
The Beast in the Jungle 89

The Beatles 180, 186
Beatty, Warren 7
Being There 109
Benedek, Laslo 37
Benjamin, Richard 63
Benning, Annette 181
Bentley, Wes 182
Beuka, Robert 4, 103, 111, 129–130
Bewes, Timothy 74
"The Big Bright Green Pleasure Machine" 134
The Big Shave 119–120
Birch, Thora 181
The Birds 105
Birthday Boy 86
Biskind, Peter 198*ch*6*n*8
Blue Velvet 109
Bonnie and Clyde 7, 10, 39, 43, 44
Bordwell, David 155, 159
Brackman, Jacob 1–2, 5, 8, 30–39, 47, 78, 133, 164, 179, 192
Brando, Marlon 37, 45
Brickman, Paul 19, 131
Brooks, Mel 55
Buchan, Magnus 184
Buffalo Springfield 10
Bunker, Archie 179
Burton, Richard 15, 54, 60

Carnal Knowledge 2, 40–41
Carringer, Robert L. 17, 19, 21, 64, 100, 105, 106, 198*ch*6*n*8
Carver, Raymond 192
Cassel, Seymour 184
Catch-22 (film) 2, 40–41
The Catcher in the Rye 26, 35, 51–52
Caulfield, Holden 26
Changas, Estelle 28, 31, 46, 79, 90–91, 123, 125, 128
Chaplin, Charlie 167–168

208　Index

Charlie Wilson's War 41
Citizen Kane 22, 24
The Coen Brothers 173
Coles, Robert 24, 125, 171
Cooley, Aaron 18, 19, 74, 81, 84, 133
Cooper, Chris 182
Cooper, Dominic 188
Coppola, Francis Ford 30
Corliss, Richard 15, 16, 29, 35, 46, 52, 107, 150, 199*ch*10*n*1
Cort, Bud 177
Costner, Kevin 174
Cousins, Mark 46, 48
Cox, Brian 184
Crawford, Joan 128
Crowther, Bosley (*The New York Times*) 1, 26–27, 29
Cruise, Tom 19, 131
The Crying of Lot 49 70–71

Daniels, William 77, 99, 102, 116
Demme, Jonathan 30
Democratic National Convention (Chicago 1968) 23, 35, 180
Denby, David 46, 91
DeNiro, Robert 45
Dirty Harry franchise 44
Donner, Richard 44
Dreyfuss, Richard 140, 143
Duvall, Robert 73
Dylan, Bob 8

Eagan, Daniel 40
Eastwood, Clint 44
Easy Rider 20, 23, 39, 43, 193
An Education 176, 186–190
8½ 141
Embassy Pictures *see* Levine, Joseph E.
E.T. 30
"Everybody's Talkin'" 74

Fabe, Marilyn 162
The Faces 184, 185
Fairbank-Hynes 187
Farber, Stephen 28, 31, 46, 79, 90–91, 123, 125, 128
Fell, Norman 140
Fellini, Federico 141
Fiddler on the Roof 180
First Presbyterian Church of Santa Barbara 155
Fischl, Eric 85–86, 115
(500) Days of Summer 9–10, 176–177
Flaubert, Gustave 50
Fleming, Victor 17
Fonda, Henry 55
Fonda, Jane 55

Fonda, Peter 20, 23
Ford, John 16, 116
The Fortune 41
Fosse, Bob 10
Foster, Jodie 44
Foster, Mark 173
The 400 Blows 162
Free Speech Movement (Berkeley) 140

Gale, Edra 141
Gamble, Mason 187
Gelmis, Joseph 42, 46, 160
Get Smart 55
Giannetti, Louis 9
Gibbs, James 189
Glamour 31
Goddard, Paulette 167
The Godfather 30, 44–45
The Godfather, Part II 45
Gone with the Wind 1, 17, 29
Gordon, Ruth 178
Gosford Park 43
Gould, Elliott 63
The Graduate (film) box-office 1, 17, 28–29, 37; budget 16, 53–54, 59–60; childhood motifs 92, 102, 146–147, 149, 158, 165, 192; cinematography 70, 76–78, 80, 83, 95–96, 102, 104–105, 116–118, 120, 129–130, 136, 138–139, 155; "conversation" motifs 81, 100, 116, 117, 119–120, 121–127, 132–135, 139, 143, 148–149, 192; cyclical motifs 11, 25, 72–73, 75, 129, 131, 142–143–144, 150, 152, 166–168; darkness motifs 95, 111, 112, 113, 120, 121–124, 126–127, 136, 148, 151, 152; "drifting" (as stasis) motifs 25, 71–72, 75, 111–112, 113–118, 137, 142, 146, 154–155, 161–168, 190–193 199*ch*10*n*3; editing 70, 71, 74, 87, 92–93, 97–98, 102–103, 105, 113–116, 118, 124, 128, 129, 134, 137, 146, 147, 159–160, 161–168; Freudian motifs 85–87, 88–90, 91, 92–93, 101, 106–111, 113, 114–116, 118–120, 126; materialist social conformity motifs 10–11, 18–19, 26–28, 36–40, 42–43, 72, 74, 84–85, 94–95, 100–101, 104–106, 111, 114, 117, 119–120, 131, 132–133, 139, 143–144, 145–148, 152, 158–168, 171 181–182, 190–193, 199*ch*10*n*3; medieval quest motifs 96–97, 136, 151, 152, 155, 156, 160–161, 165, 166, 176; misogynist motifs 90–92, 107–108, 111, 128–129, 132, 135, 181–182, 190; motion (as freedom) motifs 56–57, 129–130, 131–132, 137, 141, 142, 151, 154–155, 161–168, 190–193; performance anxiety motifs 99–101, 105–111, 119–120, 129, 133, 139, 143, 151, 183; "plastics" motifs 20–22, 24, 81, 97, 109, 148–149, 165,

Index

181, 190; point of view 7–9, 18, 31–33, 46–49, 64–65, 72–73, 77, 79–80, 82, 88–93, 95, 99–102, 106–107, 112, 114–116, 118, 120, 123–127, 131, 138–139, 140, 141, 142, 152, 156–168, 175–176, 177, 178, 179, 180, 181, 182, 183, 185–190, 191–193; predatory violence motifs 88–90, 95–96, 97, 107, 110, 111, 128, 160; production design 71, 87, 89, 100, 114, 155, 181; silence motifs 72–73, 79, 113, 127, 128, 136, 161, 164, 177; water motifs 21, 52, 76–77, 83, 85–86, 102–103, 104–105, 113–118, 128, 135–136, 138, 147, 184; Western motifs 31, 44, 155–156, 160, 165, 166, 176; *see also* Nichols, Mike

The Graduate (novel) 15, 17, 50–58, 69, 70, 71, 76, 92, 102–103, 106, 109, 111–112, 138, 141, 150, 156, 160, 161, 172, 191

The Graduate (screenplay) 54–58, 69–70, 103, 105, 106, 109, 112, 132–134, 138, 141, 150, 160, 161, 164, 171, 174, 180, 198*ch*4*n*1

The Graduate (stage play) 9, 171–172

"*The Graduate, Part II*" 175

Greeley, Andrew M. 27

Griffith, Melanie 41

Grodin, Charles 63

Grusin, Dave 88

Hackman, Gene 10, 73
Hamilton, Murray 94, 140, 149
Hanks, Tom 41
Hanley, William 55
Harold and Maude 176, 177–180, 184
Harris, Mark 5, 34–35, 45, 50, 63, 70, 83, 156, 157, 200*ch*15*n*4
Harris, Radie 64
Haynes, Todd 173
Henry, Buck 6, 16, 50, 52, 55–58, 65, 88, 90, 92, 103, 104, 105, 106, 108–109, 112, 120, 132–134, 138, 141, 150, 160, 161, 164, 171, 174, 175, 183
Hesse, Hermann 171
Higgins, Colin 178
Hill, Lee 6, 27, 29, 41, 173, 176
Hiller, Arthur 63
Hitchcock, Alfred 92, 105, 181
Hoberman, J. 63
Hockney, David 115
Hoffman, Dustin 1, 6, 10, 15, 45–46, 50, 51, 58, 60, 61–64, 65, 70, 73–74, 88, 92, 102–103, 104, 105, 107, 108, 110, 118, 125, 133, 149, 157–158, 160, 163–164, 165, 167, 183
Hollywood Strip 130, 132
Home School 9, 172–173
Hornby, Nick 186, 189–190

Howard, Ron 26, 35, 95, 135–136, 196*ch*2*n*43, 199*ch*12*n*10

In the Heat of the Night 7
Indiana Jones franchise 44
It's Complicated 174

James, Henry 89
Jaws 94, 140
Jewison, Norman 7, 180
John Birch Society 143
Johnson, Lyndon B. 4, 8, 22, 34, 171, 193
Johnson, Terry 172
Jonze, Spike 173
Jules and Jim 114

Kael, Pauline (*The New Yorker*) 1, 3, 23, 28, 29, 78, 133
Kashner, Sam 24, 61
Kauffmann, Stanley (*The New Republic*) 1, 30, 31, 51, 156
Kazan, Elia 91
Kennedy, Robert F. 180, 199*ch*9*n*4
Kent State 180
Kerouac, Jack 52
King, Martin Luther, Jr. 180
Kolker, Robert 43

Léaud, Jean-Pierre 162
Lehman, Ernest 60
Lenny 10
Levine, Joseph E. 1, 16, 30, 38, 59–60, 140
Life photograph of Dustin Hoffman in unemployment line 73
Lucas, George 44
Lumet, Sidney 16
Lyman, Rick 26, 114, 135, 196*ch*2*n*43, 199*ch*12*n*10
Lynch, David 109

MacLaine, Shirley 174
MAD magazine 58
Man, Glenn 5, 7, 43, 45, 47, 48, 73, 103, 104, 166
Manson murders 180
M*A*S*H* (film) 43, 175
The Matrix 30
May, Elaine 58
McGrath, Charles 26
Meikle, Jeffrey L. 21
Mellon, Joan 167–168
Mendelssohn 157
Mendes, Sam 9, 173, 176, 180–182, 191
Meyers, Nancy 174
Midnight Cowboy 10, 74
Minnelli, Vicente 16

210 Index

The Miracle Worker 16
Mitchell, Margaret 17
Modern Times 167
Moe's Books (Berkeley) 141
Molina, Albert 188
Monaco, Paul 72, 97
Monush, Barry 27
"Mrs. Robinson" 18, 135, 137, 144, 147, 152
Mulligan, Carey 186, 187
Murray, Bill 183, 185
Museum of Modern Art (New York) 26

Nashville 43
National Film Registry 40
"Neighbors" *see* Carver, Raymond
Nelson, Peter 55
The Newlywed Game 129
Nichols, Mike 15, 23, 27, 50, 52, 54, 55, 58–59, 80, 104, 183, 199*ch*10*n*1; college publicity tour 2, 8, 71; negative satirist 4–5, 24–25, 29, 34–49, 156, 166–168, 173, 174, 175, 184, 186, 191–193; production history of *The Graduate* 16, 60–65, 84, 106, 108–109, 110, 114, 116, 123, 124, 132–134, 157–158, 160, 161, 163–164, 165; *see also The Graduate* (film)
Nichols, Paul 58
Nilsson 74
Nixon, Richard 180

Oscar Awards 1, 5, 10, 15, 28, 54, 60
O'Steen, Sam (editor) 16, 59, 64–65, 97, 104, 114–115, 118, 124, 128, 129, 145, 148, 151, 157, 160, 161

Pacino, Al 45
Pakula, Alan J. 10
Parsley, Sage, Rosemary and Thyme (album) 65
Peace Corps 32, 193
Penn, Arthur 7, 16
Peschkowsky, Michael Igor *see* Nichols, Mike
Philadelphia Evening Bulletin 31
Pickles, Vivien 178
Play It Again, Sam 142
The Player 175–176
Poitier, Sidney 7
Pomerance, Murray 48, 83
Potente, Franka 154
Prescott, Orville 51, 53
Psycho 92–93, 109
Pynchon, Thomas 70–71

Quart, Leonard 4
"A Quick One (While He's Away)" 184

Radcliffe Camera 189
Rambo franchise 44
Ramis, Harold 173
Reality Bites 174
Reck, Tom S. 28, 35, 91, 123
Redford, Robert 10, 15, 61, 62
Reiner, Rob 174–175
Risky Business 19, 131
Robbins, Tim 175
Ross, Herbert 142
Ross, Katharine 32–33, 62, 129, 133, 163–164, 165, 167
Rumor Has It... 174–175
Run Lola Run 154–155
Rushmore 9, 176, 182–187
Russian Revolution 58
Ryder, Winona 174

Salinger, J. D. 35, 51–52
San Francisco–Oakland Bay Bridge 130, 140, 152, 200*ch*13*n*2, 200*ch*14*n*1
Sarris, Andrew 1, 29
Sarsgaard, Peter 188
"Scarborough Fair" 18, 137, 140–143, 152
Scherfig, Lone 9, 176, 186–190
Schickel, Richard 29, 46
Schlesinger, John 10, 74
Schuth, H. Wayne 6, 38, 41, 71
Schwartzman, Jason 183, 185
Scorsese, Martin 44, 119
Scott, A. O. 174–175
Segal, George 55, 63
Selznick, David O. 17
Serpico 184
sex, lies and videotape 109
Shadow of a Doubt 181
Shandling, Garry 9
Short Cuts 43
Shumway, David R. 72, 73, 115
Siddhartha 171
The Silence of the Lambs 30
Silent Majority 140, 180
Silkwood 41
Simon, John 1, 28, 29
Simon and Garfunkel 4, 18, 42, 65, 72, 74, 88, 110, 111, 114, 115, 122, 134, 135, 137, 140–143, 144, 151, 152, 157, 164, 167
The Simpsons 9
Soderbergh, Steven 16, 109, 173
The Sound of Music 1, 17, 29
"The Sound of Silence" 4, 42, 65, 72–73, 74, 108, 111, 115, 137, 163
Sounds of Silence (album) 65
Spacey, Kevin 181
Spielberg, Steven 30, 94
Splendor in the Grass 91
Star Wars 17, 44

Stevens, Cat 179, 184
Stiller, Ben 174
Stillman, Whit 173
Streep, Meryl 41, 174
Students for a Democratic Society (SDS) Takeover of Columbia University 1, 35
Sturges, Preston 27
Sunset Boulevard 54
Superman 44
Surjik, Stephen 174
Surtees, Robert (Cinematographer) 16, 60, 64–65, 70, 77, 95, 104, 110, 114, 116, 120, 136, 138, 142, 163
Suvari, Mena 181
Sylbert, Richard (Production Designer) 2, 16, 24, 53, 59, 60, 61, 83, 87, 99, 100, 105, 106, 114, 155, 161

Tanaka, Sara 185, 187
Taxi Driver 44
Taylor, Elizabeth 15, 54, 60, 63, 92
Telegraph Avenue (Berkeley) 130, 141
Thompson, Emma 186
Thomson, David 6, 23, 28, 31–32, 39, 51
Three's Company 140
The Tiger Makes Out 63
Time's "Man of the Year" 61–62
"Trouble" 179
Truffaut, François 114, 162
Turman, Lawrence 6, 16, 29, 36, 53–56, 58, 59–60, 62, 65
Turner, Kathleen 171
Tykwer, Tom 154

United Methodist Church of La Verne (CA) 155, 157–158
University of California–Berkeley 130, 140, 146

University of Chicago 58
University of Southern California 140, 146, 200*ch*13*n*2
Updike, John 192

Vadim, Roger 55
Vietnam War 1, 18, 119

Wachowski, Andy 30
Wachowski, Larry 30
Wall Street 19
Warhol, Andy 30
Warner, Jack 61
Wayne's World 2 9, 174
Webb, Charles 6, 9, 16, 23, 24, 32, 50–56, 58, 65, 69, 70, 71, 76, 92, 102–103, 106, 108–109, 111–112, 119, 124, 138, 141, 142, 156, 160, 161, 171–173, 174, 200*ch*15*n*4
Webb, Marc 9, 10, 176–177, 191
Weiss, Miriam 48
Weitz, Paul 173
Welles, Orson 22
The Who 184
Who's Afraid of Virginia Woolf? 1, 15, 40–41, 54, 55, 61, 91–92, 96
The Wild One 27
Wilder, Gene 63
Williams, Linda Ruth 6, 17, 25, 70, 171, 199*ch*10*n*3
Williams, Olivia 184–188
Willingham, Calder 55
Wilson, Elizabeth 58, 79, 115, 120
Wise, Robert 17
Woodstock 180
Working Girl 41
Writer's Guild of America 55
Wyler, William 16, 116

www.ingramcontent.com/pod-product-compliance
Ingram Content Group UK Ltd.
Pitfield, Milton Keynes, MK11 3LW, UK
UKHW041958140426
5217IPUK00015B/859